D0948511

URBAN GROWTH POLICY
IN A MARKET ECONOMY

STUDIES IN URBAN ECONOMICS

Under the Editorship of

Edwin S. Mills
Princeton University

URBAN GROWTH POLICY
IN A MARKET ECONOMY

George S. Tolley

Department of Economics
The University of Chicago
Chicago, Illinois

Philip E. Graves

Department of Economics
University of Colorado at Boulder
Boulder, Colorado

John L. Gardner

Department of Housing
and Urban Development
Washington, D.C.

With contributions by

Donald R. Haurin

Oded Izraeli

J. Vernon Henderson

Barton Smith

Peter Zadrozny

ACADEMIC PRESS   New York   San Francisco   London   1979
A Subsidiary of Harcourt Brace Jovanovich, Publishers

ACADEMIC PRESS, INC.
111 Fifth Avenue, New York, New York 10003

United Kingdom Edition published by
ACADEMIC PRESS, INC. (LONDON) LTD.
24/28 Oval Road, London NW1 7DX

Library of Congress Cataloging in Publication Data
Tolley, George S. Date
Urban growth policy in a market economy.

(Studies in urban economics)
Includes bibliographical references.
1. Cities and towns--United States--Growth--
Addresses, essays, lectures.   2. Urban economics--
Addresses, essays, lectures.   I. Graves, Philip E.,
joint author.   II. Gardner, John L., joint author.
III. Title.   IV. Series.
HT123.T63   301.36'3'0973   78-8838
ISBN 0-12-692850-9

Contents

I
FRAMEWORK FOR THE ANALYSIS OF POLICY

1
The Economic Analysis of Policies Concerned with Where People Live   3
GEORGE S. TOLLEY and JOHN L. GARDNER

V
EXTERNALITIES AND THE SPATIAL
DISTRIBUTION OF THE POOR

10
Urban Implications of the Welfare System and
Minimum Wage Laws   137
BARTON SMITH and GEORGE S. TOLLEY

VI
LABOR COMPENSATION AND EXTERNALITIES

11
A Theory of Money Wages   151
GEORGE S. TOLLEY

12
Externalities and Intercity Wage and
Price Differentials   159
ODED IZRAELI

VII
IMPLICATIONS

Preface

Increasingly there have been calls for estimates of the effects of policies aimed at influencing where people live and work. Yet few definite estimates have been made. The lack of estimates prevents a reasoned approach to policy formulation. Environmental effects are a case in point. A few years ago, environmental effects were virtually ignored. Then, almost explosively, public discussion began to imply that they should be a prime concern. More recently, concerns about energy have led some to feel that energy supersedes the environment in importance. The relative prominence given to issues surges and recedes continually, as witness the changing emphasis given to no-growth policies, the flight to the suburbs, integration, and the changing distribution of jobs between various regions.

The swings in opinion about what is important locationally call attention to the need for objective estimates of effects of urban growth policies. A reason often given for failure to estimate effects of policies concerned with where people live and work is that knowledge is too limited to permit precise estimates. However, the feasibility of making estimates is greater than commonly believed. Knowledge about locational behavior is accumulating. For analysis of policies, it is not necessary to entirely explain the spatial structure of the economy. The information needed is only that required to predict the change brought about by a policy. One of the greatest barriers is the lack of previous attempts to make estimates, even on a rough, order-of-magnitude level.

This book represents an attempt to present a framework for rational analysis of urban growth policies and to develop techniques for estimating city size and national income effects associated with alternative policies.

Much of the work reported here grew out of a grant from the Economic Development Administration, made through the Center for Urban Studies of the University of Chicago. Additional support was received from the National Science Foundation. However, these agencies are not responsible for the views expressed. The atmosphere of intellectual endeavor at The University of Chicago provided a setting without which the book could not have been completed. Help and encouragement have come from individuals too numerous to acknowledge properly by singling out a few persons, particularly since each of the chapter authors would have a long list of names to add. To all of the people who have contributed to the research, we wish to express our appreciation and thanks.

I
FRAMEWORK FOR
THE ANALYSIS OF POLICY

1

The Economic Analysis of Policies Concerned with Where People Live[1]

GEORGE S. TOLLEY
JOHN L. GARDNER

The question of where people should live has always been a source of active differences of opinion. Why the question excites so much interest could be a topic for investigation in itself. Perhaps one explanation is that people make a subjective identification with a certain type of place, whether it be a small rural community or a large city, based on nostalgia for childhood or where, at one point in his life, a person strongly desired to live. Unconsciously a person may feel that policy should favor that certain type of place. A more practical reason for lively interest is that the geographical distribution of population influences the distribution of political power. Existence of these attitudinal and political overtones increases the need for objective analysis.

Interest in possibilities to influence where people live has risen to the point of undertaking policies to influence the distribution of population as between different regions, between rural and urban areas, between cities of various sizes, and between central city and suburb. A great many new policies of this type are under discussion. These policies involve complex

[1] Portions of this chapter are from G. S. Tolley, "The Welfare Economics of City Bigness." *Journal of Urban Economics* **1**, 1974, 324–345.

economic issues that have for the most part received only casual consideration. The purpose of this book is to contribute to serious economic analysis of policies influencing where people live.

Policy Issues

COMMON VIEWS

Interest in policies designed to create jobs in particular geographic regions of the country goes back at least to the moves to support reclamation of arid lands in the 1900s and to proposals promoting nonfarm jobs in America during the agricultural depressions of the 1920s and 1930s. Among the more recent antecedents, interest in the 1960s centered on Appalachia and development effects for other regions that spun out of the Appalachian effort. The interest of the 1970s is centering more on the Sunbelt versus the Midwest and Northeast, particularly the center cities in the latter areas. Another difference in emphasis which reflects the changing times exists today. Accompanying expressions of dissatisfaction with social and environmental by-products of growth has come the suggestion to retard development of some areas where economic growth threatens a community's quality of life. Now both job creation and job retardation are entering the discussion of regional and local development policies.

Increasing concentrations of population in larger cities have heightened this concern since the physical environment is seen to be of low quality in big urban areas. Crime, riots, and protest are most conspicuous in large cities. Some observers have emphasized the effects of housing segregation, zoning, and other impediments to movement making for concentrations of black and low-income groups in central cities. The eroding tax base combined with ever more pressing demands for public services exacerbates fiscal problems facing large cities. Hence, the view has become more widespread that the bad things happening in large cities must be caused by their largeness.

The changing focus of policy discussions reflects in part the ever-shifting trends in urbanization and regional growth patterns characteristic of a dynamic economy. The percentage of the population that lives in urban areas has risen from 55.3% in 1940 to 72.8% in 1974. Since the 1970 census, the rate of growth of the central cities has become negative, for the first time in this century. While the population in the suburban ring grew by 8.4% between 1970 and 1974, the central city population of the United States declined by 1.9%. The central city decline is not evenly distributed, falling most heavily on the older, industrial cities of the Northeast and Midwest. Racial concerns have been voiced regarding the growth of nonwhite population relative to white population in central cities, with white growth being negative (-5.1%) and nonwhite growth positive (6.3%) over the period 1970–1974. The details of these and other spatial changes remain the object of ongoing extensive documentation. There has been, however, all too little analysis of why the changes take place. Even more important, there has been a lack of analysis of what the implications of these changes are in quantitative terms for the welfare of the nation.

The interest in policies to influence growth of particular parts of the country shows every sign of continuing. To judge from study groups and task forces, interest in this type of policy—in short, *population distribution policy*—is mounting. For example, the report of the President's Commission on Population Growth and the American Future, which received great publicity, was concerned with the desirability of the present rate and spatial distribution of urban growth in the United States. The commission recognized that regardless of the overall rate of growth of the national economy, criteria for setting policies to influence the distribution are needed. The commission report is only one of several major studies that have addressed population distribution questions.[2]

Although the studies are too far-ranging to summarize here, one of the strands running throughout them is almost a theme on the disadvantages of big cities. Warranted or not, the following ideas are expressed:

- Growth of the cities is seen to be at the cost of an increasingly inhospitable urban environment. Air and water pollution, the level of noise, and visual despoliation have virtually become part of the definition of urbanization. As cities grow, more time and effort are required to gain access to work, retail outlets, and recreational facilities, due to increasing distances between home and these destinations per se and to increasing congestion on the roads.
- The studies tend to accept the hypothesis that the urban psychosocial environment deteriorates with increasing city size. High crime and delinquency rates, alienation and anomie are seen as characteristics of life in the largest cities. Ethnic and racial separation are believed to be more pronounced in larger than in smaller cities.
- The viewpoint is expressed that the political structure of larger cities lacks adequate representation for the poor of the inner cities as well as strong political institutions which could serve suburban residents in matters of region-wide concern.

[2] See, for example, U.S. President's National Advisory Commission on Rural Poverty [12]; U.S. Advisory Commission on Intergovernmental Relations [7]; U.S. National Commission on Urban Problems [10]; National Committee on Urban Growth Policy [3]; U.S. National Goals Research Staff [11]; U.S. Commission on Population Growth and the American Future [8]; Task Force on Land Use and Urban Growth [6]; U.S. Domestic Council, Committee on Community Development [9; two in a continuing series of biennial reports to Congress required under the Housing and Urban Development Act of 1970].

- The fact that the most rapid growth occurs on the outskirts of major metropolitan areas is viewed as depriving central city residents of easy access to jobs in the dynamic, growing (and usually higher paying) suburban employment sector.
- On the other side of the coin, several of the studies see growth of large urban areas as sapping rural towns of vitality and leaving poverty, unemployment, and impoverished governments.

The study groups have generally recognized some advantages of economic activity at a large scale: a reduction in per capita costs of providing sewer, water, electrical, and some other services where the per capita length of feeder lines is related to density; a broader range of goods and services available in retail markets; and a more diverse array of employment opportunities. However, the impression is that these advantages are outweighed in the largest cities by the costs itemized above. The premise is that the disadvantages are inevitable consequences of large, highly concentrated population centers. Limiting growth is seen as a means for preventing the further worsening of these conditions.

The studies are at times monumental in bringing together information and opinions. Yet, without downgrading their contribution, one can assert that population distribution as an issue remains hard to get a hold of. Simplifying only a little, discussion typically focuses on only one or more problems having a geographic dimension, as for instance, some of the big city ills just listed, or difficulties being experienced by small towns in decline. From this partial analysis emerges the suggestion that a different geographic distribution of people would help solve the problems. A usual idea is that keeping big cities from growing while fostering the growth of smaller towns would contribute to solving the problems. From this idea are likely to flow vague recommendations that loan and public works policies should be undertaken to direct the location of jobs and people away from large urban centers. Similarly, no-growth policies are seen as appropriate ways of stopping environmental deterioration in urban places. National, state, and city land use controls, again sometimes vaguely defined, may be recommended to guide patterns of community growth.

THE ECONOMIST'S REACTION

The first reaction of many economists to the idea of adopting explicit policies to influence where people live and work is to favor letting the market accomplish the task, that is, to have no explicit policy. Most discussions of policies concerning regional and urban growth have been at an opposite pole, entirely ignoring the role of markets in achieving goals. There has been very little serious concern with the question of what markets do and do not accomplish. Only recently has the identification of sources of market failure been recognized as important in the analysis of policies to affect the sizes and growth of cities. There is discussion of the possibilities that (a) individuals impose costs or benefits upon other individuals or firms, the magnitude of influence being associated with city size, and (b) these social costs or benefits of migration are not fully reflected in private wage differentials between cities. If so, this would amount to a market incentive for a population distribution that is other than optimal. The aggregate real national income could be increased by having a different distribution.

Another feature of almost all discussions has been their qualitative nature. Frustrating nebulousness is encountered about the specifics of policies, and in particular about the dollars and cents of possible public inducements to alter the distribution of population. Little is known about how specific government measures would influence location, and even less is known about how the results would affect social goals.

This book contains several contributions to the analysis of policies concerned with location. After reviewing policy alternatives, this first chapter considers possible reasons for attempting to influence where people live, using national economic efficiency as the criterion. This is done by considering, in turn, three main questions:

1. What is the relationship between city size and labor supply and demand? This question leads to considering geographic variations in wage levels, with and without externalities.
2. How do externalities affect city size? Here, attention turns to the quantitative effects of congestion, pollution, economies of scale, and specific features of the taxation and unemployment compensation systems which influence city size.
3. In view of the existence of externalities, what would the benefits of alternative city sizes be? Analysis of this question requires attention to the gains from successive additions or subtractions from the size of a city in the presence of externalities.

A quantitative approach to evaluation of policies is suggested. This approach is embodied in many of the studies which comprise the central sections of the book. The final section of the book draws together the theory and empirical findings in an evaluation of policy alternatives.

A TAXONOMY OF TOOLS

Many of the ills emphasized in policy discussions involve costs to some individuals which are imposed unwittingly by the acts of others. Such private externalities have been of interest in economics at least since Pigou

[5]. Public financing problems brought about by dissociation of benefits and costs in government expenditure and tax decisions involve institutional externalities, of more recent concern but none the less externalities.

Recognition that externalities are involved clarifies issues and organizes the discussion. Two types of policies emerge: (a) policies directly bearing on activities that impose costs on others, either by introduction of pricing measures or through direct regulation, and (b) policies which affect the distribution of populations between cities, as recommended in many of the study group reports. Table 1-1 lists representative policies of each type. The optimal pricing schemes (I-A of Table 1-1) are recommended largely by economists but have received less support in the public policy process, which tends to favor nonprice externality policies (I-B of Table 1-1) and approaches involving jobs and population (II of Table 1-1).

The policy mix recommended by the Population Commission is similar to that pursued through such agencies as the Economic Development Administration and Department of Labor through the 1960s and currently being deemphasized. These include grants and loans for local public works designed to improve the business environment, loans for industry

TABLE 1-1

Policies Affecting Population Distribution

I. Externality policies
  A. Optimal pricing of urban services and amenities
     Highway congestion taxes
     Pollution taxes
     Reform of property taxes and the pricing structure for local public services
     Industry and public sector taxes and subsidies related to external economies of scale
  B. Nonprice policies
     Low-polluting fuel requirements
     Industry and vehicular emission standards
     Urban highway and mass transit construction

II. Policies aimed at population movements
     Public works
     Subsidies for industry relocation
     Migration subsidies based on city size
     Individual taxes based on city size
     Taking account of distributional goals in federal expenditure policy
     Federal transportation subsidies
     Reform of interstate inequities in the welfare system
     Zoning to limit growth
     Planned urban developments
     Land banks

and commercial enterprises that locate in depressed regions of the country, and technical and planning assistance to local governments. Included also are job-retraining programs giving potential migrants from depressed areas skills necessary to compete in urban labor markets and creating a better skilled labor force within the depressed areas which might attract new firms. Although these programs have been pursued as matters of policy for over a decade, few evaluations of them have been attempted.

The policies in Table 1-1 involving taxes on pollution or congestion or on entering a city as a migrant have not figured prominently in public discussion but are suggested by an economic analysis of the effect of such externalities on equilibrium versus optimum city sizes. In the case of environmental degradation, the tax per unit of emissions into the air or water would be equal to the value of damage done by a marginal unit of emitted materials. For transportation, the tax would take the form of highway use charges, varying in amount with the size and rate of highway use at different times and locations.

Another possible tax approach at the conceptual level would be geared to the externalities resulting from adding a person to a metropolitan area's population. In this case the tax would be imposed on in-migrants or persons living in the area where the negative externalities exist. Migration taxes or subsidies have been suggested previously by economists. Only recently has much attention been given to the fact that regional differences in income and property tax rates and welfare payments create incentives to migration. The Economic Development Administration's policy of making low-interest loans available for construction in depressed areas is an example of this sort of policy, in this case directed toward industry rather than individuals. On the whole, however, systematic tax and subsidy schemes have been rejected in public discussions not only because of high administrative costs including monitoring of emissions and congestion and collection of tolls or taxes, but also due to current limitations on analytical capacity to determine how much the optimal charges should be. Additional reasons having to do with "equal treatment" and attitudes that regulation and tax policies should be kept separate add to the difficulties of adopting such policies. Apparently, on the basis of objections such as these, the various study groups have all come to favor environmental policies involving direct regulation of producers and households.

An observation, emphasized especially by the National Goals Research Staff, is that many current public policies are already having a major effect on the distribution of population and on relative growth rates of cities and regions within the United States. One such implicit policy is the allocation of large defense contracts, which for several decades has stimulated firms to locate in the western and southern states and has been a major factor in individuals' decisions to relocate to these regions. At present, no systematic apparatus exists for reviewing the implications of location decisions of federal facilities from the point of view of their relative impact on incomes and on population distribution throughout the country.

A second group of policies relates to the intraurban tax structure, motivated by economic studies showing that existing taxes on housing distort the spatial distribution of population. Reliance on the property tax to finance local services gives high-income residents incentives to suburbanize, excluding low-income residents who bring demands for services without ability to pay. The urban personal property tax has been estimated to be equivalent to an excise tax over 25% on the value of housing services in the jurisdictions where it is applied [1, 4]. Because the occupancy value of rental housing is subject to income taxation (imposed on rents collected by the landlord) but the occupancy value of owner-occupied housing is not, new housing on the urban fringe (primarily owned single-family) appears less expensive relative to new housing in the central city (primarily rented multifamily) than it should, considering the relative costs of the resources involved. Availability of VA and FHA mortgage insurance for single-family housing tends to reinforce this. Laws permitting condominium ownership of apartments in multifamily buildings have only just begun to redress the distortion. Thus, existing property and income taxation practices can carry with them a disincentive to investment in the construction and rehabilitation of housing in the central cities, along with a relative incentive to land-extensive, single-family housing construction on the edges of metropolitan areas. The effect exacerbates the problems listed at the outset. Proposals for reform of the urban tax system, therefore, belong appropriately in a discussion of measures for dealing with the adverse consequences of urban growth. The National Commission on Urban Problems, among the study groups, gave major emphasis to prospects for such reform.

The remaining policies in Table 1-1 have as their general goal restricting development in a coordinated manner around large population centers that would otherwise grow by spreading and absorbing more of the surrounding countryside. Such policies have been suggested in the context of no-growth discussions[3] and land use instruments. Policies of this type were considered extensively and were found particularly promising

---

[3] Meadows *et al.* [2]. For reactions to this work see Weintraub, Schwartz, and Aronson [13].

by the National Commission on Urban Problems and by the National Committee on Urban Growth Policy, among the recent study groups. Zoning authority to restrict large areas of land to agricultural, open space or very large-lot residential use could be applied with existing types of administrative statutes, although coordination of the many political units with zoning authority around typical urban areas poses a potential barrier to success of this approach. More novel are proposals for a system of land use controls which would encourage coordinated development of whole communities or cities, rather than separate, individual decision making by zoning boards on each parcel of land. Federally assisted acquisition of undeveloped suburban land to be held in nonurban use is yet another kind of policy which could be applied for these ends.

Reviewing the policies listed in Table 1-1, many opportunities exist for externality policies dealing directly with the ills of large urban centers. However, it may also be the case that the practical and administrative difficulties rule out the far-reaching program of policies needed to deal with all of the problems just listed. For this reason, the question deserves to be considered whether policies altering the distribution of city sizes are justified. It is therefore appropriate to turn to a consideration of costs and benefits of such policies.

City Size and Market Performance

If the market economy is working efficiently, a geographic distribution of population will be brought about conducive to a maximum national income. Any policy interfering with the geographic distribution of people and jobs will result in a loss to the nation. There can be a gain only if markets are not efficient and if specific policies are adopted which will succeed in reducing the inefficiency. If these views are accepted, then a logical consequence is that the analysis of policies influencing the geographic distribution of population must consider the extent to which markets do or do not give adequate signals of gains and losses to influence people's free choices of where to live. The analysis of policies becomes a task of searching out and quantifying the effects of inadequacies of the signals.

In following this approach, it is useful to consider reasons for divergences between social or total costs and benefits and the private benefits and costs guiding market decisions. These divergences, or *externalities,* may be due to several causes, and each implies that the actual amount of activity that occurs in an area may differ from the amount which is optimum in the sense of contributing most to the nation's income. The analysis ultimately leads to the possibility of estimating how different the optimum is from the actual amount of activity observed and how great the gain would be from policies to rectify the situation.

A foundation based on the relation of externalities to market outcomes is thus needed for analyzing policies. The preceding section identified two types of policies—first, policies that take externalities as given and attempt to influence location of activity in light of the failure to completely internalize the externalities in market decisions and, second, policies that frontally attack externalities. Basic concepts for analyzing these two types of policies are developed in the next two sections.

Best City Sizes Given Externalities

THE MAIN ARGUMENT

Figure 1-1 shows marginal products from employing non-location-fixed resources in City A and in the rest of the economy. The distance between the left and right vertical axes is the total amount of non-location-fixed resources in the economy. Amount in City A is measured from the left,

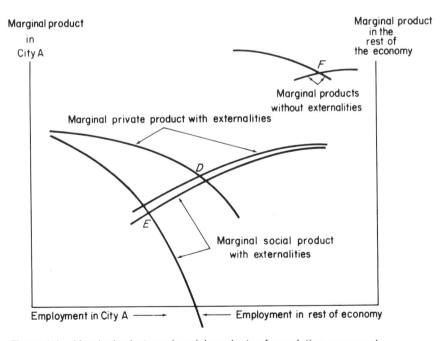

Figure 1-1. Marginal private and social products of population movements.

and in the rest of the economy from the right. A consequence of pollution and congestion is that *marginal social product with externalities* lies below *marginal private product with externalities*. If resources flow to equalize remuneration, the division of resources between City A and the rest of the economy will be at point D, where marginal private products are equal instead of at point E, where marginal social products are equal and where the total product of the economy would be maximized.

The marginal private and social product curves are determined by production function considerations. Let the output of a producing unit be $x_i = x_i(n_i, s_i, Q)$, where the amount of non-location-fixed factors employed by the producing unit is n_i. Individual acts s_i of the producing unit contributing to pollution and congestion also affect its output. Furthermore, output of producing units is affected by a totality Q which reflects pollution or congestion resulting from all the individual acts. A relationship $Q = Q(s_i \cdots s_n)$, which is a production function for Q, determines the total physical effect of the individual acts.[4]

Pollutants may be emitted either by the production activities of firms or by the household and commuting activities of persons hired. Household and commuting activities are production activities of families. For example, housing-plus-access is a commodity which families produce with their own time using purchased inputs including buildings and automobiles. In the present analysis there is no need to distinguish between outputs produced by firms or by families, but the outputs of both must be included since chimneys of factories and homes, and exhaust pipes of trucks and family automobiles, are all sources of pollution.

The emitting of pollutants may be viewed as an input s_i in the production function for goods and services produced by polluters. Emitting of pollutants has the essential attribute of an input that a change in amount of emitting changes amount of output of product that can be obtained from given amounts of all the other inputs. If a producer were reducing the emission of pollutants, he could choose a combination of actions of substituting other inputs for emissions (such as installing a precipitator or switching to cleaner, higher cost fuel) and producing less output, which would be likely in view of high marginal costs. Whatever the combination

---

[4] Although this approach is consistent with literature on technical externalities, we are unaware of previous attempts both to introduce externality-causing activities explicitly as arguments of firm and household production functions and to specify additional relations such as $Q = Q(s_i, \ldots, s_n)$ showing how another argument Q is affected by these activities. There is need to estimate relationships such as $Q = Q(s_1, \ldots, s_n)$ for both pollution and congestion. Research in the physical sciences concerned with these effects is hindered by lack of guidelines from economists about what effects matter, that is, about how to define the Q and s variables.

of actions, effects of a reduction in emitting can be analyzed in the same way as would a reduction in a labor or capital input. In the absence of incentives not to emit, emitting of pollutants will tend to be carried to the point where increased emissions neither add to nor subtract from the producer's output.

Emitting of the pollutants has external effects through air quality. The effects are determined by the physical relationship indicating how quality of the air at large Q is influenced by individual acts of emitting. Air quality is an input in production functions of firms and families affecting the output from a given amount of other inputs through dirt, discomfort, and disease effects. Some of the commodities affected by air quality are not traded, involve family production, and are often discussed as being associated with the quality of living, for example, health. However, in general, air quality can be an input in the production functions for traded or nontraded commodities which are produced either by firms or families.

Air quality as an input Q is the affecting of production of commodities by air characteristics found in the environment, while emitting of pollutants as an input s_i is the affecting of the air characteristics as part of the act of producing commodities. Unlike emitting of pollutants, air quality is a Samuelsonian public good. A change in air quality ordinarily affects several parties to whom the quality cannot be individually rationed. For such discussed reasons, there are impediments to reaching group agreements among affected parties to change the amount of such a good. In the absence of individual acts to change the quality of air, its amount is given to the producing unit, and quality of air therefore acts as a production function shifter rather than a variable input.

Remarks similar to those for air pollution apply to congestion. The input s_i causing congestion is putting a vehicle into traffic at a particular time of day, which passes the same test for an input as emitting of pollutants. If someone refrained from putting a vehicle into traffic at a particular time, he could make factor substitutions (using the greater inputs required to travel at a different time of day, travel by another mode, or produce by means using less travel) and in view of higher marginal costs would be likely to produce less output. In the absence of restrictions or changes on vehicles by time of day, he has no incentive to make these adjustments.

As number of vehicles operating on a given road capacity increases, a point is reached at which further increases reduce the speed Q at which all vehicles can travel. Changes in speed are thus analogous to changes in air quality. The changes cannot be rationed individually to those whose speed is affected, and they act as a production function shifter.

In the absence of incentives to curb pollution and congestion, the increase in output in City A may be less than the amount paid to resources added to production because, accompanying the added output of the producing units due to their use of the resources, there will be increased pollution and congestion. Resources are valued according to the amount which the act of employment adds to the units' output given the existing position of their production functions, without taking account of the reduction in output due to shifts in production functions caused by the added pollution and congestion.

Due to these external effects, the remuneration paid to resources both in City A and in the rest of the economy will tend to exceed marginal contribution of the resources to output. If owners switch resources to make marginal private products equal in City A as in the rest of the economy, marginal social products will be equal only if the excess of marginal private product over marginal social product is the same in City A as in the rest of the economy. The nature of pollution and congestion is that increased pollutants and vehicles do not shift production functions at all at low amounts, but extra amounts have increasingly severe effects as levels are raised until ultimately fumes kill and there are so many vehicles that traffic cannot move. Pollution and congestion lead to increasing negative externalities, the difference between marginal social product and marginal private product becoming greater the greater are the levels of pollutants and vehicles. Since the levels tend to vary with city size, if resource owners adjust to make marginal private products equal, it is likely that the marginal social product of the resources in a large city is below that in a small city. There would be an increase in total product from switching resources to the smaller city.

In Figure 1-1, the increasing vertical difference between the marginal private and social product curves with externalities, as employment in a place increases, reflects the assumption that there are increasing negative externalities due to pollution and congestion. The curves have been drawn assuming City A is relatively large. The marginal product curves for the rest of the economy are averages of marginal products from cities of various sizes, and therefore the externalities for the rest of the economy are shown as being smaller than for City A. The assumptions about negative externalities imply the point of maximum total product at point E is to the left of the market solution at point D, showing that with increasing negative externalities total product could be increased through contraction of the large city.

MARGINAL PRODUCTS AND MONEY WAGES

To bring out why the conclusion is not affected by labor's response to externalities, details for a simple case are shown in Figure 1-2. In Figure 1-2(a), which is a benchmark showing the situation without externalities,

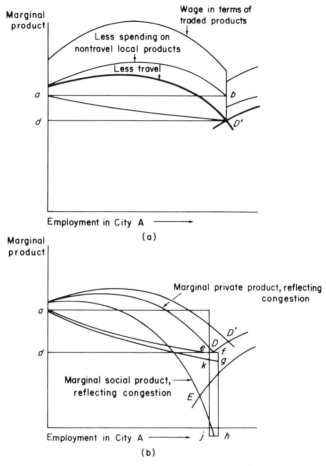

Figure 1-2. Marginal private and social products with congestion.

the topmost curve is the money wage divided by the price of traded goods, that is, the marginal physical product of labor in producing traded goods of equal market value to the bundle of nontravel local goods chosen by a person hired for an extra hour. The dark line makes the further subtraction of traded goods that would exchange for travel expenses. At city size D' persons living on the margin are spending bD' on travel. Travel expenses are progressively smaller down to zero as one considers persons closer in. The total of all travel expenses for the city is the triangular shaped area $abD'a$. The residential rent premium due to proximity to the center is ad at the center declining to zero at the margin. Thus rent-plus-travel costs are the rectangular area *adD′ ba* for the city. At any city size smaller than *D′*, the distance to the margin is less, so that a smaller rent-plus-travel cost rectangle would be drawn, with correspondingly lower travel expenses at the margin and lower rents for persons within the margin. The figure indicates the role of changing land rents as a city becomes larger making the marginal cost of travel-plus-rent the same for workers added as for those already in the city.

Because all local products have been subtracted, the dark line shows the amount of traded goods actually purchased. In Figure 1-2 the market basket demanded is assumed not to be affected by relative prices. Labor mobility then makes wages adjust to that level which enables workers to buy the same amount of traded products, after buying local products, in City A as in the rest of the economy. Thus equilibrium is at point *D′*.

In Figure 1-2(b) the curve with intersection *D′* is repeated, and the further curves show the effects of externalities due to traffic congestion. A rent-plus-travel cost rectangle can still be drawn, but for any given city size it is larger than in the upper part of the figure since congestion now adds to travel costs. Detail is exaggerated at the equilibrium point *D*. The amount of traded products purchased by a worker is represented by a small rectangle of height *e* above the *x* axis. The area *aefgka* shows the travel costs imposed by the addition of a worker at *D* owing to increased congestion, that is it is the sum of shifts in travel costs at all distances due to increased congestion. This is the externality which must be subtracted from the marginal private product curve through *D* to arrive at marginal social product. The area *aefgka* is equal to *efhje*. The curved line sloping down to the right and passing through *E* is the marginal social product showing such subtractions at every point from the curve passing through *D*. The area *efgke*, which is the extra travel cost imposed on workers at the margin, determines a downward deflection of the marginal private product curve due to congestion, that is, it determines the extent to which the curve passing through *D* lies below the curve through *D′*. This downward deflection is only part of the marginal externality, the rest of the externality being increases in travel costs for workers not at the margin. Since the external costs are subtracted from whatever private costs exist at the margin, the marginal social product curve passing through *E* must lie below the marginal private product curve passing through *D*. While the externality leads to a reduction of city size from *D′* to *D*, there is still a marginal externality at *D*. If, after labor has moved to equalize real wages, city sizes still differ as is expected due to differences in production possibilities among localities, there will still be differences in externalities among cities. If City A remains larger than average, the point *E* still lies to the left of *D*.

The conclusion holds in the more general case illustrated in Figure 1-3 where (a) market basket chosen is affected by relative prices, (b) externalities are due to traffic, pollution, or other causes, and (c) externalities may affect location-fixed as well as non-location-fixed factors through raising production costs of both local and traded products. The two sets of dark lines in Figure 1-3 correspond to the lines in Figure 1-1. Figure 1-3 indicates for the general case the relationship of the marginal private and social product curves to money wages and market basket considerations.

The topmost curve in Figure 1-3 shows how many traded products could be purchased with the money wage. The next curve, traded products actually purchased, depends on the varying ratio $\hat{k}$ of local to traded products chosen. The cost of one unit of a variable weight composite

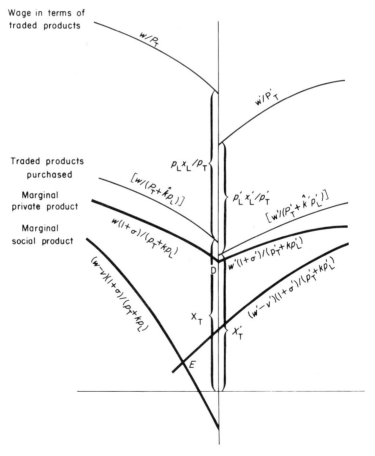

Figure 1-3. Marginal private and social products in the general case.

commodity, each unit of which contains a unit of traded products and the associated local products chosen, is $p_T + \hat{k}p_L$, and the amount of this commodity purchasable from an hour's employment is the cost per unit divided into the wage or $w/(p_T + \hat{k}p_L)$. In the denominator, substituting $\hat{k} = x_L/x_T$, factoring out $1/x_T$, substituting w for $p_T x_T + p_L x_L$ and cancelling with the w in the numerator reveals that $w/(p_T + \hat{k}p_L)$ is equal to the amount of traded products purchased x_T.

In the consideration of market baskets in Chapter 11 it is shown that the marginal private product of employment in City A is $w(1 + \sigma)/(p_T + kp_L)$, where k is a fixed ratio defining an arbitrary composite commodity and σ is the percentage wage adjustment that would make the satisfaction from the arbitrary composite commodity equal to satisfaction from the bundle of products actually chosen. If the market basket chosen is unvarying and is used to define the composite commodity, σ would be zero and k would equal $\hat{k}$. The simpler case would prevail where the curves for traded products purchased and marginal private product coincide.

To obtain marginal social product, subtract the money value of the externality v from the money wage, and express the resultant as amount of composite commodity purchasable, adjusting for the satisfaction from choosing a more desired bundle than in the composite commodity. This gives $(w - v)(1 + \sigma)/(p_T + kp_L)$ which is the lowest curve in Figure 1-3.

The exact relationships between money wages, traded products purchased, and marginal private and social products in the simpler case of Figure 1-2 are seen to be only tendencies in the general case of Figure 1-3. As in the simpler case, the higher price of local products makes money wages higher in the larger city. If externalities raise costs of local products, there may be a tendency for money wages to be higher the greater is the externality. However, the relationship is no longer exact since, generally, externalities can impinge on location-fixed factors and can raise costs of producing traded products, neither of which need affect money wages necessary to attract labor. Externalities lower marginal private product because they raise the cost of local products as in the case of Figure 1-2 and because in the more general case they may raise the costs of producing traded products. The effect of externalities in lowering marginal private product reduces city size, but externalities for any given city size remain. Thus the argument that existing large cities tend to be too large is unaffected.

CITY SIZE POLICY

The framework that has been presented suggests that externalities provide a basis for evaluating policies that affect the distribution of activity among cities. Much of the remainder of this book undertakes a more detailed analysis of externalities based on this framework.

Reducing Externalities for a Given City Size

THEORETICAL PRICE OPTIMUM

In a frontal attack on externalities, attempts might be made to put a tax or price on the activities of producing units which shift production functions of other producers. A tax or price on an externality-causing activity s_i, exactly equal to marginal effect of the activity on outputs through shifter Q, is a so-called optimal tax.

As taxes are raised from zero toward their optimal values, the marginal private product curve is shifted upward, if, as seems reasonable, the decline in externality-causing activity has the effect of reducing marginal costs of producing traded and nontraded commodities. A manifestation of the gain from reducing the externality is likely to be that the production function shift (effect on Q due to smaller s_i's in response to the tax) lowering costs, is greater than the effect of the tax as a cost raising item. The marginal social product curve is shifted closer to the marginal private product curve since the higher tax on externality-causing activities reduces the divergence between marginal private and social costs. When the optimum tax is reached, the marginal social and private product curves coincide, as depicted by the curves in the upper part of Figure 1-1.

If pollution is not industrial, the City A curves should shift up more than for the rest of the economy. The hypothesis rests on the supposition that the main determinant of upward shift is the magnitude of externality which is being reduced by imposing the tax. Since the externality is greater in City A than in the rest of the economy, the potentiality for upward shift is greater. This hypothesis implies that City A will become larger as taxes on externality-causing activities are increased. At the distribution of resources between cities existing when taxes are raised, the marginal private product of resources, being raised further in City A than in the rest of the economy, will induce a movement to City A indicating that the new equilibrium must lie to the right. Thus the equilibrium point F where taxes are high enough to eliminate externalities is at a larger size of City A than equilibrium with externalities at point D.

As discussed earlier, externalities usually thought of in connection with increasing city size raise the costs of nontraded goods, because of traffic congestion and air pollution resulting from coal burning for household heat and exhaust from automobiles. Instituting a charge for causing pollution would have a direct impact in raising costs of producing housing-plus-access and other nonexported commodities, but the lowering of costs of producing the goods due to production function shifts would be expected to exceed the charges levied. Beneficiaries of the increased output due to the pollution charge consist of the group paying the pollution charges. With the fall in price of nontraded goods, the money wage necessary to attract labor to the city is lowered, inducing more firms producing traded goods to locate in the city. On the other hand, as discussed in the following section, it seems possible that taxing pollution from exported commodities would reduce city size.

ALGEBRAIC REPRESENTATION

Let the production functions in City A be $x_T = x_T(N_T, S_T, Q)$ for traded goods and $x_L = x_L(N_L, S_L, Q)$ for nontraded goods, where N_T and N_L are amounts of non-location-fixed resources, S_T and S_L are the externality-producing activities, and $Q = Q(S_T, S_L)$ is the shifter affected by these activities. Equilibrium conditions for use of non-location-fixed factors are familarly that marginal revenue equals marginal cost: $p_T x_{TN} = w$ and $p_L x_{LN} = w$, where second subscript refers to derivative with respect to that variable. A tax on externality-causing activities is a marginal cost of engaging in them and results in similar equilibrium conditions: $p_T x_{TS} = \pi_T$ and $p_L x_{LN} = \pi_L$, where the π's are the taxes per unit of the activity engaged in.

Let $\bar{N}$ be the total amount of non-location-fixed resources in City A ($\bar{N} = N_T + N_L$). Substitute $dQ/d\bar{N}$ obtained from the expression of Q into the derivatives of the production functions with respect to $\bar{N}$, and use the equilibrium conditions to substitute prices for partials (e.g., $x_{TN} = w/p_T$). Inserting the resulting expressions for $dx_T/d\bar{N}$ and $dx_L/d\bar{N}$ into the expression for the change in the value of output from employing an extra unit of non-location-fixed resources, $p_T(dx_T/d\bar{N}) + p_L(dx_L/d\bar{N})$, gives change in value

$$w + \pi_T(dS_T/d\bar{N}) + \pi_L(dS_L/d\bar{N}) \\ + (p_T x_{TQ} + p_L x_{LQ})[Q_T(dS_T/n\bar{N}) + Q_L(dS_L/d\bar{N})],$$

which in terms of Figure 1-3 is $w - v$.

With no attempt to control externalities π_T and π_L are zero. To find the π_T that maximizes output, obtain expressions for dx_T/dS_T and dx_L/dS_T by the same steps as for $dx_T/d\bar{N}$ and $dx_L/d\bar{N}$ except that differentiation is with respect to S_T, and insert them into the maximizing condition

$$p_T(dx_T/dS_T) + p_L(dx_L/dS_T) = 0. \tag{1}$$

Rearrangement of the result gives

$$\pi_T = -Q_T(p_T x_{TQ} + p_L x_{LQ}).$$ (2)

Similarly,

$$\pi_L = -Q_L(p_T x_{TQ} + p_L x_{LQ}).$$ (3)

Here Q_T and Q_L are changes in amount of public good, and $p_T x_{TQ} + p_L x_{LQ}$ is effect of a change in the public good on value of output. If $\hat{\pi}_T$ and $\hat{\pi}_L$ are inserted into the expression in the preceding paragraph for the value of output from employing an extra unit of non-location-fixed resources, the value reduces to w, that is, private and social product coincide. The conditions $\pi_T = \hat{\pi}_T$ and $\pi_L = \hat{\pi}_L$ underlie the marginal product curves in the topmost part of Figure 1-1.

The effects on city size of varying taxes between zero and values which maximize output may be considered supposing $Q = Q(S_T, S_L)$ takes the form $Q = S_T + S_L$ with $\pi = \pi_T = \pi_L$. Increasing the tax π in City A and π' in the rest of the economy shifts the marginal private product curves. By comparing the shifts, one can deduce whether the intersection resulting from a raise in the two tax rates will be moved to the right or left, that is, to the larger or smaller size of City A. Eliminate prices and wages from marginal private product $w(1 + \sigma)/(p_T + kp_L)$ by using the equilibrium conditions, for example, $w/p_T = x_{TN}$, and differentiate with respect to π. Rearranging and dividing by marginal private product gives the percentage change in marginal private product resulting from a change in π:

$$[p_T/x_{TN}(p_T + kp_L)][x_{TNN}dN_T/d\pi + x_{TNS}(dS_T/d\pi)$$
$$+ x_{TNQ}(dQ/d\pi)] + [kp_L/x_{LN}(p_T + kp_L)]$$
$$\times [x_{LNN}(dN_L/d\pi) + x_{LNS}(dS_L/d\pi) + x_{LNQ}(dQ/d\pi)].$$ (4)

To obtain vertical shifts, the differentiation indicated in this expression is carried out holding $\bar{N}$ constant, which implies $dN_T/d\pi + dN_L/d\pi = 0$. If the ratio of consumption of traded to nontraded commodities does not change and if production coefficients are not altered, there will be no change in N_T or N_L. Although these conditions are not likely to be fulfilled exactly, they suggest that $dN_T/d\pi$ and $dN_L/d\pi$ are small. The effects of an increase in externally-causing activity on the marginal productivity of labor, x_{TNS} and x_{LNS}, are likely to be positive, whereas $dS_T/d\pi$ and $dS_T/d\pi$ and $dS_L/d\pi$ are almost surely negative (rise in tax causes reduction in the activity), making the terms containing these derivatives negative. The main reason for the gain from a tax on externality-causing activities appears to be that the positive $dQ/d\pi$ terms, giving increments to production from reducing the externality-causing activity, are greater than the negative terms containing $dS_T/d\pi$ and $dS_L/d\pi$.

As an example, where externalities emanate mainly from local goods (large $dS_L/d\pi$), such as automotive pollution and congestion caused by commutation of city residents, taxing the externalities would cause a city to have cleaner air and lower rent gradients, and money wages would not be as high relative to wages in smaller cities as now. More manufacturers of labor-intensive transportable goods would locate in big cities instead of being driven to places of lower wages as they are at present. The city would become larger.

As an example of externalities from export production (large $dS_T/d\pi$), a pulp mill producing traded goods, if required to pay a charge for pollution, might be forced out of business in a given locality. While the improved environment would lower the wage necessary to keep labor in the area, the new industry attracted by the lower wages might not result in as much employment as the pulp mill.

PRICING IN PRACTICE

Even if city size is reduced, unless externalities impinge one city to another, the gains from eliminating externalities accrue within the city where they occur, and so there should be local incentives, for example, through city government, to take action against them. If eliminating externalities would be in the city's as well as in the nation's interest, the question of why residents of a city do not take action accordingly arises. Lack of awareness of adverse effects of pollution and congestion hardly provides a reason in view of the publicity they receive. Among several reasons are conflicts of interest within a city and resistance to paying for things for which no charge has traditionally been made. Other impediments result from difficulties in charge systems including costs of collection and lack of knowledge of what the charges should be.

The impediments suggest that, whereas there may be further progress in internalizing externalities, their complete internalization is unlikely. If so, there could be a role for both of the major policy directions, namely, taking account of externality differences in public decisions affecting the allocation of resources among cities, and finding ways to internalize externalities within a city.

References

1. Joint Economic Committee. *Impact of the Property Tax: Its Economic Implication for Urban Problems*. Washington, D.C.: U.S. Government Printing Office, 1968.
2. Meadows, D. *et al. Limits to Growth*. New York: Universe Books, 1972.
3. National Committee on Urban Growth Policy. *The New City*. New York: Frederick A. Praeger, Incorporated, 1969.

4. Netzer, D. *Economics of the Property Tax.* Washington, D.C.: Brookings, 1966.

5. Pigou, A. C. *The Economics of Welfare,* 4th ed. London: Macmillan and Co., 1932. (Originally titled *Wealth and Welfare.* London: Macmillan and Co., 1912.)

6. Task Force on Land Use and Urban Growth. *The Use of Land: A Citizen's Policy Guide to Urban Growth.* New York: Thomas Y. Crowell Company, 1973.

7. U.S. Advisory Commission on Intergovernmental Relations. *Urban and Rural America: Policies for Future Growth.* Washington D.C.: U.S. Government Printing Office, 1968.

8. U.S. Commission on Population Growth and the American Future. *Population and the American Future.* New York: New American Library, Signet Books, 1972.

9. U.S. Domestic Council, Committee on Community Development. *National Growth and Development.* Washington, D.C.: U.S. Government Printing Office, 1972, 1974.

10. U.S. National Commission on Urban Problems. *Building the American City.* Washington, D.C.: U.S. Government Printing Office, 1968.

11. U.S. National Goals Research Staff. *Toward Balanced Growth: Quantity with Quality.* Washington, D.C.: U.S. Government Printing Office, 1970.

12. U.S. President's National Advisory Commission on Rural Poverty. *The People Left Behind.* Washington, D.C.: U.S. Government Printing Office, 1967.

13. Weintraub, A., Schwartz, E., and Aronson, J. R. (Eds.). *The Economic Growth Controversy.* White Plains, New York: International Arts and Science Press, Inc., 1973.

2

Comparing the Gains and Costs of City Growth

GEORGE S. TOLLEY

The preceding chapter indicated that, if externalities are not fully internalized, city sizes will not be carried to the point where marginal benefits equal marginal costs. Some cities may be too big, and some may be too small. Numerous policies have been proposed in one way or another for altering the city sizes that would prevail in an unfettered market situation. The present chapter is concerned with how to use the ideas of the previous chapter operationally to gain quantitative insights about such policies.

The approach is to postulate a policy that will have a given effect on city size. The example used is a growth-retarding policy. Retardation of growth implies sacrificing privately perceived gains. These gains are reflected in willingness to bear the costs of greater daily travel mileage as a city grows. In addition to the privately perceived gains, one should consider external gains or costs of the growth that are not taken account of in private decisions. In this chapter, density changes are used as an example of external effects.

The chapter shows by example how order of magnitude estimates can be developed for comparing costs and gains of policies affecting city size. The chapter does not provide an evaluation of policies per se but rather illustrates a method that can be used to analyze policies in light of the extensive further list of externalities with which the remainder of the book is concerned.

Private and Social Benefits and Costs

The total change in income resulting from altering the location of activity as between urban areas is the sum of the increases in income for areas where economic activity is expanded minus the sum of the income decreases for areas where economic activity is diminished. The invisible hand assumption is that individual actions are carried to the point where extra gains just equal extra costs. If this assumption were fulfilled, the output of each city would be carried to the point where the cost of additional units of output was equal to the value of additional output. The market economy would achieve the spatial distribution of activities making the greatest contribution to national income. Any policy altering this distribution would have the net effect of decreasing national income. For cities reduced in size by a policy, output would be diminished by more than costs. For cities whose size was augmented, output would be raised by less than their increase in costs.

If the invisible hand assumptions were fulfilled, parts (a) and (b) of Figure 2-1 would each contain only one curve. In part (a) of Figure 2-1, for a city reduced in terms of originating income from A to C, suppose that each unit of reduction in income entails reductions of output by a dollar, indicated by movement along the horizontal line AC. Cost reductions would consist entirely of reductions in private costs, which would be progressively reduced moving along the marginal cost curve AB. The excess of the output reduction over the cost reduction would be the area ABC. By similar reasoning in part (b) of the figure, for a city increased in its income originating from F to H the excess of the cost increase over output increase would be the area FGH. The decrease in national income from a policy affecting the distribution of activity would be the sum of the ABC areas for cities reduced in size plus the sum of the FGH areas for cities increased in size.

There are many reasons why the invisible hand assumption is not fulfilled. In part (a) of Figure 2-1, a situation is shown where net costs are imposed on others when a city grows. The costs are largely unperceived by the individuals and firms causing them and are not taken into account in their actions. Pollution and congestion are examples of these largely unperceived external costs imposed on others when there is additional out-

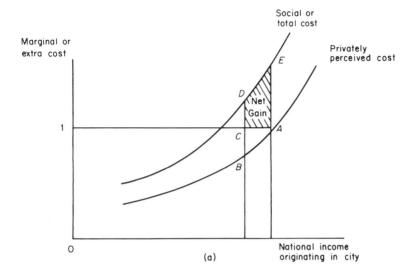

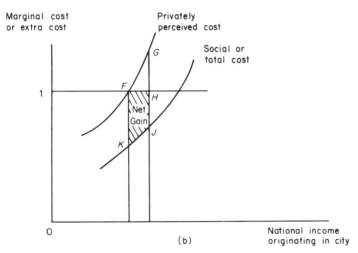

Figure 2-1. Changes in city size.

put in a large city. In Figure 2-1(a), the external cost imposed on others from an additional dollar of output in the city at its market equilibrium size is AE. Instead of there being a net cost to reducing the size of the city from A to C, there is a net gain. The cost reduction is now given by movement along the higher curve *ED*. The net gain from the reduction in city size is the difference between the private cost area *ABC* and the external gain area *ABDE*, or the shaded area *ACDE*.

The effect of the policy for the city in question can be estimated as the net sum of the two parts just noted. With regard to external costs *ABDE*, the change in city size (originating income) is unlikely to greatly affect marginal external costs *AE* for most realistic policies, since policies cannot realistically be expected to change sizes of large cities by more than a few percent. The change in external costs can thus be estimated as marginal external cost *AE* times change in output *AC*. The other part of the policy effect, which is the excess of the change in output over the change in private costs, is the area *ABC* previously considered. The effect on income *ACDE* from changing the size of the city is thus change in external costs *ABDE* minus the excess of change in output over change in private costs *ABC*. Estimating the area *ABC* requires quantifying how private costs vary with level of activity. Estimating the area *ABDE* requires quantifying externalities.

Figure 2-1(b) depicts a situation where there are external economies making costs less than privately perceived costs. Economies of scale are frequently cited as a phenomenon associated with city size. The economies can be internal or external. An example of an external economy is the effect of an increase in city size increasing density and thereby reducing costs of delivery and pickup. Pupil transportation and waste pickup services are two of many examples of functions whose cost is reduced by an increase in density. Economies due to density are external or unperceived in private decisions. People's bids for land, which determine density, reflect only the gains and costs to themselves taking as given the conditions facing them in the city. The reduction in costs of travel by other individuals, firms, or government entities due to greater density is not a part of the calculation influencing any individual actor's decision. Density is a production function shifter having the technical attributes of a public good. It shares the problem encountered with such goods that the full gains from having the good are not reflected in individual market decisions in the absence of government or other outside arrangements. Density is only one of several reasons for external economies of scale encountered at some stages of city growth. A later section discusses the order of magnitude of this density effect. In part (b) of Figure 2-1, the gain from increasing city size from *F* to *H* is *FHJK*, estimable as external economy *FGJK* less excess of additions to private costs over additions to output *FGH*.

Hopefully a population distribution will reduce city sizes for which there is a gain from city size reduction and will increase city sizes for which there is a gain from expansion. These are the situations depicted in Figure 2-1. The gains could, however, be negative if the relationship between private and social costs happened to be reversed. In part (a) of the figure, the social cost curve might lie below the private cost curve, and in part (b) of the figure social cost might be above private cost. For unemployment effects and for institutional or public finance effects, the relationship between social and private costs might vary geographically by region but not necessarily in any systematic way by city size. Thus these effects might make social costs greater or less than private costs.

Distance to Work

The preceding section indicates that the estimation of effects of population distribution policy subdivides into a concern with (a) external effects and (b) changes in private or direct costs from changing the amount of economic activity in an area. Among the reasons for changes in private costs is commuting and related daily travel. In a small town, these costs are small, and they increase with increasing city size. The rise in daily travel costs is one of the limiting considerations determining city size. The cost advantages from having some kinds of production in a large city are sufficient to compensate for large daily travel costs, but the rise in costs due to daily travel eventually raises the cost of additional output in the city relative to that in smaller cities. Daily travel costs appear to be the main reason why most of the nation's economic activity is not located in one huge city.

Complaints of residents of cities and general indignation over environmental conditions in larger cities have given impetus to recommendations that attempts be made to foster a growth pattern away from larger cities. Such recommendations could be justified on national income grounds as indicated above if the reduction in external environmental costs more than offsets the loss due to the greater reduction in output than in private costs, that is, if *ABDE* exceeds *ABC* in Figure 2-1. When city size is reduced, or when a city is kept from growing as much as it otherwise would, it is kept away from equilibrium point *A*. As reflected in market costs of resources indicating their opportunity returns, the labor and capital resources excluded from the city are producing less private returns elsewhere than if they were admitted to the city.

Suppose that the growth of an SMSA of 6 million persons is stopped for a decade, during which time its population would otherwise grow by 10%. In Figure 2-1, the city is kept at point *C* instead of being allowed to go to point *A*. If daily travel were the only reason for upward slope of the marginal cost curve, an estimate of the effects on the travel would enable estimation of the area ABC.

The number of persons living in a ring of width dr located r miles from the central business district is the area of the ring $2\pi r\ dr$ times the population density of the ring D_m. In this example the distances at issue are on the fringes of a large city where typical suburban densities may be expected to prevail, suggesting a reasonable assumption is a value of D_m of about 1000 persons per square mile. Let c be travel cost per mile, which will be assumed here to be $.10 per mile. Let τ be the daily travel per person to the central business district and to other destinations not affected by where the family lives, expressed as the number of round trips that could be taken to the central business district if the travel mileage were expended upon such trips only. If the population consisted entirely of four-person households, and if the only effect on travel of living further away from the central business district were to increase the commuting trip of the head of the household to the central business district, τ would be $\frac{1}{4}$, that is, one out of every four people making one standard trip each day. A consideration decreasing τ is that not all work trips are to the central business district. The fact that many shopping trips and goods deliveries involve a central travel destination tends to increase τ. Bearing in mind that τ is for travel from the outlying points of the city where growth takes place, refined estimates of τ could be made from travel surveys. In this example, it will be assumed that τ does not change over the range of city growth being considered. This assumption is probably defensible for the assumed growth range of only 10%. For a greater percentage range of growth, particularly if one were considering growth of a smaller city, τ would be expected to decline as distance from the central business district increased. This effect could be allowed for by expressing $\tau = \tau(r)$. The modifications of the formulas that follow are obvious and could be handled in exact numerical analysis.

Since the mileage for a round trip to the central business district is twice the distance to the central business district, there is extra mileage $2m - 2r$ of travel from the edge of the city over travel from a ring at distance r. Let m_1 refer to the distance to the edge of the city that would prevail if the city reached private equilibrium. The city size corresponding to m_1 is at point A in Figure 2-1(a). The mileage $2m_1 - 2r$ is extra travel it would be worthwhile to undertake from closer distances r and still cover the costs of output produced by persons living at distance r. For distances to which the city is not allowed to grow, the cost of traveling $2m_1 - 2r$ miles is a measure of the net gain foregone from not having people live at distance r. The sum of extra costs from the actual margin m_0, to which the city is constrained by a population distribution policy, up to the private equilibrium margin m_1, is the cost ABC in Figure 2-1(a). The cost is then the integral from m_0 to m_1 of the extra mileage $(2m_1 - 2r)$ times cost per mile c times number of standard trips per per person τ times population at that distance $D_m 2\pi r\ dr$. Assuming 250 work days per year, the yearly cost is obtained by multiplying by 250 to obtain

$$1000\pi c\tau D_m \int_0^{m_1} (m_1 - r)r\ dr \qquad (1)$$

which equals

$$1000\pi c\tau D_m[m_1(m_1{}^2 - m_0{}^2)/2 - (m_1{}^3 - m_0{}^3)/3]. \qquad (2)$$

Suppose the edge m_0 to which the city is constrained is 25 miles from the central business district. Under the assumption that additional growth would take place at suburban density of 1000 persons per square mile in a circular expansion, the area required for a growth of population of 600,000 would be such that the added area times the density would equal the added population, the condition is $(\pi m_1{}^2 - \pi m_0{}^2)\ 1000 = 600{,}000$, or $m_1 = (600/\pi + m_0{}^2)^{1/2}$. Given a value of m_0 of 25, the solution for m_1 is 28 miles.

All the needed values have now been given. Inserting the values into the foregoing centered expression indicates as the area ABC a yearly loss of $43 million, due to the movements along private costs curves if growth of the city is restricted by 10%.

Density

While city scale effects require attention to slope of the privately perceived cost curve determining the area ABC as just considered, most of the analysis of effects of population redistribution involves external or unperceived costs making a difference between height of private and social curves and determining the area $ABDE$. External or unperceived costs will be of concern in the remainder of the chapter.

As was pointed out in the opening section of this chapter, one reason for difference between private and social costs is the effect of city growth on density. Starting from very small towns and contemplating larger ones, average density of a town must rise as the increasing distance to work makes residential land near work places more valuable inducing the construction of denser housing including multifamily structures. Whether average density continues indefinitely to increase is moot. For an existing large city, the new growth on the city's edge will be at a suburban density which is exceeded in increasing magnitude by the higher densities prevailing nearer the center. Only if the further increase in density nearer the center induced by city growth overcomes the decrease due to the lowering effect on average density of the growth at the edge, will average density of the city increase. Buildings already in place which would have to be torn down to increase density will impede the density response. The possibility of development of new sub-centers within the city, instead of continuing to increase the densities in proximity to existing centers and subcenters, could further retard average density response. For these reasons, one at the least expects an eventual slowing in the increase in average density as a city grows, and conceivably there could be a fall.

For a city with a single center, the average density is determined by a density gradient beginning at the surburban density at the edge of the city and rising continuously up to maximum density at the center. If the city is not too large, density may rise by a constant exponential amount over the entire range:

$$D_r = D_m e^{kr}, \tag{3}$$

where D_m is density at the edge, m is the site of the city measured as the distance between the edge and the center, r is the distance from the edge going toward the center of the city and D_r is density measured as persons per square mile at the distance r.[1] If the city is circular, the population in a doughnut shaped ring is $D_r 2\pi r \, dr$ or substituting out the expression for D_r just given, $D_m d^{kr} 2\pi r \, dr$. Summing over all the rings between the margin and the center, the total population N of the city is $N = \int_0^m 2\pi D_m e^{kr} r \, dr$. Carrying out the integration gives

$$N = 2\pi D_m (e^{km} - 1 - k_m)/k^2. \tag{4}$$

Dividing population N by the city area A gives the average density of the city $\bar{D}$, or $\bar{D} = N/A$. To find out how average density is affected by city growth, differentiate $\bar{D}$ with respect to N and multiply by $N/\bar{D}$ to obtain the percentage change in average density resulting from a 1% increase in population, $(d\bar{D}/dN)(N/D) = 1 - (dA/dN)(N/A)$, which is a 1% increase in population minus the percentage change in city area. The problem thus reduces to finding the effect of population growth on city area. Again assuming the city is circular, its area A is $2\pi m^2$. Differentiating the area with respect to m and then multiplying by N/A reveals that the percentage increase in area resulting from a 1% increase in population $(dA/dN)(N/A)$ is $2(dm/dN)(N/m)$. Substituting this result into the equation for $(d\bar{D}/dN)(N/D)$, the percentage change in average density is

[1] For early evidence on density gradients see Richard Muth [2], and for more recent studies see various issues of the *Journal of Urban Economics*.

$$(d\bar{D}/dN)(N/D) = 1 - 2(dm/dN)(N/m). \tag{5}$$

To find the percentage increase in the distance m between the margin and the center as a result of the 1% increase in population, take the differential of the equation for population $N = 2\pi D_m(e^{km} - 1 - km/k^2)$, letting N and m vary. The result is

$$dN = (2\pi D_m/k)(e^{km} - 1) \, dm. \tag{6}$$

Solving for dm/dN and multiplying by N/m gives

$$(dm/dN)(N/m) = [1/k_m] - [1/(e^{km} - 1)], \tag{7}$$

which, inserted into Eq. (5), reveals the percentage change in average density resulting from a 1% change in population to be

$$(d\bar{D}/dN)(N/D) = 1 - 2\{[1/km] - [1/(e^{km} - 1)]\}. \tag{8}$$

Because of the possibility that the assumed shape of the density function is not suitable for predicting effects of growth of a very large city, a numerical example will be given for a city of 1 million persons. In the formula for population

$$N = 2\pi D_m(e^{km} - 1 - km)/k^2, \tag{9}$$

a population of about 1 million will be obtained by assuming a suburban density D_m of 1000 persons per square mile, increase in density per mile k going toward the center of .2 and distance m from margin to center of about 10 miles. Applying the value of km of 2 in the expression just given for $(d\bar{D}/dN)(N/D)$ indicates that the elasticity or percentage change in density resulting from a 1% change in population is .3.

The next task is to find the effect of change in density on costs. Whereas density is often found to be significant in studies of local government expenditures, systematic investigation of effects of density on costs has apparently not been undertaken. For purposes of a numerical example, a reasonable value of the elasticity of costs with respect to density is $-.1$. This is not an exact estimate but is a judgment suggested as being realistic, based on studies of waste collection costs and of education expenditures undertaken at the University of Chicago and on a review of other studies reported by Werner Hirsch [1].

Combining the foregoing results, the elasticity of percentage change in costs resulting from a 1% increase in population, due to effects on density, is the elasticity of costs with respect to density times the elasticity of density with respect to population, that is $-.1$ times .3, or $-.03$. The costs affected include all production involving significant daily travel in the city such as commuting already considered, much business pickup and delivery and a variety of local services provided by governments. For purposes of the example, suppose that one-third of the income produced in the city is subject to cost reduction. Then the elasticity of total costs, including both the commodities affected and those not affected, is one-third of − .03 or − .01. If the total income produced in the city is $2.5 billion, the effect on production costs of growth of the city population by 10%, or one-tenth, is one-tenth times − .01 times $2.5 billion or a cost savings of $2.5 million. In comparison with the example of the previous section and examples to be given later, it should be remembered that the result here is for a city of 1 million while the other examples are for a city of 6 million.

Conclusion

The example of an external effect used in this chapter has been density, in connection with which it has been postulated that the growth of a smaller city will have gains. Policy conclusions, if any were to be drawn, would pertain to smaller cities and would indicate unfulfilled gains from further expansion. However, the analysis of this chapter is partial because it does not consider other externalities. These additional externalities, most of which involve costs, will be the concern of the remainder of the book. In Chapter 13, the externalities will be brought together in an overall assessment using the general method developed in the present chapter.

References

1. Hirsch, W. *The Economics of State and Local Government.* New York: McGraw-Hill, 1970.
2. Muth, R. *Cities and Housing.* Chicago: Univ. of Chicago Press, 1969.

II
THE SCALE QUESTION

3

Scale Economies, Externalities, and City Size

BARTON SMITH
GEORGE S. TOLLEY

This chapter provides an introduction to scale economies and discusses how they affect equilibrium, and optimum city size. Since internal scale economies in producing a good or service imply a breakdown in competition leading, usually, to governmental provision, the thrust of this discussion will be toward external scale economies in the private sector. Internal economies will be considered in the context of the public sector with pricing, taxation and related issues taken up at that point.

External Scale Economies and City Size

External scale economies involve a firm bestowing by its activities benefits upon others, usually in the form of lower factor costs. These external benefits are like a public good in that the benefit to any individual is not affected appreciably by the number of those benefiting. Hence, the total value of these externalities becomes larger, the larger the population they fall upon. Therefore, a particular activity may have a greater effect in a heavily populated urban area than in a smaller community.

Such scale economies are usually associated with increases in the density of population and economic activity rather than total city size. The costs of providing electricity and telephone service to a city of one million covering, for instance, an area the size of Maryland would be greater than serving that same population contained within the bounds of present day Baltimore. Most of the economies of scale associated with "city size" can really be traced to the benefits of closeness and hence might more correctly be referred to as urban density economies or agglomeration economies.

If scale or agglomeration economies do exist whose nature resembles that of a positive externality, does their existence entail a nonoptimal market determined city size? To answer this question a simple model will be constructed in which a city is treated similarly to an industry producing one good. Here the good is a composite of outputs of all producers in the city. Two factors of production will be considered, land (L) and capital (K), which represent respectively the fixed and mobile resources available to the city. The city is assumed to face a perfectly elastic demand curve for its products. It is assumed that land is fixed in supply and that there are constant returns to scale associated with the size of the city's output.

One can draw cost curves, depicted in Figure 3-1, for the city as it produces more goods using greater quantities of mobile resources including labor, with the fixed supply of land.

Even though there are constant returns to scale, the cost curves are up-

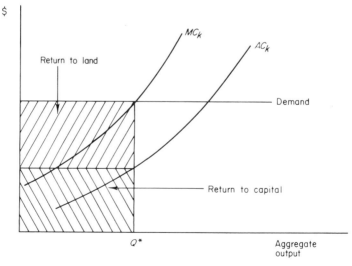

Figure 3-1. Costs and city size.

ward sloping here because land is fixed in supply and, as output increases, the price of land is bid up. The optimum output level is at Q^*, where the marginal cost of an additional unit of production by adding more mobile resources just equals its value or price. The private market equilibrium size will also be at this level. To see this, recognize that new firms will have an incentive to enter the city as long as the total average cost of production consisting of both capital and land costs is less than the price of the good. The emphasis on *total* average costs is important. Ellis and Fellner [1] proved that the marginal cost of adding more mobile factors when there are constant returns to scale is just equal to the average costs of all inputs together. This can be shown using a Cobb Douglas production function $Q = AK^\alpha L^{1-\alpha}$. The marginal cost of increasing Q by adding more K equals $MC_K = P_K K/Q\alpha$, and average capital cost $AC_K = P_K K/Q$. Land's share, $P_L L$, will equal $(1 - \alpha)Q$ and capital's share, $P_K K$, will equal αQ, assuming the price of Q is 1. It can be shown that $(MC_K - AC_K)Q$ is just equal to the return of land.[1] Therefore, $P_L L/Q = MC_K - AC_K$. But the total average cost of production (capital plus land costs) is equal to $(P_K K + P_L L)/Q = AC_K + (MC_K - AC_K) = MC_K$. Hence, the total average cost is just equal to the marginal cost of an additional unit of output by adding new capital to the city. But if this is the case then the private market equilibrium is in fact the social optimum. What is happening is that average costs from the firms' point of view are rising with city size, but they do so merely because of rising land rents with land fixed in supply. The externality, rising land prices to other firms, is pecuniary.

Now suppose that there exist scale economies, but that land is fixed in supply. The cost curves still must be upward sloping since otherwise the optimum size of the city would approach infinity. Therefore, for a finite optimum city size to exist, the economic restraint of fixed land must at some point outweigh the effects of economies of scale and the cost curves of the city must begin rising.

The city's equilibrium output (or size) will not coincide with the optimum in this case. The cost curves rise with rising land prices outweighing cost-diminishing economies of scale. The rising land prices are pecuniary effects, but the economies of scale represent a real social benefit imposed on others, a technological externality. It can be shown that social and private costs diverge, and that MC_K no longer equals the total average cost of production on the basis of which private location decisions are made.

A simple way to describe this scale economy effect is to distinguish between the city's aggregate production function and that of the firm.

[1] $(MC_K - AC_K)Q = \left(\dfrac{1}{\alpha} - 1\right)(P_K K/Q)Q = (1 - \alpha)P_K K/\alpha = (1 - \alpha)Q =$ Land's share.

$Q = AK^\alpha L^\beta$ for the city as a whole

$q = ak^{\alpha'} l^{\beta'}$ for individual firms (in range of equilibrium),   (1)

where the latter is homogeneous of degree one but the former need not be. It will be assumed that $\alpha + \beta > 1$ due to an external scale economy. Capital and land will receive their private marginal products and for simplicity it will be assumed that land's return will also equal its social marginal product (though this need not be the case). Thus,

$$P_K = \alpha' q/k = \alpha'(Q/K) \quad \text{and} \quad P_L = \beta' q/l = \beta(Q/L). \quad (2)$$

The *private decision rule* is that new firms will continue to enter the city until the total average cost equals the price of the good (assumed to equal 1), that is, until $(P_K K + P_L L)/Q = 1$. But since $P_L L/Q = \beta$, the private maximizing rule becomes $\beta + (P_K K + Q) = 1$. However, the *social maximizing rule* is that the marginal cost of increasing output by bringing in additional capital should just equal the price of the good, that is,

$$MC_K = 1 \quad \text{or} \quad \frac{1}{\alpha}\frac{P_K K}{Q} = 1. \quad (3)$$

If the social and private decision rules are the same then,

$$\beta + \frac{P_K K}{Q} - \frac{1}{\alpha}\frac{P_K K}{Q} = 0 \quad \text{or} \quad \beta - \frac{1-\alpha}{\alpha}\frac{P_K K}{Q} = 0. \quad (4)$$

If $\beta = 1 - \alpha$, then $P_K K/Q$ will equal α (since $P_L L + P_K K = Q$), and this equation is true. This is the case of constant returns to scale. However, if $\beta > 1 - \alpha$, that is, if the city's production function is homogeneous of degree greater than 1, exhibiting scale economies, then the left hand side of the equation will be greater than zero. In this case, $P_K K/Q < \alpha$, and hence $\beta - (1 - \alpha)(P_K K/Q\alpha) > 0$, since $\beta > (1 - \alpha)$, and $(1/\alpha)(P_K K/Q) < 1$. This indicates that the total average costs perceived by potential entrants to the city are greater then the social marginal costs of the additional output and the city will be too small. The scale economies shift the private average cost curve above the social marginal cost curve just as negative externalities tend to shift it below the social marginal cost curve.

If the assumption of a fixed supply of land is relaxed the same basic conclusions still hold. If land is perfectly elastic in supply then the cost curve of the city will be continuously downward sloping as long as the scale economies persist, and the optimum city size will approach infinity. However, if land is in fact inelastic in supply, as can be conceived in the case where the costs of new land acquisition is the increased transportation costs at the periphery, then rising land costs may finally outweigh the scale effects and lead to rising cost curves. But, as Lave [4] has pointed out, the introduction of transportation costs and land price gradients do not in themselves create any market distortions. Each new entrant fully considers the additional costs he must face in terms of increased transportation costs. What an entrant does not consider is the higher land costs that will be imposed on firms and residents already in the area. But again, these higher land costs are merely a pecuniary effect or transfer and therefore no social externality exists. If, however, there are scale economies (positive externalities) or perhaps congestion costs associated with transportation (negative externalities, as suggested by Lave), then these social benefits or costs not considered by the potential entrant represent true externalities and will create a divergence between the private and social cost curves leading to nonoptimality.

Private Sector Illustrations

Examples of real world scale phenomenon which are represented by the foregoing model are many. An important example of external economies whereby one actor shifts the production functions of other actors arises from the advantages to firms of being in labor markets where there is a wide variety of persons to draw upon. In larger labor markets with their greater variety of labor, people and tasks can be better matched. When a person leaves a job, there is likely to be less vacancy time until a replacement is found in view of the larger pool to draw from. A firm coming into an area increases the size of the local labor market enabling more people to live and work there. The better matching of people and jobs and the reduced vacancy times are production function shifters for all firms, increasing the amount they can produce for given expenditure on inputs. The firm deciding to locate in the town will typically have little or no awareness of the benefits conferred on other firms.

Communications may lead to similar external economies. In a place where there are many firms engaged in similar activities, having many suppliers and many customers, information about purchases and sales is more readily available than in isolated places. This information advantage may lead a firm to locate where there are already similar firms. The benefit from so doing will be greater than appears to the individual firm, because the information network is enlarged, redounding to the benefit of firms already in the area.

Greater specialization in production is achieved in larger cities, whenever the minimum city size needed to support one unit of a particular kind of productive factor is surpassed. Restaurants, sports, and theater, and the variety in these activities are sometimes cited as reflecting advantages of cities. These can be viewed as the result of greater division of labor on the product side made possible with expanding city size, which is essentially the same phenomenon that occurs for division of labor in retailing, services, and inputs for industry. The phenomenon can be analyzed as a rise in local demand curve as city size increases so a portion of the demand curve comes to lie above the downward sloping average cost curve for a product. The rise in demand curve makes it possible to cover costs leading firms to form to produce products previously unprofitable.[2] That the first productive unit can charge monopolistic prices for its services until a second producer enters should be noted; this implies that the cost curve continues to fall due to specialization even after the critical population size needed to support one unit is surpassed.

In a more concrete vein, larger cities imply a reduction in average transport costs associated with pickup and delivery of interfirm goods. Incentives to save on transport costs lead to tendencies for suppliers and customers for intermediate products at all stages of production to locate together. The fact that one supplying industry, for example, steel, has many customer industries and that one customer industry, such as automobiles, has many supplying industries leads to a compounding of effects.

These effects are reinforced by the density implications of city largeness, as discussed earlier. As an example, an increase in density will reduce transport costs within the city, if the gains from reduced delivery distances are not offset by congestion costs. As a town grows, increased commuting time raises the value of being near the center. Consequently, land prices are bid up giving incentives to increase the density of land use, and an indirect result then is that delivery and pickup times involved in providing various private and public services are reduced. The change in density will act as a production shifter, changing the amount of services that can be supplied for a given amount of inputs. In the case of density, the delivery and pickup services whose costs are affected are not necessarily to and from the center of town. The costs are those involved in any daily route activity such as transportating pupils to and from school, performing garbage pickup, and delivering goods to residences and stores scattered about the town. The economy comes from the fact that, with greater density, fewer travel costs are incurred between units served so

---

[2] A further issue is raised by variety per se: Does simply having a wider array of products to choose from increase satisfactions? If so, there is an external or unpriced effect for which producers of a new product are not compensated. Usual demand analysis throws no light on the question since it assumes a fixed number of commodities available. A subjective hypothesis is that the effect of variety per se definitely exists but has quantitatively minor externality effects. The hypothesis stems from the belief that the products themselves and not the potential for choosing among them are the major source of satisfaction.

that more services can be performed per unit of travel cost inputs. In an earlier work by Tolley [5] it was tentatively estimated for a city of 1 million persons that growth of population by 1% would reduce costs of total output of the city by .01% due to the induced increase in density. An implication is that an extra worker coming to the city adds about 1% more to total product than indicated by his market wage. More reliable estimates including a range of town sizes would require more detailed study of variation in density with respect to population and additional estimates of how costs vary with density. Possibly for small towns the density effect on costs is pronounced, but becomes less pronounced at larger city sizes when density is so high that travel cost between stops has fallen to a small fraction of total costs.

The externalities considered to this point all accrue locally in the town experiencing growth. A national, as opposed to a local, externality is implied by the hypothesis advanced by some that increased size of city leads to greater innovation (see Jacobs [3]). A production function for innovations can be conceived in which explanatory variables are inputs deliberately devoted to producing the innovations, various scale factors specific to the innovative effort (e.g., size of universities and research projects), and considerations not specific to the innovations which may influence them. A hypothesis apparently is that these latter considerations may be associated with city size. If true, production functions for innovations will be shifted as cities grow, so that there are external economies conceptually similar to those for density, labor markets, and communication already discussed. How important city size is relative to other factors influencing innovations and how important the innovation externality may be relative to other external economies and diseconomies remains unresolved at the present time.

Data limitations present a severe problem in estimating scale economies. It seems, however, that very rough estimates can be made from existing data to help evaluate their importance for policy issues associated with city growth. What is desired is the relationship between city size and the price (or average costs) of goods and services excluding the effects of rising factor prices inelastic in supply. As has already been shown, the total AC curve of the city must be rising where rising factor prices outweigh falling average costs due to scale economies. Therefore, in order to estimate the extent of the scale economies the effect of those rising pecuniary returns must be excluded.

Ideally, then, one would substract out the effect or rising land prices and the prices of other resources fixed in supply. However, the data required for this adjustment are not available. This obstacle can be partially overcome by examining wage data for cities of different size rather than land value data. If labor is perfectly mobile, it will not receive any pecuniary benefits from city growth. It will neither gain nor lose. Consequently, rising money wages must go to compensate labor for both rising prices attributable to pecuniary rent increases and for rising or falling real costs of urban living. If we substract the effect of rising wages from the changes in price, we can then roughly ascertain the magnitude of urban scale economies. If the concern is the "net" effect of city growth then, of course, rising real costs of urban living should not be excluded. However, since social costs such as crime, pollution, and congestion are to be treated separately and since the concern here is the scale economies alone, then the entire effect of rising wages should be eliminated with one minor exception. That part of higher wages that go toward paying additional transportation costs should not be excluded. Budget studies provided by the Bureau of Labor Statistics indicate that the amount would be quite small in comparison to the total change in wages as city size gets larger. Hence, one can be reasonably confident that its exclusion will not lead to any major error. Also, since the effect of rising industrial land prices (which also is quite small) is not excluded, this will tend to offset the upward bias in estimating economies of scale due to excluding the entire increase in wages associated with larger cities.

Considering these and other issues, Israeli concluded that there is strong empirical evidence for the presence of scale economies for the entire private sector.[3] He ran regressions of various price indices upon the population excluding the effect of wage increases. The results indicated an elasticity of prices with respect to population of about − .03.[4] That is, a 10% increase in population of a city of 6 million (about the size of Chicago) with an approximate level of private value added of 18 billion dollars would create .003 times 18 billion or 54 million worth of external benefits in the form of lower prices. This estimate is an underestimate since it is based on a price index weighted heavily on the prices of nontraded goods (locally produced consumer goods with a local market only). The prices of these goods including wage effects rise substantially with city size, whereas goods marketed nationally would be expected to have invariant prices with city size. Consequently, the prices of nationally marketed goods *excluding* wage effects must fall even more with increasing city size. Israeli's results do not explicitly show but implicitly suggest that the elasticity of prices excluding wage changes with respect to population for nationally marketed goods is approximately − .07. This is based on an assumed elasticity of prices including wage effects with respect to population of 0.0 and an estimated elasticity of wages with respect to population

[3] See Chapter 12.
[4] In essence, this represents an elasticity of real average costs with respect to population. All pecuniary effects are excluded.

of from .07 to .09. Assuming that one-third of the total value added is marketed nationally then scale economy benefits from a 10% increase in population would be .003 times 12 billion plus .007 times 6 billion, or 78 million dollars.

Public Sector Illustrations

Though the discussion of external scale economies in the preceding section has been limited primarily to the private sector, the analysis presented at the beginning of this chapter applies to the public sector as well. Consider a residential community which provides certain basic services that have many characteristics typical of a public good, where the per capita cost of these services decreases as the population increases. As population expands, land prices will increase as families are forced to move further out. Assume that individuals are charged the average cost of these social services. Then the cost any one individual will consider in deciding to live in the community is the average cost of the social services he consumes plus the sum of the transportation and land costs (which is equal to the total transportation cost per person from the edge of the community) he must incur to live there.

As population increases in the community, the average cost of the social services will fall but the average land and transportation costs will rise. The sum of these two most likely will form a U-shaped cost curve illustrated by *AC* (private) in Figure 3-2. Families will enter until average

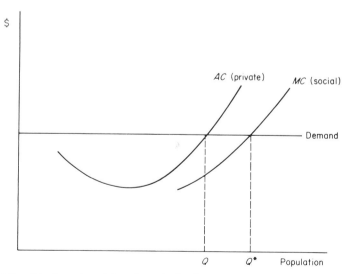

Figure 3-2. Private and social costs and city size.

costs, given by the height of this curve, equal the value of living in this area indicated by the height of the demand curve. This occurs at city size Q. However, from the social point of view the optimum decision rule is that the marginal social cost of one new entrant should be equal to the value placed on living there. But the marginal social cost is equal to the marginal cost of providing the social services plus the marginal cost of additional transportation. The latter is just equal to an additional trip from the edge of the city. However, since the marginal cost of social services is less than the average cost, the overall marginal social cost—MC (social) in the figure—will be less than AC (private) and hence the market determined level of population will be less than the optimum level, Q^*.

As before, the private average cost curve is rising despite falling costs for social services because transportation and land costs are rising faster, outweighing the effects of the former. Since no congestion costs are assumed, there are no externalities associated with transportation costs and rising land prices since the former is fully considered by the new entrant and the latter is merely a pecuniary transfer. What remains, falling costs of social services, represents the only social cost externality, bestowing positive benefits upon the current residents. Thus, the presence of this positive externality will result in a less than optimum city size.

As a final note from the diagram, one can see that had the community been pricing at marginal cost for the services provided, then the private and social decision rules would have been the same and optimality would have been reached. Such a scheme would create one difficulty, however, since the community would be running a continual deficit, not covering total costs. In order to cover the deficit and still retain an optimum population taxes must be charged such that they do not intervene or distort private location decisions. This could be accomplished by either imposing a local site value tax or by creating a uniform national tax revenue structure to cover such expenses.

The public sector, while exhibiting some *external* scale economies due to density effects as just indicated, differs from the private sector in that many of the goods produced by government are characterized by *internal* scale economies. Indeed, as emphasized in price theory, this is the usual justification for their collective provision.

Utility outputs and local road and rail services are examples of outputs serving as intermediate inputs to virtually all firms and households in a city which, due to indivisibilities, may continue to exhibit a downward sloping cost curve to extremely large city sizes. How the pricing of such outputs affects national income via city size effects, and what prices should be to give incentive to maximize national income, are not completely solved questions. The usual idea is that marginal cost pricing should be followed. Yet, with marginal cost pricing, the output in question might fall short of covering its total costs. In this event, an issue deserving investigation is whether the losses should be borne by the residents of the city where they occur or by the nation at large. If borne by residents of the city, the attractiveness of the city to labor may be affected altering the amount of industry locating there. The method of financing will thus affect city size, and the unresolved issue becomes which method will result in the greater national income.

It may be that the method of financing giving greatest gain is one where the price faced by persons deciding whether to live in the town equals marginal cost, with losses covered either out of national revenues or by site taxes in the town in question. Site taxes are on land only and not on buildings, and thus are not the same as traditional property taxes. Local reliance on property taxes probably goes only a fraction of the way in meeting the suggested way of covering losses, since buildings are typically a larger component of total property value than is land. A hypothesis therefore is that the present method of financing local services imparts a tendency for the services to be priced above marginal cost, indicating an unrealized source of gains from expanding a town which has not yet exhausted the scale economies in providing the services.

A similar pricing problem arises in connection with increasing division of labor as a city expands, as discussed in connection with the private sector. The aggregation of goods and services for purposes of analysis draws attention away from their limitless variety, which is reflected in a variety of tasks in making them. Specialization in these tasks can lower the costs of performing them, providing the demand is great enough to exhaust the initial economies of scale in specializing. Examples are provided by the increasing specialization found in retailing, services, and inputs for industry found as city size increases. There is a size of market at which a given specialization just becomes profitable, for example, selling pianos, but at that point there is room for only one piano store. A further doubling of size of market is likely to be needed to make it profitable for a second piano store to operate. An instructive exercise would be to find, for different towns and cities, those firms serving local markets which are one or few in number and hence facing downward sloping demand curves. Their monopoly or oligopoly position is limited by the competition from non-specializing firms or alternative supply sources out of town, for example, one can order a piano by mail or travel to other places to buy it. The existence of increasing division of labor as a city expands thus implies that there will always be imperfect competition, making for pricing tendencies keeping the output from expanding to the point where marginal gain equals marginal cost. However, potential competition exerts a restraining influence. Whether cities are seriously undersized as a result of the imperfect competition associated with increasing division of labor remains to be investigated empirically.

As in the case of the private sector, some limited progress has been made in determining the magnitude of scale economies in the provision of public services. Gardner examined scale economies associated with public services, holding quality constant (by use of various quality demand shifters) and concluded that though many components of the public sector did not display scale economies, some important ones did: fire protection, the provision of sewer services, and the provision of sanitation services.[5] This general finding is substantiated by several others.[6] Gardner's regressions suggest that scale economies in parts of the public sector could be quite substantial. For instance, a 10% population increase for a city of 1 million would bestow benefits of 11 million dollars to previous residents in the form of lower fire protection costs per year and similarly the gains attributable to scale economies in the provision of sewer facilities would be nearly 13 million dollars. These effects seem quite large and it should be remembered that these represent real social savings, not merely pecuniary effects. Were they construed as representative of the entire public sector the magnitude of the positive externalities associated with city size would be enormous. However, these results are at best tentative and, indeed, Gardner even finds that the public sector as a whole shows definite signs of net scale diseconomies, though the shape of the cost curve is somewhat hard to rationalize.[7]

As the reader must now suspect, some of the economies and diseconomies have been at best tenuously quantified, and others have not been quantified at all. A hypothesis is that many of the external economies are gradually exhausted as city size increases. Meanwhile, the environmental diseconomies are notably lacking in small towns and rise progressively with increasing city size. Pending more quantification, the tentative conclusion may be warranted that external effects tend to make small towns too small and large cities too large. Thus, in our examples of scale economies a city size of 1 million has been used suggesting that such cities are too small, while in other discussions throughout the book a city of 6 million is used to illustrate the negative environmental externalities suggesting that such cities are too large.

---

[5] See Chapter 4.

[6] See, for example, Hirsch [2].

[7] Considering the studies together we suggest that a 1% increase in city size might reduce average costs of some activities (e.g., education, waste collections, business communication, and transportation) by .03%. This might mean a cost savings on the order of $2.5 million from expanding a city of 1 million population by 10%.

References

1. Ellis, H. and Fellner, W., External Economic Diseconomies." *American Economic Review,* 1943, 493–511.
2. Hirsch, Werner Z., "The Supply of Urban Public Services." *Issues in Urban Economics,* H. S. Perloff and L. Wingo, Jr. (Eds.). Baltimore: Johns Hopkins Press, 1968. Pp. 477–525.
3. Jacobs, J. *The Economy of Cities.* New York: Random House, 1969.
4. Lave, L. R., "Congestion and Urban Location." *Papers and Proceedings of the Regional Science Association* **25,** 1970, 133–150.
5. Tolley, G. S., "National Growth Policy and the Environmental Effects of Cities." *Journal of Environmental Economics and Management,* forthcoming.

4
City Size and
Municipal Service Costs[1]

JOHN L. GARDNER

This chapter reports on research to identify determinants of municipal expenditure levels in the United States. A major goal has been to determine jointly the role of income and wealth levels, city size variables which influence service costs, and characteristics of community decision making relevant in the determination of expenditure levels. An additional goal has been to develop a method for identifying determinants of the levels of municipal service costs from observations on expenditures rather than on service output variables. In the following exposition, the proposed model is sketched, and then selected regression results are presented, the latter oriented particularly toward revealing the influence of city population size as a shifter of the municipal service cost functions.

[1] This study is an outgrowth of conversations between the author and George Tolley, Terry Clark, and Yi Wang. The formal modeling approach of the first part of the chapter was suggested by Inman [3]. The decision structure variables and the 51-city survey are discussed more fully in Clark [1]. A study with similar objectives with respect to economies of scale in provision of municipal services is Hirsch [2].

Modeling the Municipal Expenditure Decision

A basic assumption of the analysis is that through exercise of a majority voting procedure, the wishes of the median-income family govern the setting of expenditure levels in a city. The decision is postulated to be made in such a way as to maximize the utility function,

$$U = a_0(X_1 - x_1)^{a_1}(X_2 - x_2)^{a_2} \cdots (X_S - x_S)^{a_S}(Z_m - z)^b \qquad (1)$$

subject to the median-income family's budget constraint,

$$I_m - T_m^* = Z_m + T_m, \qquad (2)$$

where

X_s = level of the sth municipal service provided to each resident family in the city, for $s = 1, 2, \ldots, S$,

Z_m = expenditures on goods and services other than municipal services $1, 2, \ldots, S$ consumed by the median income family,

I_m = median family income in the city,

T_m = taxes paid by the median-income family to the city government to support services $1, 2, \ldots, S$,

T_m^* = taxes paid by the median income family to higher levels of government (i.e., county, state, federal),

the symbols a_i, x_i, z, and b are constants.

The X_s variables represent municipal service output levels, assumed provided equally to every family in the city, for example, level of public safety, expected yearly loss from fire damage to a given value of capital stock, or purity of sewage-treatment-plant effluent. Since such variables are difficult to quantify and measure, it is desirable to deduce properties of expenditure functions from the constrained maximization hypotheses.

Provision of the municipal services is assumed to be governed by linear cost functions of the form

$$E_s = c_{s0}X_s + \sum_{k=1}^{K} c_{sk}Y_{sk} + c_{s,K+1} + u_s, \qquad s = 1, 2, \ldots, S, \qquad (3)$$

where

E_s = minimum expenditure required to provide level X_s of the sth service to each family,

Y_{sk} = cost–function shifters for the sth service ($k = 1, 2, \ldots, K$),

c_{sk} = constants ($k = 0, 1, 2, \ldots, K, K + 1$),

u_s = random disturbance, representing the combined influence of unspecified factors on E_s.

In this formulation, municipal services are assumed not to be public goods in the sense that a given service level can be provided at constant total cost, regardless of the number of families served. Instead, population size is one of the possible shifters of this service cost function indicated by Y_{sk} in Eq. (3); an increase in population size may either shift the function up (a diseconomy of city growth) or down (an economy), the pure public goods case being an extreme case of the latter type of response.

Taxes are assumed to be collected from each of the N families in the city according to the tax formula

$$T_n = f + g \times (I_n - T_n^*), \qquad (4)$$

where T_n represents the tax paid to the city, T_n^* the tax paid to higher levels of government, and I_n represents the income of the nth family.

Assume that the government balances its budget:

$$R + \sum_{n=1}^{N} T_n = N \sum_{s=1}^{S} E_s, \qquad (5)$$

where R, intergovernmental revenue collected by the city government. Then the budget constraint faced by the median voter can be expressed in such a form as to involve the independent variables but not the E_s variables. This can be seen by combining Eqs. (4) and (5) to produce

$$R + \sum_{n=1}^{N} [f + g \times (I_n - T_n^*)] = N \sum_{s=1}^{S} E_s, \qquad (6)$$

from which

$$g = (1/\bar{I}^*) \left(\sum_{s=1}^{S} E_s - \frac{1}{N} R - f \right), \qquad (7)$$

where $\bar{I}^* = (1/N)\sum_{n=1}^{N}(I_n - T_n^*)$ = average income net of taxes paid to higher levels of government. Combining this in turn with Eqs. (2), (3), and (4) yields as a form of the median family's budget constraint

$$I_m^* = Z_m + f + (I_m^*/\bar{I}^*)$$
$$\times \left[\sum_{s=1}^{S} \left(c_{s0} X_s + \sum_{k=1}^{K} s_{sk} Y_{sk} + c_{s,K+1} + u_s \right) - \frac{1}{N} R - f \right], \qquad (8)$$

where $I_m^* = I_m - T_m^*$ is the income of the median-income family, net of taxes paid to higher levels of government.

Necessary conditions for a constrained maximum are now found by writing the Lagrangian based on Eqs. (1) and (8) and differentiating successively with respect to each of the X_s variables and Z_m. The result is an $S + 2$ equation system consisting of the equations

$$0 = \frac{a_s U}{X_s - x_s} - \lambda(I_m^*/\bar{I}^*)c_{s0},$$

$$0 = \frac{bU}{Z_m - z} - \lambda, \tag{9}$$

and the budget constraint Eq. (8), where λ is a Lagrange multiplier. From Eqs. (9) and (10)

$$0 = \frac{a_s}{X_s - x_s} - \frac{b}{Z_m - z}\left(\frac{I_m^*}{\bar{I}^*}\right)(c_{s0}), \qquad s = 1, 2, \ldots, S \tag{10}$$

from which

$$(a_s/b)(Z_m\bar{I}^*/I_m^*) - (za_s/b)(\bar{I}^*/I_m^*) = (X_s - x_s)c_{s0}, \\ s = 1, 2, \ldots, S \tag{11}$$

from which, finally,

$$E_s = (a_s/b)(Z_m\bar{I}^*/I_m^*) - (za_s/b)(\bar{I}^*/I_m^*) \\ + \sum_{k=1}^{K} c_{sk}Y_{sk} + (s_{s,K+1} - x_s c_{s0}) + u_s, \qquad s = 1, 2, \ldots, S. \tag{12}$$

These are structural equations for the S types of municipal expenditures. A system of equations which jointly determines the E_s variables together with the adjusted median family's expenditures on goods and services $(Z_m\bar{I}^*/I_m^*)$ is formed by Eq. (12) and the identity

$$R/N + \bar{I}^* = (Z_m\bar{I}^*/I_m^*) + f \times (\bar{I}^*/I_m^* - 1) + \sum_{s=1}^{S} E_s, \tag{13}$$

which is derived from Eq. (8).

The linear form of Eq. (12) makes it directly usable as a regression function. The indicated estimation procedure is two-stage least squares, since $(Z_m\bar{I}^*/I_m^*)$ is an endogenous variable of the system. In the first stage, $(Z_m\bar{I}^*/I_m^*)$ should be regressed on all of the exogenous variables of the system, including average income $(R/N + \bar{I}^*)$. In the second stage, expenditures E_s should be regressed on the calculated values of $(Z_m\bar{I}^*/I_m^*)$ from the first stage, on the ratio of average to median disposable income in the city $\bar{I}^*/I_m^*$, and on the explanatory variables which appear in the cost function. It is of interest also that shifters of the utility function might also be added to the list of regressors, in the form of an expansion of the variable x_s both in the utility function, Eq. (1), and in Eq. (12).

An expression for the sum of municipal expenditures in all categories can be derived easily from Eqs. (12) and (13). The indicated regression method is ordinary least squares, regressing $\Sigma_{s=1}^{S} E_s$ on average income, the ratio of average to median income, and all the exogenous cost- and utility-function shift variables from all the equations.

Variables and Data

In applying this framework, data were compiled for 51 cities, for nine different municipal services. The services were selected because they are provided by all the municipal governments in the sample. Expenditures in three service categories were separated into capital and current. The 51 cities were selected on the basis that information on local decision-making was available for them based on interviews conducted by the National Opinion Research Center. For the dependent variables, figures on municipal expenditures were obtained from issues of *City Government Finances*, a yearly publication of the U.S. Bureau of the Census, for fiscal years 1965 through 1970. For each service, the dependent variable was average yearly municipal expenditures divided by the number of families in the city in 1960, taken from U.S. Census of Population reports.

Considering the independent variables, average family disposable income, in dollars, for the year 1959, was the instrumental variable in the two stage regressions. It was calculated from figures on aggregate personal income reported in the 1962 City and County Data Book, and from data on intergovernmental transfers and governmental revenues in the 1966–1967 issue of *City Government Finances*. Aggregate disposable income of each city was estimated as aggregate personal income in 1959, less estimated tax payments from the city to the state and federal governments. The two tax amounts were estimated by assuming that the portion of the revenue of the federal or state government originating in each locality was proportional to the aggregate personal income of that locality.

The right-hand endogenous variable, average private family expenditure (corresponding to $Z_m \bar{I}^*/I_m^*$ in the theory) was estimated as city personal income plus intergovernmental revenue of the city less taxes paid by city residents to all levels of government. [This amounts to assuming that $f = 0$ in Eq. (13).]

Two wealth variables were included, median educational attainment of persons 25 years old or older in 1960, and assessed taxable property per family, taken respectively from 1960 census reports and from Table 18 of the 1967 *U.S. Census of Governments*. They were assumed, respectively, to be measures of human and nonhuman capital in each city.

The ratio of average to median family disposable income was included, as suggested by the theory. Estimated tax payments by local residents to state and federal government were subtracted from median income figures for 1959 taken from the 1960 census reports, to obtain the denominator.

The 1960 population of the city (and its square) and 1960 population density, together with 1969 average hourly wages of production or nonsupervisory workers in manufacturing, were included as shifters of the municipal service cost functions. The source for the manufacturing wage variable was U.S. Bureau of Labor Statistics Bulletin 1370-7, *Employment and Earnings Statistics for States and Areas, 1939–69*.

Three variables were included to characterize the decision-making structure in each of the cities. Percentage of Irish was included in recognition of the fact that this group has been disproportionately involved in city government, and hypothesizing that the more a given segment of the population tends to supply manpower for governmental agencies, the more that sector will favor governmental expansion. The data were taken from 1960 census reports.

Political leadership and business leadership variables were based on results of interviews with community leaders in each of the 51 cities. Informants were asked to identify the persons particularly influential in local decision making; the actors who were identified were categorized. Factor analysis was then performed to reduce the categories to a manageable number. Two leadership groups emerge: (1) actors identified with the business community—Chamber of Commerce, newspaper, industrial, retail, and financial leaders; (2) political figures such as leaders of the Democratic and Republican parties, labor unions, and agencies of the local government. The variables included in the regressions are the factor scores for each city on these two scales.

Results and Conclusions

Regression coefficients were computed using both two-stage least squares and ordinary least squares methods. The coefficients differed only negligibly between the two sets of results; the two-stage estimates are tabulated in Table 4-1.

At least one of the variables in each category just described—income and wealth variables, community leadership variables, and cost variables—is significant for each of the services for which analysis was done, although the specific variables within each group which are significant differ from service to service. In the regressions for expenditures for

TABLE 4-1

Regression Results[a]

Independent variables	Highways			Police	Fire
	Total	Capital	Other		
Constant	−100.	−99.	−2.0	−27.	23.
	$(-1.6)^{\triangle}$	$(-2.2)^*$	$(-.068)$	$(-.61)$	$(.71)$
Average private family expenditure (in thousands)	−.81	−5.0	4.2	6.5	15.
	$(-.077)$	$(-.64)$	$(.83)$	$(,88)$	$(2.5)^*$
Median education	18.	17,	.59	−.69	−6.6
	$(2.8)^{**}$	$(3.7)^{**}$	$(.20)$	$(-.15)$	$(-2.0)^*$
Average/median family income	−9.5	−14.	4.6	−1.1	−2.3
	$(-.70)$	$(-1.4)^{\triangle}$	$(.72)$	$(-.12)$	$(-.30)$
Taxable property per family (in thousands)	.83	.42	.41	3.4	1.6
	$(.73)$	$(.50)$	$(.77)$	$(4.2)^{**}$	$(2.7)^{**}$
Manufacturing wage	1.2	−1.2	2.5	7.5	3.8
	$(.11)$	$(-.14)$	$(.45)$	$(.92)$	$(.61)$
Percent Irish	−.24	−1.5	1.3	.95	3.9
	$(-.094)$	$(-.80)$	(1.0)	$(.52)$	$(2.9)^{**}$
Business leadership	.0081	2.9	−2.9	−1.2	−1.7
	$(.002)$	$(.85)$	$(-1.3)^{\triangle}$	$(-.37)$	$(-.70)$
Political leadership $(\times 10^6)$	−.46	−.39	−.070	−.85	−.96
	$(-.86)$	(-1.0)	$(-.28)$	$(-2.3)^*$	$(-3.5)^{**}$
Density (in thousands)	−1.7	−.71	−.96	1.6	.32
	$(-1.4)^{\triangle}$	$(-.78)$	$(-1.7)^{\triangle}$	$(1.8)^*$	$(.50)$
Population (in thousands)	.018	.032	−.014	.071	.079
	$(.82)$	$(2.0)^*$	$(-1.4)^{\triangle}$	$(4.6)^{**}$	$(1.6)^{\triangle}$
Population squared (in millions)					−.000095
					$(-1.5)^{\triangle}$
R^2	.40	.50	.26	.66	.65

(Continued)

[a] *Dependent variable:* Yearly municipal expenditures per family, 1965–1966—1969–1970 average. *Method:* Two-stage least squares.

$^{\triangle} p < .20.$

$^* p < .1.$

$^{**} p < .01.$

TABLE 4-1 (Continued)

Independent variables	Financial administration (1)	(2)	General control (1)	(2)
Constant	−5.7 (−.45)	−2.4 (−.19)	−20. (−1.0)	−12. (−.64)
Average private family expenditure (in thousands)	5.2 (2.4)*	4.2 (1.8)*	6.0 (1.7)*	3.6 (1.0)
Median education	−.26 (−.20)	−.18 (−.14)	.20 (.09)	.38 (.20)
Average/median family income	1.5 (.53)	3.1 (1.0)	−2.0 (−.44)	1.7 (.38)
Taxable property per family (in thousands)	.48 (2.0)*	.49 (2.1)*	.31 (.83)	.34 (.97)
Manufacturing wage	−4.1 (−1.7)*	−3.7 (−1.5)△	.20 (.05)	1.1 (.32)
Percent Irish	−.34 (−.74)	−.40 (−.77)	1.8 (2.1)*	1.6 (2.1)*
Business leadership	−1.7 (−1.7)*	−1.4 (−1.5)△	−1.7 (−1.2)	−1.1 (−.78)
Political leadership (×10⁶)	−.25 (−2.3)*	−.25 (−2.3)*	−.35 (−2.0)*	−.35 (−2.2)*
Density (in thousands)	.29 (1.1)	.24 (.94)	−.21 (−.52)	−.32 (−.85)
Population (in thousands)	.0070 (1.5)△	−.020 (−1.0)	.016 (2.2)*	−.046 (−1.6)△
Population squared (in millions)		.000037 (1.5)△		.000086 (2.2)*
R^2	.52	.56	.45	.53

Independent variables	Sewerage Total	Capital	Other	Sanitation	Parks and recreation
Constant	−160. (−2.7)*	−96. (−2.0)*	−65. (−2.6)	22. (.69)	−101. (−2.0)*
Average private family expenditure (in thousands)	−15. (−1.4)△	−9.6 (−1.1)	−5.3 (−1.2)	3.0 (.53)	15. (1.8)*
Median education	21. (3.4)**	15. (3.1)**	6.0 (2.4)*	−1.1 (−.35)	3.2 (.62)
Average/median family income	−31. (−2.2)*	−25. (−2.1)*	−6.8 (−1.2)	5.9 (.80)	10. (.92)

(Continued)

TABLE 4-1 (Continued)

Independent variables	Sewerage			Sanitation	Parks and recreation
	Total	Capital	Other		
Taxable property per family (in thousands)	1.5 (1.4)$^\triangle$	.96 (1.1)	.58 (1.3)	1.4 (2.5)*	.73 (.77)
Manufacturing wage	20. (1.7)$^\triangle$	7.5 (.85)	12. (2.6)*	−6.3 (−1.1)	3.4 (.35)
Percent Irish	−1.6 (−.64)	−1.7 (−.89)	.13 (.13)	1.1 (.83)	−1.1 (−.54)
Business leadership	−8.2 (−1.8)*	−6.1 (−1.7)*	−2.1 (−1.1)	−4.5 (−1.9)*	−3.3 (−.86)
Political leadership (×10⁶)	.12 (.24)	.16 (.41)	−.040 (−.19)	−.44 (−1.6)$^\triangle$	−.91 (−2.1)*
Density (in thousands)	.35 (.29)	.34 (.36)	.015 (.03)	−.53 (−.85)	−1.2 (−1.1)
Population (in thousands)	.16 (1.7)	.081 (1.2)	.076 (2.1)*	.075 (1.6)$^\triangle$	.039 (2.1)*
Population squared (in millions)	−.00018 (−1.5)$^\triangle$	−.000094 (−.98)	−.000089 (−1.8)*	−.000080 (−1.3)	
R^2	.44	.39	.37	.44	.47

Independent variables	General public buildings			Total nine common functions	Total three capital outlay	Total nine functions less three capital
	Total	Capital	Other			
Constant	43. (1.3)	37. (1.2)	5.5 (.56)	−300. (−1.6)$^\triangle$	−150. (−1.8)*	−150. (−1.2)
Average private family expenditure (in thousands)	23. (4.1)**	17. (3.3)**	6.1 (3.7)**	48. (1.5)$^\triangle$	9.6 (.01)	48. (2.2)*
Median education	−6.4 (−1.9)*	−4.0 (−1.3)	−2.3 (−2.4)*	28. (1.5)$^\triangle$	28. (3.4)**	−.51 (−.04)
Average/median family income	−17. (−2.3)*	−16. (−2.4)*	−.63 (−.30)	−30. (−.76)	−51. (−2.8)**	21. (.75)
Taxable property per family (in thousands)	−.71 (−1.1)	−.77 (−1.4)$^\triangle$	.069 (.38)	9.7 (2.9)**	.64 (.42)	9.1 (3.9)**
Manufacturing wage	−11. (−1.8)*	−10. (−1.7)*	−1.2 (−.65)	18. (.52)	−2.6 (−.17)	21. (.87)
Percent Irish	1.7 (1.2)	1.4 (1.1)	.35 (.88)	5.5 (.73)	−2.0 (−.59)	7.5 (1.4)

(Continued)

TABLE 4-1 (Continued)

Independent variables	General public buildings			Total nine common functions	Total three capital outlay	Total nine functions less three capital
	Total	Capital	Other			
Business leadership	−.89	−.24	−.65	−21.	−2.8	−18.
	(−.35)	(−.10)	(−.89)	(−1.5)$^{\triangle}$	(−.45)	(−1.9)*
Political leadership	−.80	−.61	−.19	−4.9	−.82	−4.1
($\times 10^6$)	(−2.8)**	(−2.3)*	(−2.3)*	(−3.1)**	(−1.2)	(−3.8)**
Density (in thousands)	−1.5	−1.5	−2.2	−3.0	−2.0	−1.0
	(−2.2)*	(−2.4)*	(−.11)	(−.82)	(−1.2)	(−.41)
Population	.012	.0091	.0033	.22	.056	.16
(in thousands)	(1.0)	(.83)	(.94)	(3.3)**	(1.9)*	(3.6)**
Population squared (in millions)						
R^2	.43	.36	.50	.56	.48	.70

the nine common functions taken as a group, all three of the income–wealth variables and both of the leadership structure factor score variables are significantly different from zero, at the 20% level. It was anticipated that the signs of these coefficients would be positive, since a relatively high value of this ratio implies a relatively low price of municipal services to the median voter. Further work appears to be necessary to determine why the negative signs appeared; whether the median-voter assumption can be retained or an alternative specification of the community decision-making procedure is needed.

A major goal of this chapter is to characterize the role of scale effects as determinants of municipal service costs. At least one of the relevant variables—density, population size, and its square—is significantly different from zero in the regressions for each of the services except highways. A typical pattern is a negative coefficient for density and positive for population size; that is, as a city grows, the effect of increasing density is to reduce costs per family, whereas the effect of increasing population size is to increase costs per family. Some rough magnitudes may be given. Consider two hypothetical cities of identical population size, one of which has a density 5000 persons per square mile greater than the other. (This is about one-third of the range of densities observed in the 51-city sample.) The denser city would then be expected to have aggregate service costs roughly $15 per family lower than the more sparsely populated city, attributable to the following sources:

highways:	$8.50 less per family in the denser city
police:	8.00 more
fire:	1.60 more
sewer:	1.75 more
sanitation:	2.65 less
parks and recreation:	6.00 less
financial administration:	1.45 more
general control:	1.05 less
general public buildings:	7.50 less.

The effect of increasing city population size appears to be an increase in costs for all the expenditure categories. For highways, police, and general public buildings, the population squared term is not significantly different from zero (i.e., costs per family increase at a uniform rate through the entire range of population sizes studied). For fire, sewer, and sanitation expenditures, the function increases to a maximum in the range of 400,000–500,000 population size and then decreases, indicating possibly first diseconomies and then economies of increasing city size for these services. On the other hand, for financial administration and general control, the effect is the opposite: Costs per family decrease as population size increases to about 270,000, and then costs per family increase, indicating diseconomies of city growth in these categories. These results on scale effects are clearly of importance from the point of view of considering alternative regional growth policies.

References

1. Clark, T. N., "The Structure of Community Influence." *People and Politics in Urban Society,* 6, Harlan Hahn (Ed.). *Urban Affairs Annual Reviews.* Beverly Hills: Sage, 1972. Pp. 283–314.
2. Hirsch, W. Z. "The Supply of Urban Public Services." *Issues in Urban Economics,* H. Perloff and L. Wingo, Jr. (Eds.). Baltimore: Johns Hopkins Press, 1968. Pp. 477–525.
3. Inman, R. "Four Essays in Fiscal Federalism." Unpublished Ph.D. dissertation. Harvard University, 1972.

III
ENVIRONMENTAL
EXTERNALITIES

5

The Environment and City Size

GEORGE S. TOLLEY

Air pollution, leading to external effects that emitters do not take into account, has received attention as one of the chief reasons why social cost may lie above private cost. There is a tendency for air pollution concentrations to increase with city size, although the relationship with city size is far from exact.[1] One expects to find a tendency for concentrations to increase with city size, for all three major sources of air pollution: industrial establishments, which emit gases because of fuel use and because of the chemical reactions connected with particular manufacturing processes; household heating; and motor vehicles. Pollution, as reflected in its measurement as the physical amount of substance *per volume of air,* is not a matter of absolute amount but of amount relative to air being diluted. The

[1] Various measures of air pollution concentrations are available in published EPA documents. Using yearly average mean value of micrograms of suspended particulates per cubic meter, values in 1966 for the largest cities were: New York with 134, Los Angeles with 199, and Chicago with 124. While the highest count occurred in a somewhat smaller city (Steubenville, Ohio with 254) and a few special cases fairly large cities had relatively low counts (e.g., Honolulu with 35 and Miami with 49), there is a distinct tendency for the measure of air pollution to vary in positive association with city population. For nonurban areas, the modal value was 38 μg per cubic meter. The lowest value, 9, was in White Pines County, Nevada.

growth of a city brings more and more emissions relative to the air available for dilution in a vicinity.

The air being polluted is a vast ocean whose molecules are in motion. Pollutants are released continuously into the air and begin to diffuse, so that concentrations of pollutants are highest near pollution sources and diminish as one moves away from them. There are many pollution sources, separated geographically, within any city. One effect of city growth is to lead to increased emissions from existing sources, such as in the industrial parts of the city, at the electricity-generating plants, and on the streets and highways where traffic volume is increased. Another effect of city growth is an increase in the number of sources, particularly from new houses and new roads removed from the center of the city. The pollution from the new sources spreads to the nearby existing sources, thereby increasing pollution concentrations in spite of the fact that new sources are somewhat removed from existing sources. If there is enough city growth to have an effect on residential and industrial density, sources of pollution will also tend to crowd together. Because there will then be less opportunity for dilution between sources, pollution concentrations in the city will further increase.

Cities of a given population vary in amount of pollution for a number of reasons, including types of industry, types of fuel, degree of reliance on automobile transportation, and weather differences. These reasons for differences may be compounded by complex interactions between types of pollutants and sunlight, as for example when smog is created. These reasons for variation in amount of pollution other than city population complicate the task of interpreting empirical evidence on pollution and city size, and they also complicate the task of constructing analytical pollution models.

Most scientific concern with how air quality is affected by pollution has been devoted to physical models for polluting phenomena, with applications limited to particular metropolitan areas. Combining urban theory with physical principles from these models, it might be possible to construct simple analytical models indicating how pollution can be expected to vary with city size. The models would have to indicate how pollution concentrations grow at particular points taking account of lack of uniformity of pollution across the city.

Such models do not yet exist. The only measures comprehensively available to compare pollution levels among many cities are readings at a single downtown point. Increases in pollution at such downtown points as cities grow understate the increase in pollution nearer pollution sources and overstate the increase for areas in the city not much affected by increases in emissions. If pollution increases most near existing sources, then the downtown measure underestimates the pollution increase where the pollution does the most harm, as will be brought out later. Based on downtown readings, an extra worker added to a city may be judged to increase suspended particulates by .0001 μg per cubic meter.[2] Let ds_i/dn refer to the increase in pollution concentration at the ith location in the city. If ds^*/dn is the increase in downtown pollution reading per unit increase in employment, an approximation is that this increase is applicable to all locations, or $ds_i/dn = ds^*/dn = .0001$ for all i. Error from this approximation will be considered later.

To find effects on national income, these physical pollution changes must be translated into costs. The costs of pollution consist of the sum of (a) the value of damages caused, plus (b) the costs of defensive expenditures undertaken to avoid damages. Those affected by pollution make choices between allowing damages to occur and undertaking defensive expenditures to prevent the damages, thus determining how costs are split between the two components. For materials, the costs of more rapid corrosion are an example of damages. Use of more resistant paints and more frequent painting are examples of defensive expenditures. The unhappiness caused by dirty homes, clothes, and faces are examples of damages, whereas the extra cleaning, laundering, and bathing are examples of defensive expenditures. The discomfort due to tears and unpleasant smells caused by pollution are examples of damages, whereas climate control devices provide examples of defensive expenditures. Suffering due to ill health, work days lost, or impaired in efficiency, and years of life lost are examples of damages. Medical measures connected with disease caused by air pollution may be viewed as a combination of damages and defensive expenditures undertaken to avoid further damage. Movement of an industrial plant to a location in another city which would be a higher cost location in the absence of pollution and spreading out of residences within a city to avoid pollution are examples of defensive expenditures taking the forms of locational changes.

Figure 5-1 depicts the costs. Each dashed line shows the total value of damages given a particular level of defensive measures. Because of the possibility of reducing the deleterious effects of pollution through defensive expenditures, higher concentrations lead to increased defensive expenditures, so that there is movement to higher dashed curves at higher pollution levels. The dots indicate the locus of actual damages given the

[2] Assume that growth of a metropolitan area to 1.5 million workers (6 million population in view of nonworking family members) adds 150 μg of suspended particulates per cubic meter over what prevails in a small isolated community. An estimate of the marginal effect is then that each extra worker added to the city increases the measure of suspended particulates by 150 divided by 1,500,000 or .0001 μg per cubic meter.

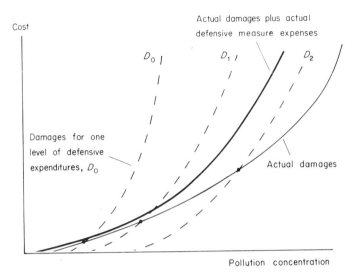

Figure 5-1. Air pollution cost.

increasing defensive expenditures. To these actual damages are added the amounts of the defensive expenditures undertaken at each pollution level, to arrive at the thick solid line showing the costs of pollution. The costs of pollution rise increasingly with pollution level, although the rise is not as great as it would be if there were no defensive expenditures. Notwithstanding the defensive expenditures, at a sufficiently high pollution level the costs would rise virtually without limit, as human life became sustainable only with gas masks.

Let g_i be the increase in cost to a family resulting from a one unit increment in air pollution in the ith location, as determined by the slope of the thick schedule of actual damages plus actual expense of defensive measures shown in Figure 5-1. For the reasons brought out, g_i will become progressively larger at higher pollution concentrations. An approximation is that the increase in costs resulting from an increment in pollution has the same estimated value g^* in all grids in the city, or $g_i = g^*$ for all i. Based on analyses of property values, an estimate of g^* is that an increment of 1 μg of suspended particles per cubic meter increases cost to a family by \$2.40 to \$4.80 per year, or by an average value of \$3.60 per year.[3]

[3] There has been considerable interest in measuring the deleterious effects of air pollution on land values. See, for a recent review of the literature, Smith [4]. For Chicago, Anderson and Crocker [1] have estimated that an additional μg per cubic meter detracts about \$48 from sale price of a residential house and lot. Since this is capitalized value, a yearly equivalent value would be \$2.40 to \$4.80 per property.

The information on costs must be combined with the information considered earlier on how pollution is affected by city growth. By multiplication, the increase in costs of air pollution in the ith location resulting from an expansion of city employment by one worker is equal to the number of families n_i times the increase in costs g_i resulting from an increment to air pollution ds_i/dn caused by the expansion of employment, giving a cost for the one location of $n_k g_k(ds_i/dn)$. For the entire city, the cost is the summation over all grids, given as the true cost of adding a worker $\Sigma n_i g_i(ds_i/dn)$.

Using the approximations just noted, it can be seen that the estimated increase in air pollution cost from adding a worker to the city reduces simply to $Ng^*(ds^*/dn)$, where N is the total number of families in the city. Insertion of the coefficient values that have been noted for g^* and ds^*/dn, for a city of 6 million persons having 1.5 million one-worker families, gives the estimated cost of adding a worker as 1.5 million times $3.60 times .0001, or $540. If eliminating a 10% growth in population would prevent the addition of 150,000 workers to the city, the saving in air pollution costs would be $540 times 150,000, which equals $81 million.

The difference per family between the true cost and the estimated cost is $\Sigma(n_i/N)g_i(ds_i/dn) - g^*(ds^*/dn)$, which is obtained by subtracting the estimated cost from the true cost and dividing by the number of families. If all locations experience the same increase in pollution as at the downtown and if the cost of additional pollution were the same at all locations, then clearly the estimated cost and the true pollution cost would coincide, that is, the foregoing difference would be zero. Suppose half the locations receive no increase in pollution, while the other half, near polluting sources, receive an increase in pollution twice that downtown. Suppose further that the half receiving the increase in pollution, being already heavily polluted, is at point on the thick schedule showing pollution costs in Figure 5-1 with a steeper slope than the average of cases to which the estimated slope g^* applies. The supposition that the slope for the heavily polluted areas is 5 times g^* provides a liberal allowance for error in slope, since observations on heavily polluted areas themselves enter into the statistical estimate of g^*. Under these suppositions, the true pollution cost for the heavily polluted areas is 2 times 5, or 10 times the estimated cost per residence. The true cost, considering the city as a whole, is thus an average of half the observations at zero and half at 10 times the estimated cost, making the true cost for the city 5 times the estimated cost.

Another reason the foregoing estimate could understate true cost is lack of knowledge of harmful effects of pollution on the part of those being harmed. Lave and Seskin [2, 3] have suggested that a microgram of suspended particulates may increase the death rate by 4 persons per million. Using the estimate above that a worker adds .0001 μg, the addition of a worker then increases the death rate by .0004 per million persons. This amounts to an increase of yearly deaths of .0024 for a city of 6 million persons. A liberal allowance is that the unknown consequences of loss of life and sickness from diseases caused by air pollution are $225,000 per life lost. This appears liberal because there is in fact some awareness of the deleterious effects of air pollution on health. The $225,000 figure is that which would just make the unknown costs equal to the known costs as estimated based on land values. That is, $225,000 is a $540 cost per worker divided by the increase in deaths of .0024. Put another way, it would take an unknown cost per life lost of $225,000 to make the total costs of air pollution double what they were estimated to be on the basis of the perceived costs estimated from land values.

The estimation has ignored spatial adaptation to pollution. If all pollution took place in completely automated industrial parks having no effect on residential areas which themselves emitted no pollutants, then additional growth of a city need cause no increase in pollution costs. These conditions are clearly not fulfilled. Yet there is some tendency toward segregation of heavy pollution into areas where effects on others are reduced. To avoid pollution and other disamenities, residences tend to locate away from areas of heavy industrial pollution. This may, however, result in greater commuting costs and pollution from that source. Because of land available, economies of association, and zoning regulations, industries tend to locate near one another and so have their main pollution effects only on the workers there and on the relatively few residences located nearby. For industrial pollution, therefore, there is a possibility that costs are significantly lowered by spatial adaptation. The reasoning does not suggest the costs are completely eliminated.

For residential and automotive pollution, those bearing pollution costs as a group tend to be those emitting the pollutants. There appear to be only minor possibilities for them to escape their own pollution through spatial adaptation.

For all types of pollution, more stringent environmental controls imply there will be less additional pollution with future city growth than there has been with past growth. In sum, the original $81 million estimate of cost savings from keeping a city of 6 million from expanding by 10% could be an underestimate in view of the greater costs of pollution in areas already polluted and in view of the unperceived costs by those harmed. The reasoning suggests methods for allowing for error. The estimates of error, while largely illustrative, suggest the possibility of obtaining an idea of the maximum possible costs. In the illustration given, multiplying the maximum estimate of greater costs of pollution in areas already polluted using a factor of 5, times the maximum effect of unperceived costs using a factor of 2, gives a maximum possible cost of 10 times the original estimate, or $810 million. Not quantified were neglected effects reducing costs, namely, spatial adaptation to pollution and lowering of emissions due to environmental controls.

References

1. Anderson, R. and Crocker, T., "Air Pollution and Residental Property Value." *Urban Studies* **7**, 1971, 171–180.
2. Lave, L. B. and Seskin, E. P., "Air Pollution and Human Health." *Science* **139** (3947), 1970.
3. Lave, L. B. and Seskin, E. P., "Does Air Pollution Cause Mortality?" Carnegie-Mellon and Resources for the Future, Mimeo., March, 1976.
4. Smith, V. K., *The Economic Consequences of Air Pollution*. Cambridge, Mass.: Ballinger Publishing Co., 1976.

6

Congestion and City Size[1]

GEORGE S. TOLLEY
PETER ZADROZNY

Traffic congestion is one of many types of external costs associated with the growth of large cities. The externality arises from the fact that an individual driver does not take account of the costs he imposes by slowing other drivers down. The externality could be internalized by a toll: a tax on trips raising marginal private cost of a trip by the extra costs the driver imposes on others. Vickrey [3, 4] has been a leading analyst of the effects of congestion on speed and the possibility of eliminating external costs through congestion tolls.

The analysis of congestion needs to be extended to consider more explicitly the responsiveness of commuting decisions to costs of driving at peak times. When costs of driving rise due to congestion, commuters have incentives to switch from automobiles to mass transit. Many commuters can arrange to travel at off-peak times. There is an elasticity of demand to commute by auto at peak periods.

Another need is to allow for road building responses. Because amount

---

[1] Much of the material of this chapter is reprinted from "Congestion, Road Capacity, and City Size," which appeared in R. Grieson (Ed.), *Public and Urban Economics: Essays in Honor of William S. Vickrey*. Lexington, Mass. Lexington Books, D.C. Heath Co., 1976.

of peak travel affects the marginal productivity of road expenditures, road builders can be expected to vary the characteristics of the road network in response to changes in peak demand. Capacity is likely to be expanded to accommodate increased traffic.

These extensions are of particular importance when congestion is considered as one of the environmental costs of growth of large cities. An earlier paper by Tolley [2] considered qualitatively the effects on city size of the externalities from failure to impose congestion tolls. A person migrating to city does not take account of the slowing down he imposes on others already in the city. The distortion in migration incentives depends on differences in externalities. If congestion is greater in large cities than in the rest of the economy, a person migrating to a large city raises external costs by more in the large city than he reduces them in leaving the rest of the economy. Because of the difference in externalities, a tendency is imparted for large cities to be too large; though, large cities may be too small relative to their optimal size in the presence of congestion tolls.

Using this framework, another paper [1] quantified the divergence between private and social gains from migrating to a large city under the assumptions that (1) per person travel in the city is unaffected and (2) the road network of the city does not expand in response to the migration.

The present chapter relaxes these two restrictive assumptions. First, a model is developed of equilibrium traffic speed and traffic volume for given road-building expenditures and city population. The model contains a demand schedule for auto trips and a relation which indicates how traffic speed is affected by traffic volume.

Second, road expenditures are allowed to vary in response to city size. This is done by adding a road-building decision to the model. When a city grows, additional inhabitants cause an increase in the demand to use the local road network. The road-building decision indicates how the increased demand is met through some combination of allowing congestion to increase and building new road capacity. The expanded model is used to make illustrative numerical estimates of changes in congestion due to an increase in population.

Third, the expanded model is used to consider the question: To what extent do immigrants coming into a city bear the additional transportation costs which they impose? A condition for optimal migration incentives is derived. The condition has two parts, taking account of effects of immigrants both on congestion and road expenditures, and generalizes earlier analyses.

An expression is developed for the external costs imposed by nonoptimal migration incentives. This is used to calculate numerical examples suggestive of the magnitude of external commuting costs being imposed by the growth of large cities in the U.S. economy.

Commuter Response with Fixed Capacity

Following a standard approach (see, for instance, Walters [5]) an illustration was given in a previous paper (Tolley [1]) of a congestion cost of $0.10 per mile driven in a large city, amounting to $0.50 per day per worker.

To extend that analysis, note that for the person deciding to make the trip, the cost of an auto trip of length D is the car operating cost plus the time cost of the trip or

$$p = D(c + w/s), \tag{1}$$

where p is the cost per trip, c is the car operating cost per mile, w is the wage or other amount at which the time cost per hour of travel is valued, and s is speed of travel.

The number of auto trips made at times of day when there is traffic congestion depends on the cost of making the trips. At higher costs per trip, people will be increasingly willing to bear the costs encountered in reducing auto trips at congested times. The demand schedule for auto trips at congested times can be expressed as

$$p = p(x), \tag{2}$$

showing cost per trip corresponding to a given x, where x is the number of trips per person.

The number of trips taken per person is the number of trips on the demand schedule indicated by the cost for a person deciding to make trips or

$$D(c + w/s) + t = p(x), \tag{3}$$

where t is the congestion toll per trips. Since the normal situation is to collect no congestion toll, t will be assumed to be zero.

The speed of travel s depends on the total number of trips taken by all persons. Speed also depends on characteristics of the road network such as the number of roads, their width, and arrangements provided for avoiding delays due to intersecting traffic. The relation determining speed can be written

$$s = s(v, k), \tag{4}$$

where the total amount of resources devoted to providing the road network is denoted as k, and

$$v = nx. \tag{5}$$

The symbol n refers to the total number of persons in the city, so that v is total number of trips taken in the city under the above conditions. Conditions (3), (4), and (5) jointly determine x (number of trips taken per person), s (speed of travel), and v (total number of trips), given population of the city n, the road network characteristics as determined by k, and the cost parameters D and W.

Knowledge of the relation determining speed enables estimating the cost imposed by taking a trip which a person deciding to take the trip does not pay for. To find the cost not paid for, due to the slowing down of other cars, note that the total cost of travel is traffic volume times cost per trip of $vD(c + w/s)$. The cost of an extra trip is the derivative of total cost with respect to traffic volume $d[vD(c + w/s)]/dv$ or $D(c + w/s) - (vDw/s^2)(\partial s/\partial v)$. The second part of this expression is the cost not paid for. It depends on the partial derivative $\partial s/\partial v$, which is the effect of a unit increase in traffic volume on speed. Letting e_v equal the absolute value of the elasticity of speed with respect to volume, or $-(\partial s/\partial v)(v/s)$, and expressing cost on a per mile basis by dividing by length of trip D, the cost not paid for is $(w/s)e_v$ per mile of travel or the time cost of traveling a mile multiplied by the volume elasticity.

The speed relationship is illustrated in Figure 6-1. Increased road expenditures cause the curves to shift out. Suppose road expenditures are at a level reflected by the middle curve. LM is the horizontal line segment with no congestion. Congestion begins at point M and forces speed to zero at point P. Observed speed and volume are at point N.

The slope of the speed relation at N is now approximated linearly by the slope of LN, the line passing through estimated noncongested speed at zero volume L, and the observed speed and volume N. If noncongested speed is 35 miles per hour and the observed speed is 20 miles per hour, $\partial s/\partial v$ is $(20 - 35)/v$ giving $e_v = [(35 - 20)/v] \cdot (v/20)$ or 0.75. With a value of travel time per car of \$3.00 per hour, the earlier estimate of the cost not paid for is \$0.10 per mile.

Another approximation is obtained by the slope of MN, the line passing through the point M where congestion begins, and observed speed and volume N. Suppose traffic volume at M is one-half the observed volume at N. The estimate of e_v becomes $[(35 - 20)/(v - 0.5v)] \cdot (v/20)$ or 1.5 giving the cost not paid for of about \$0.20 per mile.

The previous two approximations are underestimates of the elasticity at N. An overestimate is obtained by the slope of NP, the line passing through observed speed and volume N, and the point P where volume forces speed to zero. Suppose traffic volume at P is one-and-a-half times the observed volume at N. The estimate of e_v becomes $[(20 - 0)/(1.5v - v)] \cdot (v/20)$ or 2 giving the cost not paid for of \$0.30 per mile.

The results may be used to estimate external costs of growth of a city. For purposes of illustration, consider the effects of a 10% increase in the

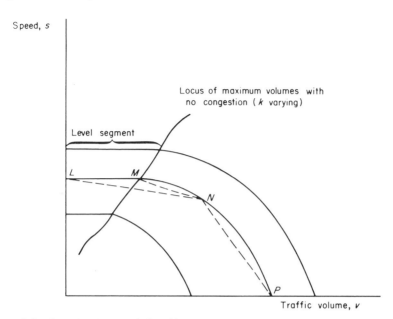

Figure 6-1. Speed–volume relationship.

population of a city of 6 million. Assume that the congestion cost is the average of the latter two estimates, or $0.25 per mile. If there is an average per worker of 5 miles each work day of driving under congested conditions and if there are 250 work days a year, a worker imposes extra travel cost on others each year of $312.50. If one-quarter of the 600,000 residents added to the city by 10% growth are workers, the total cost is $312.50 times 150,000 or about $47 million per year.

This is the estimate obtained if commuter response is ignored. One of the uses of the model of the present chapter is to take account of the response of automobile commuters to cost per trip. From the end of the next section, the elasticity of speed with respect to population is -0.86, when road capacity is fixed and when the elasticity β of travel with respect to cost per trip is -1. A 10% growth of city population reduces speed only 8.6% instead of the 15% just estimated for zero response (where β was assumed to be 0 instead of -1).

The difference in speed effects reduces the estimate of the cost of the existing number of trips per person in the ratio of speed reductions or 8.6/15, reducing the increase in cost of the existing number of trips to $27 million. In addition, there is a triangle effect associated with the change in number of trips per person. The reduction in travel leads to a saving in consumer outlays as compared to the existing number of trips which is, however, partially offset by the reduced benefit of travel. The change in net benefits per trip is the average of the change for the first and last trips cut or $\Delta P/2$, which is multiplied by the change in amount of travel ΔQ to obtain the triangle effect. The triangle effect is $0.6 million. Subtracting the triangle effect from the increased cost of existing trips gives an external cost due to 10% city growth of $26.4 million when the elasticity of demand for auto commuter trips is -1.

The Road Capacity Decision

The estimates so far have assumed no change in road-building expenditures. Ordinarily as a city grows more road building will be undertaken. The extent of this road building will determine how speed of traffic is affected by city growth. A more general framework will now be developed allowing for changes in road-building expenditures.

It is reasonable to suppose that road expenditures are influenced by the marginal benefits from them, without assuming an exact optimization is achieved. As indicated in (22) below, the total benefit from a road is the number of persons in the city times the travel benefit per person, minus the number of persons times the travel cost per person, minus road cost. Differentiating (22) with respect to k and using (3) through (5) to determine the equilibrium responses of x and s with respect to k, gives the following as the net marginal benefit of road expenditures: benefits of extra trips, nt dx/dk plus travel cost savings due to higher average speed, $nxDw/s^2 \, ds/dk$ minus the dollar of expenditure, 1. The change in traffic volume (dx/dk) is governed by (3) through (5) determining traffic flows. A road planner contemplating extra road capacity can be visualized to differentiate (3) through (5) with respect to k obtaining three equations in the derivatives dx/dk, dv/dk, and ds/dk. The solution of the three equations for dx/dk is $-(x/k) \, [e_k/(-e_v + 1/\rho\beta)]$ where e_k and e_v are the absolute values of the elasticities of speed with respect to road expenditures and traffic volume, ρ is $D(w/s)/[D(c + w/s) + t]$ or time cost as a fraction of total travel cost and β is the elasticity of demand for trips.

With perfect optimization, the road planner would choose capacity making net marginal benefit equal to zero. However, road expenditures are decided by a public process, and the benefits are difficult to evaluate precisely. Tax and borrowing decisions at the local and state levels may impart a tendency for rich communities to overbuild and for poor communities to underbuild. Growth-minded communities may tend to build beyond the point suggested by the criterion, while communities not desiring growth may deliberately underbuild. Subsidies for expressways can give incentives to build beyond the point suggested by the criterion.

Let m be the difference between the marginal benefits and marginal cost of extra road-building expenditures. Then substituting the solution for dx/dk into the expression for net marginal benefit, the relation being sought specifying road building expenditures k is

$$m = \left(\frac{nx}{k}\right) [t - p(x)/\beta][-e_k/(-e_v + 1/\rho\beta)] - 1. \qquad (6)$$

Conditions (3) through (6) determine trips per person, total number of trips, speed, and road-building expenditures for a city of given population. We are now in a position to consider how these magnitudes are affected by a change in population. Let $\dot{x}$ denote percentage change $dlnx$, $\dot{s}$ denote percentage change $dlns$, and so forth. Taking the differentials of the four conditions, dividing through by absolute values, and making divisions and multiplications as necessary to obtain elasticity expressions gives

$$\dot{x}/\beta = -\rho\dot{s}, \qquad (3')$$

where β is price elasticity of demand for trips $p/xp'(x)$ and ρ is time cost of a trip as a percentage of total cost of a trip or $(Dw/s)/[D(c + w/s) + t]$;

$$\dot{s} = -e_v\dot{v} + e_k\dot{k}, \qquad (4')$$

where e_v and e_k are the absolute values of the elasticities of speed with respect to volume and road expenditures.

$$\dot{v} = \dot{n} + \dot{x} \qquad (5')$$

and

$$(1 + e_{kv} + \epsilon e_{vv})\dot{v} + (e_{kk} + \epsilon e_{vk} - 1)\dot{k} + \dot{x}/\beta = 0, \qquad (6')$$

where e_{kv} and e_{kk} are the elasticities of e_k with respect to traffic volume and road expenditures or $e_{kv} = (v/e_k)\partial e_k/\partial v$ and $e_{kk} = (k/e_k)\partial e_k/\partial k$; similarly e_{vv} and e_{vk} are the elasticities of e_v with respect to traffic volume and road expenditures or $e_{vv} = (v/e_v)\partial e_v/\partial v$ and $e_{vk} = (k/e_v)\partial e_v/\partial k$; and ϵ is a negative number whose absolute value is less than one and specifically is $\epsilon = \rho\beta e_v/(1 - \rho\beta e_v)$.

In taking these differentials it has been assumed that t is zero which is realistic inasmuch as congestion tolls are essentially nonexistent. It has also been assumed that $\dot{m}$ is zero. This assumption will definitely be fulfilled if road expenditures are optimal ($m = 0$). The assumption that $\dot{m}$ is zero implies there is no systematic change one way or the other in the difference between marginal gain and marginal cost of road expenditure as city size increases. Economies or diseconomies of scale, in connection with average cost financing, might lead to m not being zero. Economies and diseconomies will be considered later in this chapter.

Equations (3') through (6') determine the percentage changes in trips per person, speed, traffic volume, and road expenditures ($\dot{x}$, $\dot{s}$, $\dot{v}$, and $\dot{k}$) given the percentage change in population $\dot{n}$. Equations (3') through (6') can be solved by any method applicable to linear equations. The solution for the percentage change in speed is

$$\dot{s} = -\dot{n}[(1 + e_{kv} + \epsilon e_{vv})e_k + (e_{kk} + \epsilon e_{vk} - 1)e_v]/$$
$$[(1 + e_{kv} + \epsilon e_{vv})(-\rho\beta e_k) + (e_{kk} + \epsilon e_{vk} - 1)(1 - \rho\beta e_v) - \rho e_k]. \quad (7)$$

The special case of no change in trips per person is obtained if the elasticity of demand for trips β is zero, in which case ϵ is also zero. Inserting these conditions into (7), the percentage change in speed becomes

$$\dot{s} = \dot{n}[(1 + e_{kv})e_k + (e_{kk} - 1)e_v]/(1 + \rho e_k - e_{kk}), \quad \text{if } \beta = 0. \quad (8)$$

Another special case occurs if no changes in road-building expenditures are allowed as city size changes. Then $\dot{k}$ is zero, and equation (6') is dropped. The solution for the percentage change in speed is

$$\dot{s} = \dot{n}[-e_v/(1 - \rho\beta e_v)], \quad \text{if } \dot{k} = 0. \quad (9)$$

A final special case occurs when there is no change in trips per person and road capacity does not change. Letting $\beta = 0$ in the foregoing equation gives percentage change in speed

$$\dot{s} = -\dot{n}e_v, \quad \text{if } \beta = 0 \text{ and } \dot{k} = 0. \quad (10)$$

To further examine changes in speed, the following form for the speed relation may be considered:

$$(s/\bar{s}) = 1 - a[(v/\bar{v}) - 1], \quad (11)$$

where $\bar{s}$ is maximum uncongested speed attained, when traffic is light enough so that cars do not slow each other down, and $\bar{v}$ is the maximum uncongested traffic volume, above which the cars slow one another down. Both $\bar{s}$ and $\bar{v}$ may be increased by road-building expenditures, that is,

$$\bar{s} = \bar{s}(k) \quad (12)$$

and

$$\bar{v} = \bar{v}(k), \quad (13)$$

where $\bar{s}'(k)$ and $\bar{v}'(k)$ are positive.

Taking the partial of (11) with respect to v and using the substitution from (11) that $-a[(v/\bar{v}) - 1] = (s/\bar{s}) - 1$ gives $\partial s/\partial v = (s - \bar{s})/(v - \bar{v})$. Using this result in the definition of e_v gives

$$e_v = [(\bar{s}/s) - 1]/[1 - (\bar{v}/v)]. \quad (14)$$

Substituting (12) and (13) into (11), differentiating with respect to k, and substituting in the expressions for $(s/\bar{s})$ and $(s/\bar{s}) - 1$ obtained from (11) gives $\partial s/\partial k = (s\bar{s}'/\bar{s}) + (v\bar{v}'/\bar{v})(\bar{s} - s)/(v - \bar{v})$. Using this result in the definition of e_k gives

$$e_k = \eta + \pi[(\bar{s}/s) - 1]/[1 - (\bar{v}/v)], \qquad (15)$$

where $\eta = k\bar{s}'/\bar{s}$ is the elasticity of uncongested speed with respect to road expenditures and $\pi = k\bar{v}'/\bar{v}$ is the elasticity of maximum uncongested traffic volume with respect to road expenditures. The values of η and π are determined by (12) and (13), as $\bar{s}'$ is the first derivative of (12), and $\bar{v}'$ is the first derivative of (13).

Using (11) we can evaluate e_{vv}, e_{vk}, e_{kk}, and e_{kv} in terms of e_k, e_v, η, and π. The following two relations help simplify these derivations: (a) $e_k = \eta + \pi e_v$ which follows from substituting (14) into (15), and (b) $e_v = a(v/s)(\bar{s}/\bar{v})$ which follows from (11) and (14) along with some algebraic manipulation. This form of e_v simplifies the task of taking logarithmic differentials. Recalling that a is a constant, s is a function of v and k, and that $\bar{s}$ and $\bar{v}$ are functions of k only, we can readily calculate e_{vv} after taking logarithms of $e_v = a(v/s)(\bar{s}/\bar{v})$. This yields

$$e_{vv} = 1 - e_v. \qquad (16)$$

Similarly $e_{vk} = -e_k + \eta - \pi$ and using $e_k = \eta + \pi e_v$. This implies

$$e_{vk} = -\pi(1 + e_v). \qquad (17)$$

In order to calculate e_{kv} and e_{kk} use $e_k = \eta + \pi e_v$. It will be assumed that (12) and (13) are constant elasticity functions. This has the advantage of allowing for diminishing returns to road-building expenditures and it implies that η and π are constants. Differentiating logarithmically gives $e_{kv} = \pi(e_v/e_k)e_{vv}$ which together with (16) implies

$$e_{kv} = \pi(e_v/e_k)(1 - e_v). \qquad (18)$$

Similarly we can derive $e_{kk} = \pi(e_v/e_k)e_{vk}$ which together with (17) implies

$$e_{kk} = -\pi^2(e_v/e_k)(1 + e_v). \qquad (19)$$

The conditions for observed traffic $\bar{s}/s = 35/20$ and $\bar{v}/v = 0.5$ inserted into (14) give $e_v = 1.50$. Consider the increase in road expenditures that would be necessary to maintain the same speed if traffic volume were increased. The assumption that a 10% increase in volume would require a 10% increase in road expenditures to maintain the same speed implies that e_k equals e_v. Since $e_k = \eta + \pi e_v$, with $e_k = e_v = 1.50$, the assumed values of η and π must then be consistent with $1.50 = \eta + 1.50\pi$. As road expenditures are increased, there is some optimum division of expenditures as between increasing uncongested speed and traffic volume possible before congestion is encountered. This division determines the relative values of η and π. Intuitively, it seems likely that most effort would be devoted to increasing the capacity to handle traffic at existing speeds, rather than attempting to increase maximum speed as city size increases. In obtaining a numerical result here, it will be assumed that all additional road expenditures are devoted to increasing traffic volume with no increase in maximum speed, that is, $\eta = 0$, $\pi = 1$. Using (16) through (19), the following values are then obtained: $e_{vv} = -0.50$, $e_{vk} = -2.50$, $e_{kv} = -0.50$, and $e_{kk} = -2.50$.

The values in the preceding paragraph can be used to estimate how speed will change as city population increases. From (10), if thé elasticity of demand β is 0 and if road expenditures are not allowed to change, the percentage change in speed resulting from a 1% increase in population $\dot{s}/\dot{n}$ is -1.50. From (9) if β is -1 and the ratio ρ of time cost to travel cost is 0.5, still retaining the assumption that road expenditures do not change, $\dot{s}/\dot{n}$ is -0.86. From (8) if β is zero but road expenditures are allowed to change, $\dot{s}/\dot{n}$ is -1.06. From (7) if β is -1 and road expenditures are allowed to change, $\dot{s}/\dot{n}$ is -0.66.

Road Taxes for Optimal Migration Incentives

To use these results to examine the effects of population redistribution on national income, let y refer to all income earned by a person in the city in question other than the net benefits b of using the city's congested roads, so that $y + b$ is all income earned in the city including net benefits of using its roads. Let y' refer to the income the person would earn if he were outside the city in question, where y' is all income from being elsewhere including benefits from using any roads in other cities. Labor will have incentives to migrate until the benefits from an extra person moving to the city in question are zero, implying $b + y - y' = 0$, or $b = y' - y$. The effect on national income is the change in benefits from road use dB/dn plus other income earned in the city minus total income the person could earn elsewhere, or $dB/dn + y - y'$. Substituting b for the difference between y and y' as expected in view of migration incentives gives the effect on national income when a person moves to the city:

$$dB/dn - b, \tag{20}$$

that is, the difference between the marginal effect of a person on road benefits and the benefit b a person receives from the road when he moves to the city.

Confining attention to that part of the road system which is congested, the benefit to a person from using the roads when he moves to a city is

$$b = \int_0^x p(X)dX - xD(c + w/s) - k_n. \tag{21}$$

The first term on the right hand side is the area under the demand curve of a person to travel on the roads from zero trips up to the actual number of trips taken. It is the sum of the amounts that he would be willing to pay to use the road system and is greater than his travel expenditures due to willingness to pay higher prices per trip at smaller numbers of trips. The second term on the right hand side is the travel cost borne by a person using the roads. It is the cost per trip $D(c + w/s)$ times x, the number of trips per person. The third term k_n is the person's contribution to road expenditures. It is the amount his taxes are higher because of provision of the roads.

The total benefits from using the roads are

$$B = n \int_0^x p(X)dX - nxD(c + w/s) - k. \tag{22}$$

The first two terms on the right side of (22) are equal to the population n multiplied by the first two terms of (21) which are travel benefits and travel costs in the expression for individual benefits, and the third term k is the total cost of providing the roads. To find the effect on the road benefits of an extra person entering the city, differentiate (22) with respect to n:

$$\begin{aligned}dB/dn = &\int_0^x p(X)dX - xD(c + w/s) - dk/dn \\ &+ n[p(x) - D(c + w/s)](dx/dn) \\ &+ (nxDw/s^2)(ds/dn).\end{aligned} \tag{23}$$

When road capacity expands optimally due to an increase in city population, we can relate the changes in trips per person dx, average speed ds, and total road expenditures dk to the changing city population dn using equations (3′) through (6′). Hence for given road contributions per person k_n we can view road benefits per person b and the change in total benefits due to an extra person entering the city dB/dn to be determined by the city population n. In other words—mathematically speaking—$db/dn - b$ is a function of the city's population n for given k_n, and it correctly measures the addition to national income of a person entering the city only when it is evaluated at the level of population consistent with the zero net migration condition $b = y' - y$. Subtracting (21) from (23) allows us to write (20) explicitly as

$$dB/dn - b = (xDw/s)\dot{s}/\dot{n} + (k_n - dk/dn), \qquad (24)$$

where percentage change notations $\dot{s}$ and $\dot{n}$ have been substituted for ds/s and dn/n. Suppose that k_n is a neutral tax except to the extent that it affects city population. This means that the level and method of collection of road contributions per person does not influence allocative decisions with respect to trips taken within the city. Therefore for a given city population n, the level of k_n does not affect average speed or the external cost due to the slowing down of traffic [this assumption is implicit in the fact that k_n does not appear in Eqs. (3') through (6')]. Of course, k_n affects the external cost indirectly because it is a factor determining migration into the city. Lowering k_n will stimulate migration into the city by increasing b, the benefit to a person from using the city roads. Consequently, in the absence of an optimal toll, national income will be maximized when personal contributions to road expenditures k_n determine a city population such that $dB/dn - b = 0$.

Setting the left side of (24) equal to zero and solving indicates the condition to maximize national income is:

$$k_n = dk/dn - (xDw/s)\dot{s}/\dot{n}. \qquad (25)$$

People should be charged for *the extra cost of road capacity,* dk/dn, *plus the extra travel costs imposed on other drivers due to the reduction they cause in average traffic speed,* $-(xDw/s)\dot{s}/\dot{n}$.

To derive numerical estimates of external costs of city growth assume $dk/dn = k_n$ (that is, that the city tax levied per person to finance roads equals the cost of adding to road capacity to accommodate an additional person). Then $dB/dn - b = (xDw/s)\dot{s}/\dot{n}$, indicating that to find external costs of city growth the results for $\dot{s}/\dot{n}$ obtained above should be multiplied by xDw/s. Following the earlier example, assuming that yearly congested driving per worker is 1250 miles or per person xD is 312.5 miles and that w/s is $3 per hour divided by 20 miles per hour or $0.15 per mile, then xDw/s, which is the yearly time cost of congested driving per person in the city, is $46,875. Multiplying xDw/s by $\dot{s}/\dot{n}$, as obtained for alternative response assumptions in (7) to (10), gives the effect of growth of the city by one person. Further multiplication by 600,000 gives the effect of growth of a city of 6 million persons by 10%.

The estimated effect is $42 million if $\beta = 0$ and $k = 0$, which is close to the $47 million estimate given initially. Applying other assumptions, the effect is $24 million if $\beta = -1$ and $k = 0$, $30 million if $\beta = 0$ and road expenditures are allowed to change, and $19 million if $\beta = -1$ and road expenditures are allowed to change.

In practice k_n may not equal dk/dn as assumed in these estimates. In the absence of transfers between cities such as due to federal subsidies to urban expressways, road expenditures will be self-financing within the city, and k_n may tend to equal average road expenditures per person. Real methods of financing probably come closer to charging an average than a marginal cost. If there are road diseconomies of scale with respect to city population, that is, dk/dn rises with n, with average cost pricing migrants to the city are being charged for roads less than the marginal road-building costs they impose. This means $(k_n - dk/dn)$ is negative. Using Eq. (24) there is an additional external loss by the amount $(k_n - dk/dn)$ as compared with the case where people are charged the marginal cost of road expenditures. The external costs would be higher than in the estimates just given.

Extensions of the Analysis

Further refinements are possible and might suggest reasons for obtaining higher instead of lower losses as compared to the original linear speed–volume example. All the analysis in this chapter has assumed a constant speed under congested conditions and has assumed that city growth does not affect number of miles of congested driving. Suppose congestion is due to slower speeds within a distance of 2.5 miles from work, encountered once in the morning and once in the evening for a total of 5 miles per day. Figure 6-2(a) depicts congestion costs if the congested speed is constant regardless of distance from work, with congestion cost per mile plotted on the y axis and distance from work plotted on the x axis. The area R is the total congestion cost per trip to or from work, and the area Q is the increase in costs due to growth of the city as estimated above.

Figure 6-2(b) depicts a more realistic situation where congestion is encountered at the same distance, but speed is slower the closer one is to the place of work. For simplicity linear effects are depicted in Figure 6-2(b), but the argument is the same if the lines are curved. The line rr showing congestion cost per mile would be much more steeply sloped if it were not for road expenditures undertaken to hasten traffic flow near the place of work. Extra expenditures are to be expected due to increasing traffic volume near work place, as persons living nearer and nearer to work enter the road system. On the other hand, one would not expect it to be optimal to flatten completely the travel speed gradient. These ideas are corroborated by common experience. Though there are more elaborate roads near the center of town, traffic is also slower there.

So long as the area R in Figure 6-2(a) is the same as the area R in Figure

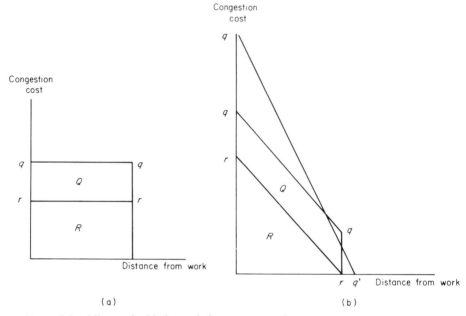

Figure 6-2. Effects of added population on congestion costs.

6-2(b), no bias in estimating total congestion costs results from the unrealistic constant speed assumption. However, eliminating the bias in the estimate of congestion costs imposed by additional population could be more difficult than eliminating bias in the estimate of total congestion cost. If congestion costs imposed by additional population were a constant amount per mile of road already congested, as indicated by line qq in Figure 6-2(b) being the same distance above rr at all points as in Figure 6-2(a), the method of estimating costs of additional population developed above would be adequate. The more likely situation is that the congestion costs with added population are depicted by $q'q'$. Congestion is encountered at a greater distance, and the increase in congestion is greater the closer one comes to the place of work. The basic reason for the position of $q'q'$ is the point already made that extra road expenditures are undertaken partly, but not completely, to reduce congestion. One would expect the largest increases in road expenditures in the places where the increases in congestion are greatest, but one would not expect the greater congestion increases to be completely eliminated. The more the increase in congestion, the greater will be the expenditures to reduce congestion but the greater also will be the increase in congestion remaining. Given the nature of the speed–volume relation and the nature of the existing road network, the increase in congestion will be greatest near the work place. As shown, the area between rr and $q'q'$ representing the true costs of congestion resulting from added population could well be greater than the area between rr and qq used in the examples.

As another consideration, it was assumed in this section that persons moving to a city were charged for the extra road expenditures due to their entry. Real methods of financing probably come closer to charging an average rather than a marginal cost. In the absence of transfers between cities, which only accentuates the conclusion that follows if the transfers are due to federal subsidies to urban expressways, financing of roads so that the road authority breaks even represents average cost financing. If there are diseconomies of scale to additional road expenditures, people in the city are being charged for roads less than the marginal road cost imposed by an additional person. The congestion situation depicted in Figure 6-2(b) is suggestive of reasons for diseconomies of scale. When new entrants come to a city, the road system is expanded to accommodate greater travel distance as the city expands, and *in addition* road expenditures are undertaken near places of work to reduce added congestion there. If the road capacity for greater travel distances from the edge of the city could be provided at constant cost, the added expenditures to reduce congestion at the city center would imply an increasing cost situation considering the road system as a whole. Since density decreases at greater distances from the center, diseconomies of scale are probably eventually reached even in providing for the greater travel distances. A hypothesis for further consideration is that new residents of large cities pay less than the marginal costs of expanding the road system, further increasing the negative externalities connected with roads above those estimated in this chapter.

Thus while the existence of a nonzero price elasticity of demand for travel and a response of road construction decisions to increasing population both act to reduce the negative congestion externalities from increasing city size, as estimated in the earlier parts of this chapter, the possibility that new residents do not pay the full marginal cost of new road capacity is an offsetting effect increasing negative externalities.

Conclusion

To illustrate the external congestion costs associated with growth of large cities, the growth of a city of 6 million persons by 10% (roughly a decade of growth of the Chicago SMSA) leads to external costs on the order of $42 million per year if the customary type of speed volume relationship is assumed, where there is neither change in road capacity nor any response of auto commuters to higher travel costs. Using the model developed in this chapter, if the elasticity of auto commuting with respect to the cost per trip is − 1 (still assuming no change in road capacity), the external costs of the 10% growth are brought down to $26 million.

The congestion resulting from growth of a city will increase the marginal benefits from adding to road capacity, leading road decision makers to expand the carrying capacity of the existing road network as the city grows. The marginal benefits are determined by a road production function showing (a) how increases in traffic volume reduce speed below free-flow speed and (b) how road-building expenditures can be used to increase the free-flow speed. Road-building expenditures reduce the congestion resulting from growth of cities. In the simple case of no response of amount of auto commuting to costs, the elasticity of speed with respect to population is reduced from − 1.5 with no change in road expenditures to − 1.06 if the change in road expenditures is allowed for. In the more general case of a response of auto commuting to costs, if the commuting response elasticity is unitary, the elasticity of speed with respect to population is reduced from − 0.86 to − 0.66.

For optimum migration incentives, people should be charged for the external congestion costs they impose plus the costs of extra road capacity built if they come to a city. The major estimate of this study is that the external congestion costs from 10% growth of a city of 6 million population are $19 to $30 million dollars per year if changes in road capacity are allowed for. It is likely that migrants do not bear the full costs of extra road capacity, and so the external costs of city growth due to increased traffic are probably higher than indicated by this estimate.

Beyond these specific results, a contribution of this study is to explain urban congestion as an equilibrium phenomenon determined by commuter response to travel cost, the physical relations governing speed, and road builder behavior.

Another contribution is to add to the ability to evaluate urban policies in a number of areas including congestion tolls, road finance, and city size. Most discussions of such policies have been at best qualitative. The present study has developed means for considering the benefits in quantitative terms.

References

1. Tolley, G. S. "Population Distribution Policy," *Increasing Understanding of Public Problems and Policies*. Pp. 52–59. Chicago: Form Foundation, 1971.

2. Tolley, G. S. "Welfare Economics of City Bigness." *Journal of Urban Economics* **1,** 1974, 324–345.

3. Vickrey, W. S., "Pricing in Urban and Suburban Transport." *American Economic Review* **53,** 1963, 452–465.

4. Vickrey, W. S., "Congestion Theory and Transport Investment." *American Economic Review,* **59,** 1969, 251–260.

5. Walters, A. A. "The Theory and Measurement of Private and Source Costs of Highway Congestion." *Econometrica* **29,** 1961, 676–699.

7
Effect of Taxation of Externalities on City Size

J. VERNON HENDERSON

A popularly held idea is that cities, in particular big cities, are too large and that optimum size cities would be smaller.[1] Nonoptimality arises because of unpriced production or consumption externalities such as noise, air, or water pollution and congestion, which, if properly priced, would lead to a reduction in city sizes. This chapter argues that taxing externalities optimally may lead to either a decrease or an increase in city size. This ambiguity will be seen to arise from viewing the city as a joint production–consumption unit. For illustrative purposes, we shall consider an analysis of air and water pollution.

The first task is to formulate the problem correctly. The usual analysis states that if production of a good results in external diseconomies, optimally taxing this good will result in a decline in the production, and hence a decline in the size of the city producing the good. In view of the work of Plott [9], Tolley [12], and Schall [11] on externalities, it will be shown that even this conclusion concerning reduction of production is just one of several possible conclusions arising from a more generalized analysis.

[1] See Sandquist [10] or Mills and de Ferranti [7]. Mills and de Ferranti also question the standard conclusion.

Furthermore, even if the size of the economic sector producing a good declines, this says nothing about the direction of change in efficiency or in the size of a city as a whole, which is a consumption as well as production unit and one of many cities in an economy and perhaps one of multiple cities producing the polluting good.

The chapter focuses on a simple case. Firms produce an export good in a city. The production of the export good results in air or waterborne emissions or pollution.[2] This pollution may affect production efficiency of firms; or, as will be the case in our principal example, it may simply enter the utility functions of people living in the city. Concerning this, one might hypothesize that since many work places are air conditioned and purified primarily to stabilize seasonal fluctuations in temperature, air pollution in general does not enter production functions or affect efficiency in a significant way. Similarly, water pollution affects minimally the efficiency of water use in industrial processes. However, they certainly affect consumption activity, directly or indirectly entering utility functions. That is, they are part of the amenity income from living in a city. While taxing the good or input causing pollution may lead to a decline in its production in the economy, the utility of people living in the city may increase since amenity income has risen because pollution will decrease. That is, the city may be a more efficient production–consumption unit. Thus, if there are multiple cities producing a good, reduction of its production (if it occurs) may be effected with an *increase* in average city size of cities producing the good but a *decrease* in the number of cities producing the good.

In order to discuss optimum city size it is very important to understand what a city is and does and how it relates to the total economy and the system of cities of which the economy is composed.

As characterized by Mills [6], in even the most simple model, cities produce an export good or bundle of goods, housing, and a commuting good. Agglomeration in cities occurs because of scale economies in producing the export good. Workers work in the city center producing the export good and commute from their home site to the city center and back each day. As city size increases, per-person-commuting costs rise due to increasing distances that workers must commute and rising congestion on the roads. As expressed by Mills [6] and by Henderson [2], these rising commuting costs with agglomeration may offset the benefits of agglomeration or scale economy exploitation in traded good production. That is, there is an efficient city size for production and consumption.

Extending this analysis, Henderson [2] then shows that if there is an ef-

<hr>

[2] See Kneese [4] for a description of the multiple forms and effects of pollution.

ficient city size where net benefits of agglomeration are maximized,[3] there may be multiple cities producing the same bundles of goods.[4] Further, as has been asserted by numerous people (e.g., Losch [5] and Beckman [1]), Henderson also develops a model accounting for the presence of different types of cities in the economy. Each type of city specializes in the production of a different export good or bundle of export goods. Henderson's [2] reasoning is as follows. If the production of two export goods or bundles of export goods involve no benefits from a common location such as utilizing a common specialized labor force or locationally fixed intermediate input, then it may be beneficial to locate the production of these goods in different cities. Locating their production together increases the labor force that must be housed and that adds to average commuting costs in the city while not increasing efficiency in the production of the traded goods. Separating the production of the two goods into different cities lowers the increase in per-person commuting costs relative to scale economy exploitation per unit of traded good output with increasing traded good production and city size. Separating the two industries of course involves further transportation expenditures due to intercity trade and a complete analysis would have to account for these costs.

The analytical framework is thus one involving a system of cities in an economy with different types of cities producing different bundles of export goods. For each city type there may be one or several cities, depending on economy or world demand for the export goods (total economy output), their costs of transportation in trade (the Loschian [5] limitation of city size), and production technology, in particular, the degree of scale economies (the extent of city agglomeration economies).

This discussion relates to the externality question and to the opening remarks in the following way. Suppose there are two types of cities in the economy, specializing in a manufactured export good and a service export good. Factors of production are mobile between all cities. The production of the manufactured good involves external diseconomies or pollution, and optimal taxation of the externalities usually will reduce output of the good in the economy, increasing output of the service good. Although manufacturing production falls, the efficiency of manufacturing cities as production–consumption units may increase with the reduction of the externality in those cities. If this is the case, and given initial mul-

---

[3] Henderson does not state the market achieves this efficient city size. His analysis and any reasons for nonoptimality are independent of the analysis in this paper or external diseconomies.

[4] This result can be derived in a Loschian [5] world where efficient city size is limited by the increasing transport costs of supplying larger and larger rural areas as a city size increases.

tiple manufacturing cities, city size in manufacturing may increase, with a reduction in the number of manufacturing cities yielding lower economy output of that traded good.[5]

In the previous paragraph it was noted that optimal taxation of externalities "usually" will reduce output of the good in the economy. Since many would prefer "always" to usually here, a brief digression appears in order. The essential notion is that the pollution generated by an industry may have unperceived adverse effects on firm production ("own" and "other" producers). This could occur through corrosion of machinery and/or deleterious effects on worker productivity (missed workdays, impaired effectiveness on the job, etc.). In such a case the true social marginal product of the polluting input can be negative. For example, a tax on high-sulfur coal might cause firms to shift to a low-sulfur coal, a switch that could raise the efficiency and output of all firms. Abstracting from unusual assumptions (inferior polluting input, complementay inputs, etc.), there is a further allocation implication—taxing the factor source of pollution while perhaps reducing use of that factor may lead to a more efficient allocation of output between firms polluting different amounts at the margin, with perhaps a rise in total output.

The City as a Production–Consumption Unit

We now turn to an examination of the optimum city (or production–consumption unit) size. Rather than dealing with the more complex situation of externalities in production considered briefly above, we assume externalities caused by production only affect consumption or production of leisure activities. The city to be considered is a representative city of the type that produces and exports good X to national and/or international markets. There may be multiple cities producing X and other types of cities exporting other goods. In addition to the export good, a variety of nontraded goods and services are produced in the city, summarized in a bundle of goods Y.

Factor inputs are labor and a resource input, N. N is purchased at a fixed price to the city from other areas such as processing towns or mines. Labor is perfectly mobile in the economy and moves to equalize utility levels. By using utility levels rather than wage rates we capture the effect of not only wage differentials between cities but also differentials in prices

[5] If the city-specialization argument is not accepted and it is viewed that cities, under our simple assumptions, would produce all goods, our argument is even stronger! Optimally pricing the good-causing externalities will only change the production ratios of goods in the economy and city. This says nothing, a priori, about the effect on city size.

of nontraded goods and amenity income or, specifically in our example, pollution.

Currently the city is in production and consumption equilibrium. Its laborers have equalized utility levels with laborers in other cities and its trade is balanced. However, the use of N in producing X causes pollution which enters people's utility functions as a public good (or bad). To move toward a Pareto-optimum, the use of N is taxed and the proceeds redistributed to the city's inhabitants. This tax is introduced holding city population initially fixed. The tax leads to a fall in N usage and X output; it also leads to a fall in pollution. We will examine at an intuitive level[6] whether in the new initial equilibrium utility levels have risen or fallen in the city and hence whether labor will migrate to or from the city, changing city size and adjusting utility levels to those prevailing in national labor markets.

Assuming X production in the economy falls, if our representative city increases in size then some other cities producing the good will either decline in size or disappear. Which cities survive and increase in size and which disappear, given our information, is indeterminant. Those cities with firms that are the worst polluters due to inefficiency or regional atmospheric stagnation, would be the ones most adversely affected and would tend to disappear.

Under certain fairly standard assumptions, it can be shown that imposing a tax on N and redistributing the proceeds will lead to a rise in utility in the city (hence in per capita utility). Intuitively this makes sense. The basic city resource is labor, which produces goods for its own consumption and to trade for other goods. Given only basic resources of labor, a Pareto-optimal tax should by definition improve welfare. We tax the use of an input the city imports. The effect of the tax is to reorder production priorities in the city away from X to Y. Since the tax proceeds are returned to labor, only substitution effects in consumption are present and as an approximation they would net out in terms of affecting utility. The loss from utilizing less imported N is of second order magnitude. The main net result is a Pareto-optimal reduction in the imported input and the accompanying positive benefits from the optimal reduction in pollution. If the production of X were to have industry-increasing returns to scale (this analysis has assumed CRS production functions) apart from pollution, and Y were to have decreasing returns to scale, then the reduction of X and increase in Y would have adverse effects on labor productivity and the production potential of the city.

---

[6] See Henderson [2] for a rigorous proof of assertions to follow which do not appear intuitively plausible.

If the reader is persuaded by the preceding argument that utility levels in the city rise or, at least, there is a strong case for their rising, we can extend the analysis to the total economy. If utility levels rise, city size should increase as labor moves to enjoy higher utility levels in that city; and it is then possible that ultimately X production in the city will rise, given the city is a more efficient production–consumption unit. However, if N is being taxed throughout the economy, then N usage and X output for the economy may well fall, as resources are shifted to less costly (social cost) production. If N is only taxed in one city, our analysis stands without further comment.

Where N is optimally taxed in all cities, for X output to fall in the economy but city size in producing X and perhaps city X production to rise, there must be a decline in the number of cities producing X. This scenario assumes multiple cities producing X. If there is only one initial city producing X and economy X production falls it still is not clear that the city population falls. Production priorities have been reordered away from X to Y in the city and it is entirely possible this reordering toward city nontraded goods will be maintained. X labor usage will fall but Y and total city labor usage will rise.

This chapter has viewed optimum city size in the presence of external diseconomies in a somewhat unique manner. The situations considered were fairly specific but the conceptual conclusions and suggestions for future work are quite general:

1. When examining external diseconomies, production conditions must be carefully reviewed before one can conclude that Pareto-optimum production of the source of the externality is less than its competitive production. Pollution could be so pervasive that the social marginal product of the input causing pollution would be negative under competition. A reduction in the input might then lead to increased output in the Pareto-optimum solution. Second, by rearranging output between firms that pollute differently or are affected differently by pollution, total output could rise following the imposition of the optimal tax.

Immediate parallels for other types of externalities spring to mind, in particular for congestion. Is the effect of optimally pricing congestion, to lower total traffic volume and hence city size? Johnson [3] has shown when traffic *density* becomes very high, traffic flow or *volume* may actually decrease as density and congestion rise (this occurs at about 11 miles per hour). Then an optimal congestion tax while lowering traffic density would increase traffic volume at a reduced price. Furthermore, by taxing vehicles differently, traffic composition might be changed at peak hours, increasing automobiles relative to trucks on intracity expressways. Recently, Mohring [8] has shown that a full analysis would compare the optimal pricing–*investment* scheme with the existing solution of gasoline taxes. Switching to a time variable congestion price would most likely reduce off-peak prices while increasing peak prices relative to the competitive price including gasoline taxes. A complete analysis would examine how average price changes for all users, how optimal capacity of roads might change, the effect of a different financing scheme, etc. Whether optimal total traffic flows and average prices rise or decline is uncertain.[7]

2. In discussing the externality–city-size question it must be realized that we are discussing city size not firm/industry output. The city produces a variety of goods and is a consumption as well as production center. The tax ultimately affects consumers and as such may well increase utility levels. Productive capacity (in the export good industry) may be reduced but so is the externality and the negative amenity income of city inhabitants. Optimal city size may increase.

References

1. Beckmann, M. *Location Theory*. New York: Random House, 1968.
2. Henderson, J. V. "The Sizes and Types of Cities." *American Economic Review* **LXIV** (4), 1974, 640–656.
3. Johnson, M. B. "On the Economics of Road Congestion." *Econometrica* **32** (1–2), 1964, 137–150.
4. Kneese, A. V. "Background for the Economic Analysis of Environmental Pollution." *Swedish Journal of Economics* **73** (1), 1971, 1–24.
5. Losch, A. *The Economics of Location*. New Haven: Yale University Press, 1954.
6. Mills, E. S. "An Aggregative Model of Resource Allocation in a Metropolitan Area." *American Economic Review* **57** (2), 1967, 197–210.
7. Mills, E. S. and de Ferranti, D. "Market Choices and Optimum City Size." *American Economic Review: Papers and Proceedings* **61**, 1970, 340–345.
8. Mohring, H. "The Peak Load Problem with Increasing Returns and Pricing Constraints." *American Economic Review* **LX** (4), 1970, 693–705.
9. Plott, C. R. "Externalities and Collective Taxes." *Economics* **33**, 84–87.
10. Sandquist, J. L. "Where Shall They Live?" *Public Interest* **18**, 1970, 88–100.
11. Schall, L. D. "Technological Externalities and Resource Allocation." *Journal of Political Economy* **79** (5), 1971, 983–1001.
12. Tolley, G. S. "Welfare Economics of City Bigness." *Journal of Urban Economics* **1** (3), 1974, 324–345.

[7] Drawing from Mohring's [8] analysis, suppose all expansion is initially gasoline financed and investment occurs so that the marginal benefits (reduction in total travel costs) of investment equal the marginal costs of investment. (This is *not* the second-best solution; from Mohring [8, pp. 700–701], marginal benefits given gasoline taxes should exceed marginal costs.) Replacing the gasoline tax with a congestion tax will raise the peak prices and lower the off-peak prices. Increasing the peak price will reduce peak usage and hence the marginal benefits of investment. Optimal capacity may fall. A complete answer would consider this, the effect upon total traffic volume of the peak increase in price but the off-peak decrease, and the substitutes (rail and bus express) for peak versus nonpeak users. Presumably the latter, which are recreationally oriented, have fewer, if any, substitutes.

IV
FISCAL EXTERNALITIES

8

Fiscal Externalities, City Size, and Suburbanization

GEORGE S. TOLLEY
BARTON SMITH

Earlier chapters have attempted to apply externality thinking to spatial issues. So far most of our attention has centered on public goods, congestion, and pollution, although some recognition has been given to scale economies external to the firm. The present chapter is concerned with two additional types of externalities. First is the externality that results from supplying local government services free to residents while financing through taxes levied irrespective of the amount of the services received by payers, as for example, the financing of education through property taxes considered by Haurin in Chapter 9. The nonexclusion version of this fiscal system is applicable to the distribution of people between cities, within any one of which there is no escape from the local tax. This chapter indicates how to measure the national income losses, the transfers between groups, and spatial relocations resulting from this system.

A partial exclusion version of this same type of fiscal system is applicable to the distribution of population between cities and suburbs. The assumption that high-income groups can exclude by forming separate communities provides a theory of suburbanization within an urban model. Exclusion of low-income residents by a part of the high-income population which suburbanizes leads to losses in national income due partly to larger commuting costs. It also leads to increases in size of partially excluding cities and to a reduction in income transfers for the nation as a whole. Some idea of the magnitude of these effects can be gained.

Concentrations of Rich and Poor without Exclusion

A usual procedure is to make available to each family within a jurisdiction a given level of local government services. Instead of charging for the services as such, taxes are levied in the form of rates applied to wealth, income, or sales. Residents, voting on the amount of service they would like, face different cost curves for the services depending on their wealth, income, or value of purchases subject to tax.

To explore implications of this system, assume that local government services subject to constant marginal cost are financed by a proportional tax on wealth. Then any resident having wealth greater than the average wealth of the jurisdiction will pay more in taxes than the cost of services received. Residents with less than average wealth will not pay as much as the cost of the services. Every resident, rich or poor, has incentives to live in that jurisdiction in which the relation between services received and taxes paid is most favorable. With sufficient mobility the outcome will be a situation where the income of people of a given skill level, counting both their earnings from work and the difference between taxes paid and value of government services received, is the same among cities. Labor flows will lead to wage differences among cities ensuring this result.

In a city where the tax base per resident is high, a given level of government services can be financed with a lower tax rate. A city with a high tax base per resident will tend to have its wage rates lowered relative to other cities by the amount of benefit bestowed by the higher tax base. Wage rate adjustment will come about through labor being attracted to the city. There is an efficiency loss because marginal product of labor in this city will be lowered below marginal product in other cities. The effect on marginal product will be greatest for labor of high skill, assuming wealth holdings are higher for higher-income groups. These groups face the largest differences in tax payments between cities and hence will move until there is a greater compensating wage difference. The equilibrium will be one where, from an efficiency point of view, cities with high tax bases per resident will be too large and will have too much skilled relative to unskilled labor.

Instead of wages of the ith kind of labor being equal as between Cities A and B, there will be a tendency for the wage minus the taxes necessary to finance a given level of public services to be equal, or $w_{iA} - r_A V_i = w_{iB} - r_B V_i$ where V_i is the taxable wealth held by a person of the ith skill and r_A and r_B are the tax rates.[1] To find the difference in wages, note that the total tax revenue, per resident in a city, is the tax rate times the amount of wealth per resident which in turn depends on the proportion of different kinds of wealth holders. The tax revenue per resident is $r_A[\Sigma p_{jA} V_j + Z_A]$ in City A and $r_B[\Sigma p_{jB} V_j + Z_B]$ in City B, where the ps are the proportions of residents in each wealth holding class and the Zs are values per resident of commercial and industrial property. These tax revenues must be sufficient to pay for the level of services s. It follows that the tax rate will be equal to the value of services divided by the bracketed term, that is,

$$r_A = s / \left[\sum p_{iA} V_i + Z_A \right] \quad \text{and} \quad r_B = s / \left[\sum p_{iB} V_i + Z_B \right]. \quad (1)$$

The difference in total tax paid between cities by the ith kind of labor is $r_A V_i - r_B V_i$ and as noted is equal to the difference in wages. The percentage difference in wages is then $(r_A - r_B) V_i / w_i$. Substituting in the values for r_A and r_B gives as the percentage difference in wages for the ith kind of labor:

$$[s/w_i] \left\{ \left[\sum p_{jA}(V_j/V_i) + (Z_A/V_i) \right]^{-1} \right.$$
$$\left. - \left[\sum p_{jB}(V_j/V_i) + (Z_B/V_i) \right]^{-1} \right\}, \quad (2)$$

which shows dependence of the percentage wage difference on proportions in wealth classes and on the ratios of value of wealth between classes.

As an illustration, suppose there are two kinds of labor and that City A contains a relatively large proportion of higher-skilled labor and more taxable commercial and industrial property per resident than does the rest of the economy (City B). Specifically, let

$$p_{1A} = p_{2A} = .5, \quad p_{1B} = .75, \quad p_{2B} = .25, \quad (3)$$

where the first group is low-skilled labor and the second group is high-skilled labor; the subscript 1 refers to low-skilled labor and the subscript 2 refers to high-skilled labor. The wealth ratios for City A are $V_1 : V_2 : Z_A = 1:3:3$ and for City B are $V_1 : V_2 : Z_B = 1:3:1$. Finally, suppose that the

[1] Voting in a city with a higher tax base may lead to choice of a higher level of public service and less difference in tax rates than would occur under identical service levels among cities. The higher level of services is offset by higher total tax payments to finance them and is a second order effect which could be included in a more extended analysis.

general level of wages of the high-skill group is double that of the low-skilled group, with local government expenditures per resident being 20% of the earnings of low-skilled labor, so that $s/w_1 = .2$ and $s/w_2 = .1$. Insertion of these values into Eq. (2) indicates that wages of low-skilled workers in City A are depressed by 4%, and wages of high-skilled workers are depressed by 6%.[2]

The loss in national income can be estimated by visualizing a reallocation of workers back to the point where their marginal products are equal in City A and City B. There will be an increase of 6% in the marginal product of the first high-skilled worker reallocated back to City B. As succeeding workers are reallocated, the marginal product in City A will rise and in City B will fall leading to successively smaller gains from reallocation until there is no gain at all on the last worker as marginal products in City A and City B become equal. The decline in the difference in marginal products as workers are reallocated will depend on the slopes of the marginal product curves for the labor in City A and City B. A reallocation of one worker will raise the marginal product in A by the slope of the marginal product curve in A and lower the marginal product in B by the slope of its marginal product curve. One worker thus lowers the difference in marginal products by the sum of the slopes. Since the reallocation of labor must be sufficient to reduce the difference in marginal products from 6% of the marginal product to zero, the reallocation times the sum of the slopes equals 6% of the marginal product. Multiplying and dividing by wages and proportions of employment in order to obtain elasticities rather than slopes, and solving for the reallocation, reveals the number of workers reallocated to be $.06\overline{N_i}/[(1/k_{iA}\eta_{iA}) + (1/k_{iB}\eta_{iB})]$ where N_i is the total number of workers of the ith category in the economy (City A plus City B), the ks are the proportions of these workers employed in each city, and the ηs are the elasticities of demand for the workers. The average gain in national income on each worker reallocated is in a linear approximation one-half the difference between the beginning gain and the ending gain or $.06w_i/2$. Multiplying the average gain by the number of workers reallocated gives the increase in national income from the reallocation of

$$(.06)^2(w_i N_i/2)/[(1/k_A\eta_A) + (1/k_B\eta_B)].\qquad(4)$$

Suppose workers of the high-skilled class receive 30% of the national

[2] The effects on wages are relative to wages that would prevail in each city in the absence of the fiscal externality. This analysis is in real terms. Due to differences in cost of producing local goods expected between cities, money wages in City A, if it is large, might be higher than in the rest of the economy both with and without the fiscal externality. For a theory of money wage differences between cities and a discussion of their relation to externalities, see Chapters 11 and 12.

income, are equally distributed between City A and City B ($k_{2A} = k_{2B} = \frac{1}{2}$
for skilled workers) and the elasticity of demand for the labor in both
cities is 3. Equation (4) gives an allocative effect of .04% of the national
income. Assuming a national income of $1 trillion, the allocative effect is
$400 million. The assumptions about proportions of workers made to this
point imply that there are three times as many low-skilled workers in City
B as City A ($k_A = \frac{1}{4}$ and $k_B = \frac{3}{4}$ for unskilled workers). Using these ks in
conjunction with earnings of unskilled workers and the estimated .04
earnings differential gives an allocative effect for the unskilled workers of
.013% of national income or $130 million.

To find effects on city size, the formula for number of workers reallocated may be used. The assumptions imply that $\overline{N}$ for skilled workers is
one-third of the labor force. Using this figure in the expression for
workers reallocated $.06\overline{N}_t/[(1/k_A\eta_A) + (i/k_B\eta_B)]$ together with the ks and
ηs noted in the preceding paragraph indicates that 1.5% of the skilled
workers are reallocated. Since one-third of the workers in the economy
are in City A, the movement of skilled workers increases the number of
people in City A by 1.5% and reduces the number in City B by .75%. Following the same method for unskilled workers indicates that 1.8% of the
unskilled workers are reallocated, contributing a 3.6% increase to City A
and a 1.8% decrease to City B. Totalling for skilled and unskilled workers,
the fiscal externality causes an increase in the population of areas with
concentrations of high income people of 5.1% and a decrease in the remainder of the country of 2.55%. These estimates are sensitive to the assumed elasticities of demand for labor, but given the factor shares for
each kind of labor the elasticities in these calculations do not seem high.

A complication in analyzing redistributive effects is the tax on commercial and industrial property. To the extent this wealth is owned indirectly by higher-income groups, it is a tax on them but is not related to
where they live. The allocative effects of the tax on this wealth are ignored, which might involve locational shifts since the tax rate on the commercial and industrial property is affected by the population movements.
In the example, about 9% of national income is being spent on the local
government services. Both high- and low-skilled groups are receiving
more in services than they are directly paying for through taxes, the difference being made up by revenues from the tax on commercial and
industrial property. In City A, the taxes paid by the low-skilled group are
20% of the cost of services they receive, and the taxes paid directly by
high skill groups are 66% of the cost of services they receive. In City B,
the taxes paid by the low-skilled group are 40% of the cost of services,
and the taxes paid directly by the high-skilled group are 120% of cost of
services.

If the tax on commercial and industrial property is borne by high-skilled groups as ultimate claimants to income from that property, the excess of what low-skilled groups receive in services over what they pay directly in taxes is a measure of the redistribution achieved from the higher to lower-income groups. In City A, 1.5% of the national income is spent on local government services for low-skilled residents for which they bear 20% of the costs. There is a transfer to them equal to 1.2% of national income. In City B, 4.5% of the national income is spent on local services for low-skilled residents who bear 40% of the costs. The transfer to them is 2.7% of the national income. Thus the total transfer to low-skilled groups is 3.9% of national income.

This system may be compared with any other scheme which would accomplish the same redistribution without giving incentives to relocate. An obvious but not necessarily realistic alternative would be a wealth tax levied at a uniform rate for all localities by the federal government. Under any such alternative, there would be no fiscal externalities causing differences in marginal products among cities. One would expect a distribution of workers changed by the amounts estimated above in connection with the allocative effects of the externalities. Note that the fiscal externality induces movement of both high-skilled and low-skilled workers to City A. This movement brings about the compensating differences in wages between cities, but it has limited effect on tax rate. The tax rate depends on proportions of workers of different skills, and since both high- and low-skilled workers move, there is little effect on their relative proportions in any city. The proportions remain indistinguishably different from .5 : .5 in City A, and they change from .25 : .75 to .24 : .76 in City B. The proportion of cost of services borne by low-skilled groups in City B rises from .40 to .403 or negligibly.

In sum, in this numerical example, the allocative cost of the fiscal externalities due to induced movements among cities is on the order of .05 to .1% of national income, and the geographic shifting has negligible effect on the amount of redistribution. In contrast, the effect on city size is pronounced as indicated by the 5% increase in population of City A in this example caused by the fiscal externality. While the example is only suggestive, the same general results have been obtained for a fairly wide range of alternative assumptions.

Exclusion through Suburbs

Incentives to form suburbs can be of several kinds including demands for a different level of public service than offered in the city, a desire to control type of neighbors and physical surroundings, and incentives to escape the support of lower-income residents that figured in the preceding analysis of intercity fiscal differences. Factors inhibiting or speeding up the rate of suburbanization include economies of scale leading to a need for critical mass of potential suburbanizers in order to form a suburb and historical events that led to existence of towns resistant to annexation.

With these qualifications in mind, the implications of the single factor of incentives to escape support of lower-income residences may be considered. Suppose high-income residents living on the edge of a city can choose voluntarily whether to be a part of the incorporated city receiving the same level of services as other city residents and paying the same tax rates, or to form into a separate jurisdiction from which low-income persons can be excluded by some such device as zoning. If they are receiving a net subsidy from more services than they pay for in their taxes, due to existence of sufficient quantities of commercial and industrial property, they will have no fiscal incentive to suburbanize. The loss in subsidy to themselves from the commercial and industrial property will exceed the savings in costs of supplying services to lower-income residents which in fact are financed from the commercial and industrial property tax revenues. However, with a continuous income distribution, there will always be some people so wealthy that their tax payments exceed value of services received. Urban theory suggests moreover that higher-income people will tend to live farthest from the center of the city so will be on the edge where the alternative of forming a suburb is real. It will be assumed here that there are always enough high-income residents to overcome any initial economies of scale and that a suburb can therefore be formed to supply public services at the same constant marginal cost as in the city.

Using the same notation as before with the subscript 2 referring to a high-income group, the tax paid by a high-income resident if he remains a part of the city is the city tax rate r_A, which equals $s/(p_1V_1 + p_2V_2 + Z_A)$, times his wealth subject to tax V_2. If he becomes part of a suburb with no lower-income people and negligible commercial and industrial property, his tax will be equal to the cost of the public services he receives s. Subtracting the tax in the city from the tax in the suburb gives the tax saving

$$I = s\{[p_1(V_1/V_2) + p_2 + (Z_A/V_2)]^{-1} - 1\}. \tag{5}$$

Assume that, given these incentives, suburbanization takes place. Then, as between the edge of the incorporated central city and contiguous land just over the line in a suburb, there will be a difference in land rents equal to the tax savings from living in the suburb. People will be attracted to the suburbanizing areas to take advantage of the tax savings. As the suburbs grow, requiring commuting to greater and greater distances, the advantages of moving to the suburbs will be diminished. When the area of suburbanization is so large that the extra travel cost to the far edge of the suburbs is as great as the tax savings, there will be no further incentive to suburbanize. The balancing of tax savings and travel costs provides a theory of the size of high-income suburbs (see Chapter 9 for more details).

Within the central city, additional land becomes available as high-income residents leave. The effect is to increase the supply of labor available to firms at the center of the city, assuming mobility of labor between this city and the rest of the nation. To attract labor, firms at the center of this city must pay a real wage which, after subtracting commuting costs, is equal to what can be earned after commuting costs in the rest of the nation. When land is vacated in the central city by high-income residents leaving, given the wages prevailing in this and other cities, labor from the rest of the country will find it attractive to move into the vacated land. Suburbanization, by increasing the supply of labor at prevailing wages, leads to an increase in employment and hence population for the metropolitan area.

To ascertain the amount of suburbanization that will take place, if there are 250 working days per year and if the extra travel to the suburbs is undertaken once a day going to work and once coming back, the extra distance will be traveled 500 times per year. The number of times traveled multiplied by ΔR the extra distance between the near edge and the far edge of suburbanization multiplied by the cost per mile of travel will equal the tax savings from suburbanization: $500 \ \Delta R \ \$.10 = I$, or $\Delta R = I/50$, where the cost of travel has been assumed to be $\$.10$ per mile. More generally

$$\Delta R = I/nt, \qquad (6)$$

where n is number of times the distance is traveled per year and t is cost per mile. The area of a circular metropolitan area experiencing growth in a suburban ring of this magnitude is increased by $\pi[(R + \Delta R)^2 - R^2]$. The increase in population of the city is this increase in area times the suburban density D_s. The population of the city without the suburban ring is the average density of the city D_A times the original are area πR^2. Dividing the suburban population by the original population gives the percentage increase in the metropolitan area population due to suburbanization $(\dot{N})$:

$$\dot{N} = (D_s/D_A)[(R + \Delta R)^2 - R^2]/R^2. \qquad (7)$$

The suburbanization process will erode the tax base of the central city as residents with high wealth who leave are replaced by residents of lower average wealth. In the central city, the tax rate necessary to supply a given level of public services will therefore rise. In the expression presented above for the tax savings from moving to the suburbs, the proportions p_1 and p_2 in the central city will change. Assume that the demand for labor is such that, for the metropolitan area as a whole, there are given proportions q_1 and q_2 of the lower-income and higher-income residents. When the city grows as a result of the suburbanization, additional numbers of both kinds of residents are attracted to the metropolitan area due to labor demand conditions to maintain the proportions q_1 and q_2. With suburbanization the number of lower-income residents in the central city, where all the lower-income persons are concentrated, is $p_1 N$ and is equal to the proportion for the entire metropolitan area times the metropolitan area population or $q_1(N + \Delta N)$, which implies $p_1 = q_1 + \dot{N}$ and $p_2 = q_2 + \dot{N}$.

Using these values for p_1 and p_2 in (5), substitute (5) and (6) into (7) and rearranging to obtain:

$$1 + (D_A/D_S)N = \{1 + (s/ntR)[[q_1(V_1/V_2) + q_2 + (Z_A/V_2) - N(V_2 - V_1)/V_2]^{-1} - 1]\}^2. \quad (8)$$

The percentage increase in population of the metropolitan area, $\dot{N}$, appears on both sides of this equation, which may be solved by iteration.

Assume the average density D_A is 6000 persons per square mile and that suburban density D_s is 1500 persons per square mile, with a distance R from the downtown to the edge of the central city of 15 miles, and with 30% of the population in a high-income group whose taxable wealth per family is four times as great as that of the rest of the families and twice the value of commercial and industrial property per family. Values noted before are cost of public services per family $s = \$1000$, number of times per year extra distance is traveled $n = 500$ and cost per mile $t = \$.10$. Using all these values in Eq. (8), the percentage increase in population due to suburbanization $\dot{N}$ is found by iteration to be 4%.

It is possible to choose values for the various parameters in Eq. (8) for which the iterations do not converge to a finite value of $\dot{N}$. The iterations reflect the changing level of taxes in the central city as suburbanization occurs. The tax changes give incentives to suburbanize still further. Putting in $\dot{N} = 0$ on the right-hand side of (8), a solution for the left-hand side value of $\dot{N}$ can be obtained which is the suburbanization that would take place under the initial incentives. Plugging this value of $\dot{N}$ back into the right-hand side, one obtains a new left-hand value indicating suburbanization in response to the eroded tax base resulting from the initial suburbanization response, which in turn can be plugged back in to calculate a further round of adjustment, and so forth. Paramater values which lead to progressively larger values of $\dot{N}$ instead of converging to a finite value indicate an unstable situation where suburbanization is explosive. Each round of adjustment is greater than the previous round, instead of less as under the stable solution. The end result in the explosive case would be to empty the central city entirely of its high-income residents. Militating against the explosive solution in reality is the fact that, instead of having two discrete income groups as assumed in this example, there is a continuum. Highest-income residents have greatest incentives to suburbanize. As suburbanization proceeds the number of people with incentives to suburbanize at any given tax rate decreases. Stability could be investigated further by assuming a continuous income distribution, with the wealth per family of those left in the city with incentives to suburbanize, decreasing progressively the greater is suburbanization.

Other possible refinements may be noted. The rise in taxes necessary to supply a given level of government services in the central city will, first, induce compensating wage adjustments between this metropolitan area and the rest of the nation, raising money wages necessary to attract labor to the city and therefore reducing somewhat the amount of labor demanded by firms in the city. Second, the increase in number of workers available at a given wage, due to the suburbanization process itself, will depress wages as firms move along demand curves for labor. This will lead to less labor being attracted to the city than on the one for one basis as people move to the suburbs, which was assumed in this analysis. Whereas the analysis here has assumed immigration equal to the full rightward shift of labor supply due to vacated land in the city, the first effect just noted is a vertical shift in the supply curve, and the second effect is movement along the demand curve to intersect with the new supply curve. A conjecture is that the magnitude of these effects is of second order. Their direction is to make the population growth of the metropolitan area less than in the analysis here. In the other direction, no movement of commercial and industrial property to the suburbs has been assumed in this analysis, nor has account been taken of the fact that with any real suburbanization some low-income suburbanization is likely to be induced by the high-income suburbanization. There are demands for employment to provide goods and services to the high-income residents, and some businesses formerly operating in the center of the city will be attracted to the suburbs by the increased supplies of high-income labor there. These considerations would increase the amount of suburbanization and population growth for the metropolitan above that obtained in the analysis here.

The number of people living in a suburban doughnut of width dr is $2\pi r D_s\, dr$. If there is one worker among every four persons, the number of workers in the doughnut is $\pi r D_s\, dr/2$. The travel cost for each worker is equal to the distance to the center r times the number of trips per year n times cost per mile t. The extra travel cost caused by suburbanization is then the integral, from the inner edge to the outer edge of the suburbs, of $(\pi D_s \, ntr^2/2) \, dr$, or $(\pi D_s \, nt/6)[(R + \Delta R)^3 - R^3]$. It is being assumed in this example that $R = 15$ miles. Inserting the other assumed parameter values into (5) and (6) using $p_1 = q_1 + \dot{N}$ and $p_2 = q_2 - \dot{N}$, it is found that $\Delta R = 1.2$ miles. The value of the integral for extra travel costs can then be determined to be $34 million per year, which is an estimate of the national income loss due to suburbanization.

If there is one worker for every four persons, about 40,000 high-income workers would move to the suburbs leaving 175,000 high-income workers in the city after the equilibrium amount of suburbanization is reached. The revenue above costs for each high-income worker, available for redistribution to low-income workers, can be calculated from (5). Assuming as before that the cost of services is $1000 per worker in the city, the loss of 40,000 high-income workers means a loss of revenue above costs available for redistribution of $10 million. If the income produced in the city is $1 billion, the decrease in amount available for redistribution is .1% of the income produced.

The results obtained for suburbanization in this section are similar to those for fiscal externalities in the preceding section, in that there are essentially negligible effects on income transfers, small but nonnegligible national income costs, and quite pronounced effects on distribution of population among cities. While strong inferences from these examples are not warranted, it may be noted that the combined effect of the intercity and suburbanization externalities is to make some cities have 5–15% more population than they would in the absence of the externalities.

9
Property Taxes and
Spatial Resource Misallocation

DONALD R. HAURIN

This chapter considers the possibility that property taxes in urban areas may be contributing to the "flight to the suburbs"[1] using a model which jointly accounts for urban land and housing rentals, property tax rates, and related variables. The first part of this chapter investigates the role of property taxes in urban residential distribution by extending the traditional model (based on the work of Muth [7], Alonso [1], and Wingo [13]) in a straightforward way. This is an obvious way to approach the problem because assuming a plausible value of the income elasticity of demand for housing, the traditional models imply that the rich will live toward the edges of a city. If transportation costs per mile fall, or if income per household rises, these models predict that the rich will tend to move out of the legally defined central city to the suburbs, a prediction which corresponds with reality.

The first part shows that if the income elasticity of demand for housing is greater than unity and if only minimal modifications of the traditional models are made to take account of the property tax, the models imply

---

[1] See Bradford and Kelejian [3]; Rothenberg [10, 11]; and Chapters 8 and 10 of this volume.

that the property tax will be progressive. This contradicts the finding of Netzer [8, p. 41] that business and residential property taxes, after federal tax offsets, are regressive throughout the income distribution. Without the offsets they are regressive up to $8000 income in nominal terms (1957 prices) and approximately proportional afterwards. Netzer [8, p. 55] finds residential taxes alone to be regressive at very low levels of income and approximately proportional thereafter with a local peak at $10,000–$15,000 income. He also notes a very progressive benefits distribution for local expenditures that are financed by property taxes [8, p. 61].[2]

Thus there is a need to develop a model that is consistent with a potentially regressive property tax and a progressive distribution of benefits, but which does not contradict the traditional models' implications concerning the flight to the suburbs. The model presented in the second part will accomplish these goals, and in addition will provide a further theoretical explanation of the flight to the suburbs, involving an expansion of the boundaries of an urbanized area, the movement of the rich to the suburbs, and the creation of social welfare losses. Examples will be given for an urbanized area such as Chicago with approximately 1.5 million households as residents. The remainder of this introduction will summarize the analysis.

The question of what determines property tax and urban service levels in a group of adjacent municipalities was initially treated by Tiebout [12]. He stated conditions under which local public goods will be provided optimally. One of the conditions was that households receive their income through a means such as dividend payments and not by commuting to a CBD. Bruce Hamilton [5] in an extension of Tiebout's work showed that suburban residents then have an incentive to form local communities, so that the political structure of a Tiebout world will be approached. This important insight will form the basis of the model presented here. The urban service to be considered will not be a pure public good in the Samuelsonian sense [11], but rather an individual consumption good provided publicly. The public sector's behavior constraint is that all recipients are provided identical amounts of the public good. Every household consumes all units allotted to it as long as it derives some marginal benefits from the good. Assuming nonsatiation, all residents will share the same level of consumption of the public good. The example taken here will be education, ignoring national external effects. Thus the model to be presented assumes two distortions: (1) a property tax in the central city, assuming full Tiebout adjustment does not take place there, and (2) a legal

[2] There is no agreement among economists on the question of regressivity. An opposing view is presented, for example, by Gaffney [4].

constraint restricting the quantity of education consumed by individual households.

The empirical relevance of a model which considers only a residential property tax and education as the only public good should be considered. In 1957, taxes on single family units and apartments comprised 55.5% of total local real property taxes. Commercial and industrial taxes comprised 28.6% of the total, and farms, vacant lots, and others, 15.9%. Also in 1957, expenditures on education by local governments were 44.6% of local general expenditures, of which it was estimated that 51% were financed by the property tax. Welfare, police, fire protection, health, hospitals, sanitation, and miscellaneous were 44.2% of expenditures, of which 48.4% were financed by the property tax. Finally, highway expenditures were 12.2% of total local expenditures of which 29% were financed by the property tax [8, p. 261]. So although the assumptions restricting the model to residential property taxes and a public good such as education are not completely realistic, these are significant components, respectively, of total taxes and expenditures of local government.

The question occurs whether people view the property tax as a full tax or as partial payment for local services when full Tiebout adjustment does not take place. Under full Tiebout adjustment, the tax payment is perceived as the cost of public services; hence there is no distortion or welfare loss. The question may be a psychological one, to which an economist can give no answer. It will be assumed here that only the amount of services demanded at a given price but not received (due to the legal constraint) constitutes the tax. If services are received in excess of demand, as for a relatively poor family, there is perceived a housing subsidy. The perceived tax or subsidy rate is this amount, divided by actual housing consumption.

In the model of the second part of this chapter, the overall equilibrium level of services in the city is derived endogenously. The rich are "taxed" in their consumption and the poor "subsidized" but each household's consumption of the service is the same. It is assumed for simplicity that services are provided at constant costs and each family has the same number of children recalling that the service is education. In equilibrium, given the number of residents, total taxes are a function of housing consumed, which is a function of perceived taxes on housing, which depend in turn on the actual education tax level. Thus there is a simultaneous solution for the actual tax rate, perceived tax rates for each group, and the amount of services per family.

The final element is the number of residents in the city. If suburban residents are in a nondistorted equilibrium while city residents are not, the city residents will have an incentive to move. As a preliminary exercise, it will be shown that the rich will live in the suburbs whenever a city–suburban boundary exists. They may use zoning as an instrument to keep the poor out if the incentive to the poor to move is of sufficient size. The rich who remain in the central city will face higher taxes than in the suburbs, while they will incur increased transportation costs if they move to the suburbs. Equilibrium city and suburban population sizes are determined by these two forces. Movement of the rich to the suburbs will reflect back upon the tax rates.

In a full adjustment Tiebout world, the entire burden of the property tax falls on the residents. Consider a city simplified by assuming zero rent at the margin. There are constant expenditures on housing and a property tax on structures and land. The question occurs whether residents (renters) or owners pay the tax, or whether it is shared between them. Figure 9-1 illustrates the situation. At the margin, S^*, the renters have to pay the full tax since land rent is zero there. Between the center and S_1, the tax could feasibly be passed fully to the landowner. But this is not an equilibrium solution since the residents that live between S_1 and S^* would then bid up the site value of land between the center and S_1. The final equilibrium will occur when site values have been bid up by the amount of the tax. All renters therefore pay fully for services received in the final equilibrium.

Relaxing the constant expenditures assumption does not change the result, but if there is some alternative use of land at the margin such that rental is positive, then a difference occurs. In this case it is possible that some of the tax could be passed on to the landowner, the proportion depending upon the relative size of rents at the margin and the tax. Of course, the tax on landowners will not affect the allocation of land if it is in inelastic supply. However renters would be subsidized in their consumption of public goods financed by the tax. The form of the subsidy is a

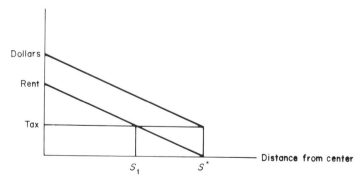

Figure 9-1. Property tax burden in an urban area.

lump sum per unit land. A distortion would result due to land being subsidized relative to structures in housing. Since argicultural rent is likely to be small relative to urban site value, the size of the distortion is likely to be small.

It will be assumed that the relevant tax rate is the observed rate, not some fraction of it. If housing is owner-occupied, the tax will be viewed as falling on housing rather than separately on land and capital. The homeowner then considers the observed tax in relation to benefits received, and so the assumption is justified.

This analysis will not consider implications of location-related amenities, environmental externalities, or multiple work places. To facilitate derivation of empirical estimates, specific production and demand functions are assumed and only two income groups are considered. The distribution of income is endogenous, but utility functions of the two groups are assumed to be independent of one another.

The first part of the chapter generalizes the Alonso–Wingo–Muth model with one income group by incorporating a property tax. This will provide a simple base to build on, and an analysis for the full adjustment suburbs in the city–suburban model. The second part presents the city–suburban model with two income groups. The equations that form the simultaneous solution will be specified and the method of determination shown. The third part presents some estimates of social costs and population distribution assuming plausible parameter values and concludes with comments on the flight to the suburbs and the regressivity of the property tax.

Model with One Income Group

The model presented in this section relates to individuals in a city, assumed to have the same incomes and identical utility functions $U(h, x, g)$, where h is the quantity of housing, x is the quantity of a composite "other good," and g is the quantity of public services provided to the individual. Their budget constraint is

$$y = p_h h + p_x x + p_g g + s\, c(y), \tag{1}$$

where p_i is the price of one unit per year of good i, s is the distance from place of residence to the CBD, c is the transportation cost per mile for the journey to work, y is income. Necessary conditions for a maximum with respect to h, x, and g are $U_h/p_h = U_x/p_x = U_g/p_g$, where, for example, $U_h \equiv \partial U/\partial h$. Assume that prices of housing and public services are such as to make utility the same at all locations; thus $dU/ds = 0$. Evaluating

dU/ds, differentiating Eq. (1) with respect to s and using the first-order conditions, it follows that

$$h(dp_h/ds) + c(y) + g(dp_g/ds) = 0. \tag{2}$$

The individual's demand function for housing is assumed to have the form,

$$h(s) = By^{\theta_1}p_h(s)^{\theta_2}, \tag{3}$$

where B is a constant, θ_1 is the income elasticity of demand for housing, θ_2 is the price elasticity of demand for housing. Such a model was analyzed by Barr and Davis [2]. They showed that in a community where all utility functions and incomes are the same, those who pay relatively more for housing will demand (vote for) a relatively smaller amount of public expenditures. Since the price of housing declines with distance from the CBD, residents relatively close to the CBD will vote for more expenditures if the demand for housing has a price elasticity greater than unity and for lower expenditures if the price elasticity is less than one. They also showed that the median voter corresponds to the household with the median property value. Thus, if $\theta_2 = -1$, everyone becomes the median voter and all demands are satisfied at the selected tax rate.

The restrictive assumption that $\theta_2 = -1$ will be made here; this implies that households do not take the property tax into account in their housing decisions.[3] A consequence of this assumption is to make the model similar to Tiebout's, which is nonspatial in nature. Incorporating this assumption into Eq. (3),

$$h(s) = B\, y^{\theta_1}/p_h(s). \tag{4}$$

Thus $p_h(s)h(s)$, yearly expenditure on housing, is invariant with respect to distance.

The unit price of public services perceived by an individual residing in the city is his total tax bill divided by the quantity of services received, that is,

$$p_g(s) = t\, p_h(s)h(s)/g^*, \tag{5}$$

where t = tax rate per dollar's worth of housing services per year. Recalling Eq. (4), $p_g(s) = t(By^{\theta_1})/g^*$, that is, p_g is the same at all locations. Equation (2) then implies

$$dp_h/ds = -c(y)/h(s) < 0. \tag{6}$$

---

[3] This assumption corresponds to published estimates.

An explicit functional form for this housing rental–distance function will be derived.

The individual's demand function for public services is assumed to be

$$g(s) = Cy^{\theta_3}p_g(s)^{\theta_4} = Cy^{\theta_3}p_g^{\theta_4}, \tag{7}$$

where C = constant, θ_3 = income elasticity of demand for services, θ_4 = price elasticity of demand for services. The total quantity of public services demanded in the city will be

$$G = gN^* = g \int_0^{s^*} N(s) \, ds, \tag{8}$$

where N^* is the total number of individuals.

The total value of public services supplied is assumed to depend on the quantity of taxes collected and on the number of residents in the city, $N(s)$, at each distance from the center:

$$G = \int_0^{s^*} N(s)tp_h(s)h(s) \, ds, \tag{9}$$

where G = aggregate quantity of the public service supplied, and s^* = distance from the CBD to the edge of the urban area. Equality of the G's in Eq. (8) and Eq. (9) is an equilibrium condition.

The housing production function is assumed to be Cobb–Douglas:

$$H(s) = AL(s)^{\alpha}K(s)^{1-\alpha}, \tag{10}$$

where $H(s)$ = aggregate quantity of housing supplied at distance s, per unit of land, $L(s)$ = quantity of land available, $K(s)$ = quantity of capital used, and A = constant.

In such a case it is well known that

$$p_l(s) = \alpha H(s)p_h(s)/L(s), \tag{11}$$

$$p_k = (1 - \alpha)H(s)p_h(s)/K(s), \tag{12}$$

where p_l and p_k are the rentals, respectively, on land and capital, and p_k is assumed to be exogenous. Solving Eq. (11) and Eq. (12) for L and K and substituting into Eq. (10) it follows that

$$p_h(s) = A^{-1}[\alpha/p_l(s)]^{-\alpha}[(1 - \alpha)/p_k]^{\alpha-1}. \tag{13}$$

Differentiating Eq. (13) with respect to s,

$$dp_h/ds = A^{-1}p_l'(s)p_l(s)^{\alpha-1}[p_k\alpha/(1 - \alpha)]^{1-\alpha}. \tag{14}$$

The quantities of housing demanded and supplied at distance s are then related by the equation,

$$H(s) = h(s)N(s), \tag{15}$$

where $N(s)$ is the number of households residing at distance s.

Land supply is assumed to be a circular area centered on the CBD; that is, if

$$L(s) = 2\Pi s, \tag{16}$$

then the area of the city is

$$\int_0^{s^*} 2\Pi s \, ds = \Pi s^{*2}. \tag{17}$$

It will be convenient to have the notation

$$p_l^* = p_l(s^*) \tag{18}$$

for the value of land rent at the edge of the city. This completes the exposition of the model.

To obtain an expression for land rent gradient, first substitute Eq. (3) into Eq. (6) recalling that $\theta_2 = -1$:

$$dp_h(s)/ds = -c(y)/[By^{\theta_1}p_h(s)^{-1}]. \tag{19}$$

Next substitute for p_h using Eq. (13) and for dp_h/ds using Eq. (14) yielding

$$[\alpha p_l'(s)/p_l(s)][By^{\theta_1}] + c(y) = 0. \tag{20}$$

This differential equation has as its solution, using initial condition Eq. (18), that

$$p_l(s) = p_l^* \exp[c(y)(s^* - s)/(\alpha By^{\theta_1})], \tag{21}$$

which is the desired expression.

To derive an expression for the density gradient, note that from Eq. (11) and Eq. (12)

$$\frac{p_l(s)}{p_k} = \frac{\alpha \, K(s)}{(1 - \alpha)L(s)}. \tag{22}$$

Solving for $K(s)$ and substituting into Eq. (10) implies

$$H(s) = A(s)\left(\frac{p_l(s)}{p_k}\right)\left(\frac{1 - \alpha}{\alpha}\right)^{1-\alpha}. \tag{23}$$

From Eq. (13) and Eq. (3)

$$h(s) = By^{\theta_1}A[\alpha/p_l(s)]^{\alpha}[(1 - \alpha)/p_k]^{1-\alpha}. \tag{24}$$

Combining Eq. (15), Eq. (22), and Eq. (24) implies

$$N(s) = \frac{H(s)}{h(s)} = \frac{p_l(s)(L(s))}{\alpha B y^{\theta_1}}.$$ (25)

Finally, combining with Eq. (21), density at each distance is given by $N(s)/L(s)$, or

$$p_l^*[1/\alpha B y^{\theta_1}] \exp\{c(y)(s^* - s)/[\alpha B y^{\theta_1}]\}.$$ (26)

To obtain an expression for the radius of the city, s^*, combine Eqs. (8), (16), and (25) to obtain

$$N^* = \int_0^{s^*} [2\Pi s p_l(s)/(\alpha B y^{\theta_1})] \, ds.$$ (27)

Substitute for $p_l(s)$ in Eq. (27) using Eq. (21) and derive

$$-c(y)Es^* + \exp[c(y)Es^*] = 1 + N^*Ec(y)^2/[2\Pi p_l^*],$$ (28)

where $E = [\alpha B y^{\theta_1}]^{-1}$. One can solve this for s^*, given the values of the other parameters.

Finally we turn to the service sector. It is assumed that the public good is provided at constant costs and output is measured by expenditures. This corresponds to measuring the output of schools by expenditures per child (or per household), as is often done, though with obvious regrets, in empirical work. From Eq. (3) with $\theta_2 = -1$, $p_h(s) = B y^{\theta_2} = $ constant. Substituting this into Eq. (9),

$$G = t B y^{\theta_1} \int_0^{s^*} N(s) \, ds = t B y^{\theta_1} N^*$$ (29)

and from Eq. (8),

$$g = t B y^{\theta_1}.$$ (30)

Taxes per household are equal to g. An implication of Eq. (30) is that taxes are progressive if $\theta_1 > 1$, proportional if $\theta_1 = 1$, and regressive if $\theta_1 < 1$. Muth [6] and Reid [9] present evidence indicating that $\theta_1 \geq 1$; therefore this simple model predicts a nonregressive property tax. To determine the tax rate, note that from Eqs. (7) and (8), the aggregate service demand for the area is $G = N^*Cy^{\theta_3}p_g^{\theta_4}$. From the assumptions of constant costs and output measured in terms of expenditures, $p_s = 1$, thus,

$$G = N^*Cy^{\theta_3}.$$ (31)

In equilibrium, combining Eqs. (30) and (31), we have $tN^*By^{\theta_1} = N^*Cy^{\theta_3}$. Therefore,

$$t = (C/B)y^{\theta_3 - \theta_1}.$$ (32)

The change in the tax rate with respect to income is given by

$$\frac{\partial t}{\partial y} = (\theta_3 - \theta_1) \frac{C}{B} y^{(\theta_3 - \theta_1 - 1)},$$

which is positive or negative according as θ_3 is greater or less than θ_1. The conclusion is that it is not necessarily true that as one's income rises the tax rate will rise, but expenditures on services, and hence total taxes will rise if $\theta_3 > 0$. The question of why different Tiebout (suburban) communities have differing tax rates is then easily explained by differences in the relative values of income elasticities of demand of housing and service.

Regarding the implicit assumptions of voting and demand behavior for the public good, the analysis shows that if the price elasticity is -1 and there is only one income group, then all residents would vote alike. This behavior is equivalent to equating aggregate supply and demand, as is done in the model, and then deriving each household's supply. When more than one income group is considered, voting behavior will not, in general, correspond to the usual methods of supply and demand analysis even if $\theta_2 = -1$. Under certain assumptions concerning the income distribution and voting methods, the analysis can be carried out.

A numerical example of the simple model will conclude this part of the analysis. Suppose that $B = .25$, $C = .10$, $y = \$10,000$, and $\theta_1 = \theta_3 = 1.0$. From Eq. (32), $t = .4$. Let $N^* = 1.5$ million, $p^* = \$100,000$ per square mile, $\alpha = .1$, and $c(y) = 100$. Then one can deduce that s^* is approximately 12 miles using Eq. (29). The total area of the urbanized area would be 452 square miles and the average density about 3320 households per square mile. From Eq. (30) each person receives $s^* = \$1000$. From Eq. (10) with $\theta_2 = -1$, expenditures on housing are $p_h h = 2500$. From Eq. (21), the rent function is $p_l(s) = \$100,000\ e^{.286(12 - s)}$.

Model with Two Income Groups

We now present a model of an urban area that contains two income groups. The number of households in each group is arbitrarily specified: N_1 members of group 1 (poor), and N_2 of group 2 (rich). The presentation follows a different sequence from that of the preceding section. First the housing production and demand sectors are defined and expressions for the bid rents for land by the two groups are derived. It is shown that under the assumptions of the model, the rich live farther from the center, and the poor nearer; the boundary will be designated s_0 miles from the center. Then assumptions on taxation and on the provision of public services are introduced and the crucial assumption is made that there are two fiscal jurisdictions, designated central city and suburban, divided at s_c miles from the center where $s_c > s_0$. That is, the suburbs contain exclusively rich households while the central city contains members of both income groups. The location of this boundary reflects a prior decision in history. The equations defining the remainder of the solution are then derived.

The assumptions of this model generalize from those made in the first part of the chapter. Equations (10)–(14) and Eqs. (16)–(18) are carried into this model without change. Let i index income groups 1 and 2. Utility is given by $U^i = U^i(h_i, x_i, g)$ and the budget constraint is

$$y_i = p_h h_i + p_x x + p_g{}^i g + c_i s. \tag{1'}$$

All households—rich and poor, central city, and suburban—have the same level of public services g^* and pay the same tax rate t per dollar of housing expenditures per year. The tax rates τ_i are perceived tax ($\tau_i > 0$) or subsidy ($\tau_i < 0$) rates for housing. As indicated in the introduction, the Tiebout assumptions will not be satisfied in a city with several income groups. Thus $\tau_i \neq 0$ if some members of both groups 1 and 2 reside in the central city in equilibrium. The perceived rate is not the same as the observed tax rate, t, because the households realize they are paying for a service. In the first section, the perceived tax rate was zero because the value of the service to the household was equal to what they paid for it. The perceived tax rates τ_i will be determined endogenously as the solution proceeds.

The maximization yields $U_h{}^i/p_h = U_x{}^i/p_x = U_g{}^i/p_g{}^i$ and

$$h_i(dp_h/ds) + c_i + g \, dp_g/ds = 0. \tag{2'}$$

The individual's demand for housing is assumed to be

$$h_i(s) = By_i{}^{\theta_1}/[p_h(s)(1 + \tau_i)] \tag{3'}$$

assuming as before, $\theta_2 = -1$. Thus yearly expenditure on housing by a household is

$$p_h(s)h_i(s) = By_i{}^{\theta_1}/(1 + \tau_i), \tag{4'}$$

which, as before, is invariant with respect to distance.

Similarly to the first model, the public service price for each income group is related to the property tax rate by an equation

$$p_g{}^i(s) = tp_h(s)h_i(s)/g^*, \tag{5'}$$

from which, recalling Eq. (4'), $p_g{}^i(s) = tBy_i{}^{\theta_1}/[g^*(1 + \tau_i)]$. The public service price is the same at all locations, given the income group $(dp_g{}^i/ds = 0)$. Equation (2') therefore implies

$$dp_h/ds = -c_i h_i < 0. \tag{6'}$$

Digressing from the model exposition to derive the land rent gradient, substitute Eq. (3′) into Eq. (6′) to find

$$dp_h/ds = -c_i p_h(s)(1 + \tau_i)/(By_i^{\theta_1}). \tag{33}$$

[This corresponds to Eq. (19) in the first model.] Substitute Eq. (13) for p_h and Eq. (14) for dp_h/ds in Eq. (33) and derive

$$p_l'(s)p_l^{-1}(s)\ \alpha By_i^{\theta_1}(1 + \tau_i) + c_i = 0. \tag{34}$$

The solution of this differential equation is a family of bid rent curves for each income group, whose form is

$$p_l^i(s) = p_l\dagger \exp[c_i(s\dagger - s)(1 + \tau_i)/(\alpha By_i^{\theta_1})], \tag{35}$$

where the members of each family are indexed by $p_l\dagger = p_l(s\dagger)$, for some arbitrary value of s. The competitive process which leads to an equilibrium rent gradient is described by Alonso [1]. Its outcome in the present case is straightforward. One of the groups—suppose provisionally that it is group 2—outbids the other for sites relatively far away from the center, between distance s_0 (at the intergroup boundary) and s^* (at the outer edge of the suburbs). Taking $s\dagger = s^*$, the rent gradient in this range is

$$p_l^2(s) = p_l^* \exp[c_2(s^* - s)(1 + \tau_2)/(\alpha By_2^{\theta_1})], \tag{35a}$$

where, as before, $p_l^* = p_l(s^*)$, the agricultural land rent at the margin. To obtain an expression for land rent between the center and distance s_0, note that

$$p_l^1(s_0) = p_l^2(s_0) = p_l^* \exp[c_2(s^* - s_0)(1 + \tau_2)/(\alpha By_2^{\theta_2})].$$

Take $s\dagger = s_0$ in Eq. (35) and derive

$$p_l^1(s) = p_l^* \exp[c_2(s^* - s_0)(1 + \tau_2)/(\alpha By_2^{\theta_2})$$
$$+ c_1(s_0 - s)(1 + \tau_1)/(\alpha By_1^{\theta_1})]. \tag{35b}$$

The whole rent gradient is depicted in Figure 9-2.

The urban area will be organized in this way, with the rich living farther from the center than the poor, if group 1's bid rent curve is steeper than group 2's at distance s_0. The slopes are $dp_l^2(s_0)/ds$ from Eq. (35a) for group 2 and $dp_l^1(s_0)/ds$ from Eq. (35b) for group 1. Calculating these derivatives and noting that $p_l^1(s_0) = p_l^2(s_0)$, a sufficient condition that group 1's curve be steeper is $c_1(1 + \tau_1)/y_1^{\theta_1} > c_2(1 + \tau_2)/y_2^{\theta_1}$. A sufficient condition for this, if $\theta_1 \geqq 1$, is that $d^2c/dy^2 < 0$—as income increases, transportation expenditures increase at a decreasing rate. This will be assumed to be the case, for the rest of this chapter. If $\theta_1 < 1$, or if $d^2c/dy^2 > 0$, the result depends on specific parameter values. (Recall the assumption that $\theta_1 \geqq 1$ based on studies of Muth [6, 7] and Reid [8].)

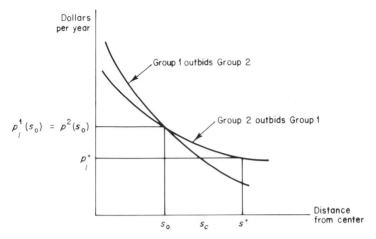

Figure 9-2. Urban land rent gradient.

To derive the population density gradient, substitute from Eq. (13) into Eq. (3′):

$$h_i(s) = By_i^{\theta_1} A[\alpha/p_l(s)]^{\alpha}[(1 - \alpha)/p_k]^{1-\alpha}/(1 + \tau_i). \qquad (36)$$

Note also that $H(s) = h_i(s)N_i(s)$; combining this with Eq. (36) and using also Eq. (23),

$$N_i(s) = (1 + \tau_i)L(s)p_l(s)/[\alpha By_i^{\theta_1}]. \qquad (37)$$

Density $N_i(s)/L(s)$ follows immediately from this. The larger the perceived tax rate, the larger the density, for a given land rental.

In view of the above discussion, we now assume that the central city contains members of both income groups, and the suburbs contain only members of group 2. It is assumed that the total population of the urban area is N^*, and since the jurisdictional boundary at s_c is arbitrary, the initial number of suburban residents (i.e., ignoring the effects of taxation) is arbitrary. Let the ratio of suburban to total residents of group 2 be represented by $\sigma_2 = N_2^s/N_2 = N^s/N_2$. Then

$$N_2^c = N_2(1 - \sigma_2). \qquad (38)$$

Part of the simultaneous solution will be to specify the number of rich who move from the city to the suburbs. For expository convenience we define this to be μN_2. The migration ratio μ is an endogenous variable. In equilibrium, the central city will then contain $N_2(1 - \sigma_2 - \mu)$ rich residents. The radius of the city and suburban area s^*, and the radius s_0 of the area occupied by income group 1 are then characterized by the solution of the two equations

$$N_2 = \int_{s_0}^{s*} N_2(s)\, ds,$$

$$N_1 = \int_0^{s_0} N_1(s)\, ds. \tag{39}$$

Returning to complete the exposition of the model, a household's demand for the public service is assumed to be

$$g_i(s) = Cy_i^{\theta_3}(p_g{}^i)^{\theta_4}. \tag{7'}$$

Aggregate demand for the service is $G_i(s) = g_i(s)N_i(s)$, expressed as a density given distance from the center. Since housing expenditures are invariant with respect to location, given income, according to Eqs. (4'), (5'), and (7'), we can write an expression for aggregate demand within the central city as a whole:

$$G = N_1 g_1 + (1 - \sigma_2 - \mu)N_2 g_2. \tag{8'}$$

Substituting from Eq. (7') into Eq. (8'),

$$G = N_1 Cy_1^{\theta_3}(p_g{}^1)^{\theta_4} + N_2(1 - \sigma_2 - \mu)Cy_2(p_g{}^2)^{\theta_4} \tag{40}$$

or, incorporating Eq. (5') and then Eq. (4')

$$G = N_1 Cy_1^{\theta_3 + \theta_1\theta_4}\{Bt/[g^*(1 + \tau_1)]\}^{\theta_4} \\ + N_2 Cy_2^{\theta_3 + \theta_1\theta_4}\{Bt/[g^*(1 + \tau_2)]\}^{\theta_4}(1 - \sigma_2 - \mu). \tag{41}$$

In equilibrium $g_1 = g_2 = g^*$ in Eq. (8'); one can use this to eliminate g^* from the right-hand side of Eq. (41), and then solve for G in terms of t and other variables.

Considering aggregate services in the central city to be equal in value to aggregate tax collections there, we have

$$G = \int_0^{s_c} tN(s)p_h(s)h(s)\, ds \tag{9'}$$

The integral separates into terms relating to group 1 (between the center and distance s_0) and group 2 (between distances s_0 and s_c). Using Eq. (4'),

$$G = N_1 t\, By_1^{\theta_1}/(1 + \tau_1) + N_2(1 - \sigma_2 - \mu)tBy_2^{\theta_1}/(1 + \tau_2). \tag{42}$$

An equilibrium condition is equality of the Gs in Eqs. (41) and (42). It will be useful for subsequent analysis to write the resulting equation as a formula for the equilibrium tax rate:

$$t = (C/B)y_2{}^{\theta_3-\theta_1}[1 + (N_1/N_2) - \sigma_2 - \mu]^{\theta_4}$$

$$\frac{(N_1/N_2)(y_1/y_2)^{\theta_3+\theta_1\theta_4}[(1 + \tau_1)^{-1}]^{\theta_4} + [(1 + \tau_2)^{-1}]^{\theta_4}(1 - \sigma_2 - \mu)}{[(N_1/N_2)(y_1/y_2)^{\theta_1}(1 + \tau_1)^{-1} + (1 + \tau_2)^{-1}(1 - \sigma_2 - \mu)]^{1+\theta_4}}. \quad (43)$$

Thus t is expressed in terms of perceived tax rates, the number of rich who migrate to the suburbs, and other parameters. Equation (43) is analogous to Eq. (32) in the first section of the chapter, the difference being a multiplicative adjustment factor.

One assumption of this analysis is that no city poor would be drawn to the suburbs. Whether the incentive would be large enough has not been determined but the implicit assumption is that the rich suburbs will zone out the poor. If zoning or some type of restrictive covenant is nearly costless to enact, the benefit of keeping the poor out will be larger than cost. Note that local labor does not enter into this model, hence the rich do not consider the nearby availability of workers to be employed in local goods production to be a benefit. An interesting solution not considered here is the existance of a suburb composed of poor who work as local laborers in nearby rich suburban communities.

To solve the system, four equations will be developed, relating to τ_1, τ_2, and μ. Equation (43) is the first of these. The next step is the determination of the perceived tax rate. The perceived tax rate on housing is

$$\tau_i = (p_g{}^i - 1)g^*/(p_h h_i). \quad (44)$$

This may be interpreted as the excess cost of services, per unit of housing expenditure. The value $(p_g{}^i - 1)$ is the excess cost per unit of services. For example, the rich in the central city will pay a price for services $(p_g{}^2)$ that is greater than the marginal cost of the services. Thus when $\tau_2 > 0$, the rich are taxed. For the poor $p_g{}^1 < 1$. Therefore if $\tau_1 < 0$, the poor are subsidized.

Substitute Eq. (5') into Eq. (44) to find

$$\tau_i = (tp_h h_i/g^* - 1)g^*/(p_h h_i)= t - g^*/(p_h h_i). \quad (45)$$

If $g^* = tp_h h_i$ as in Model 1, then $\tau_i = 0$ and we return to the Tiebout world. Substitute from Eq. (4') for $p_h h_i$ and from Eq. (42) for $g^* = G/[N_2(1 - \sigma - \mu + N_1/N_2)]$:

$$\tau_1 = t - t[N_1/N_2 + (1 - \sigma_2 - \mu)(y_2/y_1)^{\theta_1}(1 + \tau_1)/(1 + \tau_2)]/$$
$$(1 - \sigma - \mu + N_1/N_2), \quad (46)$$

$$\tau_2 = t - t[(N_1/N_2)(y_1/y_2)^{\theta_1}(1 + \tau_2)/(1 + \tau_1)$$
$$+ (1 - \sigma_2 - \mu)](1 - \sigma - \mu + N_1/N_2). \quad (47)$$

To obtain an equation for μ we must solve for the equilibrium number of rich who migrate from the city. To accomplish this, we must find the "burden" on the rich who remain in the city. It is obvious that some will move out, considering the situations of the rich on either side of the boundary before there is migration. On the suburban side, households receive in services what they demand, paying marginal cost. On the central city side, the rich households pay a price for services in excess of marginal cost and perceive a tax on housing. Thus there is an incentive for city rich to more, the offsetting costs being higher transportation costs or a change in rents. We first specify the magnitude of the burden and then develop an expression for the final equilibrium condition.

The burden to the rich in the central city consists of two parts. The first is the private welfare cost of the loss in housing services due to the perceived tax, τ_2. The second is the loss related to the consumption and taxation of the public good. The traditional consumer surplus triangle is lost as a result of the housing tax, since consumption is reduced. A similar statement can be made concerning the loss related to the consumption of services, also measurable as a consumer's surplus triangle. The major portion of the burden is created by the consumption constraint in the city, since the rich will received only g^* units of services but pay taxes on their total housing consumption. Algebraically, an approximation to the burden is $\frac{1}{2}(g_2 - g^*)(p_g^2 - 1) + \frac{1}{2}(h_2 - h^*)\tau_2 + (tp_h h^* - g^*)$ where g^2, h^2 are the undistorted values and g^*, h^* are the equilibrium values in the central city. The expression can be evaluated by substituting the values derived in the first part of the chapter for g_2 and h_2, and values from the second part for g^* and h^*. For computational convenience, an alternative expression for welfare costs is used for housing, namely $-\frac{1}{2}(\tau_2)^2 h_2 p_h \theta_2$. Since $\theta_2 = -1$, we have the burden $\frac{1}{2}(g_2 - g^*)(p_g^2 - 1) + \frac{1}{2}(\tau_2)^2 h_2 p_h + (tp_h h^* - g^*)$. Equations (17), (36), (52), (41), (45), and (46) are used to evaluate this expression.

The final equilibrium condition depends on what assumptions are made concerning immigration to the city. One may consider two extremes. The first is that no immigration will occur as the rich leave the central city. This implies that rents in the central city will fall and s_0 will become larger as the poor occupy more and more land. In this case the burden to the migrating rich would be offset by increased transportation costs and rent in the suburbs plus the decrease in land rent in the central city.

An alternative method is to assume there is immigration to the central city from elsewhere. Since this model has never specified why there is more than one income group, the proportion of rich and poor that enter is arbitrary. As easy assumption to work with is to assume that only rich households migrate. This assumption implies that in equilibrium the burden to the city rich will equal the increased transportation costs of those who migrated to the suburbs. It implies also that the burden will not change in the city, because the number of rich is the city is fixed by assumption. This formulation does miss the aspect of a cumulative movement of the rich out of the central city but it will be used here, in view of its relative ease of manipulation.

In Figure 9-3, the introduction of the public sector causes the urbanized area to expand from s^* to $s^* + \Delta s$. Equilibrium will occur when the burden of living in the city per year per household is equal to the increase in transportation costs for the rich living at the margin (i.e., $c_2\Delta s$). Thus the condition is: burden $= (c_2\Delta s)$.

There are three topics of interest that remain to be discussed. They are the number of city residents that migrate to the suburbs, the welfare cost of the property tax in final equilibrium, and whether the property tax is regressive in this model.

An approximation may be made of the amount of migration to the suburbs by considering the density function [from Eq. (37)] and the expansion of the city (determined in the equilibrium condition involving the burden). If the density function were linear, one could average the original densities at s^* and $s^* + \Delta s$ to get an estimate of the average density in the newly created suburban areas. The estimate of migration would be $\frac{1}{2}[N_2(s^* + \Delta s)/L_2(s^* + \Delta s) + N_2(s^*)/L_2(s^*)] \Delta$area. Using Eqs. (37) and (35a) this simplifies to

$$\Delta\text{area } p_l^*(1 + \tau_2) \exp[c_2\Delta s(1 + \tau_2)/\alpha By_2^{\theta_1} + 1]/(2\alpha By_2^{\theta_1}), \qquad (48)$$

where the increase in area is $\Pi(s^* + \Delta s)^2 - \Pi s^{*2} = 2s^*(\Delta s)\Pi + (\Delta s)^2\Pi$.

Another topic of interest is the measurement of social welfare costs. There are resource allocation distortions in the provision of the public service, in the consumption of housing, and in additional transportation costs

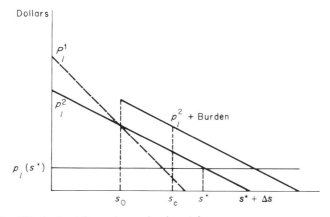

Figure 9-3. Effect of public sector on land rentals.

incurred in final equilibrium. The algebraic representation of the welfare cost triangles and transportation costs is

$$\tfrac{1}{2}(g_2 - g^*)N_2(p_g{}^2 - 1) + \tfrac{1}{2}(g^* - g_1)N_1(p_g{}^1 - 1) + \tfrac{1}{2}(h_2 - h^*)N_2\tau_2$$
$$+ \tfrac{1}{2}(h^* - h_1)N_1\tau_1$$
$$+ (\Delta \text{ average distance traveled})$$
$$(\Delta \text{ population})(c_2). \qquad (49)$$

The number of families affected may be derived from the migration equation, above. An approximation to the average increase in distance from the CBD by these families is $(s^* - \tfrac{1}{2}\Delta s) - \tfrac{1}{2}(s_0 + s_c)$. Thus the final expression for welfare cost is

$$\tfrac{1}{2}(g_2 - g^*)(p_g{}^2 - 1)N_2 + \tfrac{1}{2}(g^* - g_1)(p_g{}^1 - 1)N_1 + \tfrac{1}{2}(h_2 - h^*)\tau_2N_2$$
$$+ \tfrac{1}{2}(h^* - h_1)\tau_1N_1 + c_2 (\Delta \text{ population})$$
$$[s^* + \tfrac{1}{2}\Delta s - \tfrac{1}{2}(s_0 + s_c)]. \qquad (50)$$

The final topic is the structure of the property tax and the schedule of benefits that are derived from it. The model of the first section implied that the property tax was proportional or progressive given empirical estimates of the income elasticity of housing demand. In the model of this section, the tax rate t depends on additional parameters [Eq. (43)]. This fact, combined with distortions in housing consumption, yields the result that even if the income elasticity is unitary, the property tax may be regressive. The numerical example of the following section demonstrates this point.

This completes the exposition of the model. Means have been developed for accomplishing the goals of measuring social costs, migration, and regressivity. A numerical example using realistic parameter values follows in the final section.

An Example

A simple numerical model will be presented so that some idea of how the model behaves may be obtained. The values of a number of parameters are specified, and then the solution of the model follows.

ASSUMPTIONS

$B = .25$	$y_1 = \$10,000$	$N_1 = 500,000$
$C = .1$	$y_2 = \$15,000$	$N_2 = 1,000,000$
		$N^* = 1,500,000$

$$p_l^* = 100{,}000 \qquad c_1 = 100 \qquad N_c = 1{,}000{,}000$$
$$c_2 = 125 \qquad \sigma_2 = \tfrac{1}{2}$$
$$\alpha = .1$$
$$\theta_1 = 1.0$$
$$\theta_2 = -1.0$$
$$\theta_3 = 1.0$$
$$\theta_4 = -1.0$$

RESULTS

Equation (43) simplifies easily to yield, $t = .4$. Knowing this value, Eqs. (46) and (47) can be solved simultaneously to yield the values for the perceived tax rates:

$$\tau_1 = -.067, \qquad \tau_2 = .051.$$

With these three values, there is enough information to solve for $g^* = 1247$. We may note at this point that the undistorted values of public service consumption are:

$$g_1 = \$1000, \qquad g_2 = \$1500.$$

Also the undistorted values of housing consumption are:

$$p_h h_1 = \$2500, \qquad p_h h_2 = \$3750.$$

With this information we may solve for the implicit tax rate on provision of the public service:

$$p_g{}^1 - 1 = -.138, \qquad p_g{}^2 - 1 = .114.$$

Now that the various tax rates and levels of goods consumption have been determined, the burden to the city rich is found to be \$197 per rich household in the city. Using the value of the burden and the assumption that $c_2 = 125$, the expansion of the city may be determined to be

$$\Delta s = 1.57 \text{ miles.}$$

This implies an increase in suburban area of

$$\Delta \text{area} = 164 \text{ square miles.}$$

The number of rich who migrate to the suburbs is found to be 57,200 or slightly more than 11% of the original number of rich in the city. Finally, the social welfare cost of the property tax including spatial effects is calculated to be \$99,300,000. This may be stated as \$66 per household in the urban area. Of the total cost, the spatial misallocation resulting in increased transportation costs is 78.9%. This large percentage is to be expected since the rich migrate to avoid their private loss in consumption of the public service and do not take into account the gain of the lower income residents.

Of interest are the perceived tax rates, τ_i. In this example they average about 14% of the actual tax rate. Thus, in studies that use the observed tax rate to measure distortions, a substantial overestimate of the distortion results when the benefit of the tax is not considered. On the other hand, a lack of consideration of the spatial effects of the property tax results in a large underestimate of the welfare cost. Whether these effects have offset each other would have to be determined in an empirical study.

A final comment may be made concerning the increase in city size. The model can be solved to yield the initial values of

$$s_0 = 3.8 \text{ miles}, \qquad s^* = 15.8 \text{ miles}.$$

and it was implicitly assumed that $s_c = 7.5$ miles. The increase in total area of the urbanized area was 21.2% as a result of the migration.

The last topic of this section is the potential regressivity of the property tax and the progressivity of the benefits schedule. Suppose the situation is as indicated in Table 9-1.

TABLE 9-1

Assumptions for Regressivity Analysis

Income	Residence	Population	Tax	Benefits
$15,000	City	500,000	$1425	$1247
15,000	Suburb	572,000	1500	1500
10,000	City	500,000	1070	1247

From the results of Table 9-1 we may derive that:

Benefits	Income	Benefit/income
1247	$10,000	.125
1382	15,000	.092

Therefore, the benefits are relatively weighted toward the low-income residents, a fact which Netzer noted.

Taxes	Income	Taxes/income
1070	$10,000	.107
1465	15,000	.098

In the case of taxes, a regressive tax schedule is derived from the model. The reason is that, even with similar tastes, the consumption of housing by the poor is subsidized and as a result they pay a relatively larger tax as a percentage of income. Another potential source of regressivity lies in changes in the observed rate, t in Eq. (43). In the numerical example, it happened that the parameters yielded an unchanged t, so that this source did not come into play. The net result of the benefits and taxes is an income transfer of $174 per low-income household. The transfer is, of course, in the form of public services.

The tasks that were set out originally in this chapter were to explain the regressivity of the property tax and to develop a model that contributed to the explanation of the flight to the suburbs. In a simple model with one income group, neither result could be obtained, but the model did represent what a spatial Tiebout world would be like. The model was extended by introducing another income group and the concept of perceived tax rates. It was found that the high-income groups in the city faced a burden of making transfer payments to the poor. In response, a migration to the suburbs occurs, resulting in a substantial welfare cost in terms of transportation costs. If an alternative method of financing local public services were used, such as lump sum taxes, some of the social cost might be reduced but there would still be a spatial incentive for migration. In our case where the public good is actually a private good, the spatial incentives could be eliminated if the public sector stopped taxing and providing the good. This scheme would have a benefit equal to the full social cost that has been derived from the model, and a "flight to the city" may occur if less restrictive assumptions were placed on the model.

References

1. Alonso, W. *Location and Land Use.* Cambridge, Mass.: Harvard University Press, 1964.
2. Barr, J. L., and Davis, O. "An Elementary Political and Economic Theory of the Expenditures of Local Government." *Southern Economic Journal* **2**, 1966, 149–65.
3. Bradford, D. F., and Kelejian, H. H. "An Econometric Model of the Flight to the Suburbs." *Journal of Political Economy* **81**, 1973, 566–589.
4. Gaffney, M. "The Property Tax Is a Progressive Tax." *Proceedings of the Sixty-Fourth Annual Conference of the National Tax Association,* 1971.
5. Hamilton, B. "Zoning and Property Taxation in a System of Local Governments." *Urban Studies* **12**, 1975, 205–211.
6. Muth, R. "The Demand for Non-Farm Housing," in *The Demand for Durable Goods,* A. Harbergen (Ed.). Chicago: University of Chicago Press, 1960.
7. Muth, R. *Cities and Housing.* Chicago: University of Chicago Press, 1964.
8. Netzer, D. *Economics of the Property Tax.* Washington D.C.: The Brookings Institution, 1966.
9. Reid, M. *Housing and Income.* Chicago: University of Chicago Press, 1962.

10. Rothenberg, J. "Strategic Interactions and Resource Allocation in Metropolitan Inter-governmental Relations." *American Economic Review* **59**, 1969, 495–504.
11. Rothenberg, J. "Local Decentralization and the Theory of Optimal Government," in *The Analysis of Public Output,* J. Margolis (Ed.). New York: Columbia University Press, 1970.
12. Samuelson, P. "The Pure Theory of Public Expenditure." *Review of Economics and Statistics* **36**, 1954, 387–389.
13. Tiebout, C. "A Pure Theory of Local Expenditures." *Journal of Political Economy* **64**, 1956, 416–424.
14. Wingo, L. *Transportation and Urban Land.* Resources for the Future, Washington, D.C., 1961.

V
EXTERNALITIES AND THE SPATIAL DISTRIBUTION OF THE POOR

10

Urban Implications of the Welfare System and Minimum Wage Laws

BARTON SMITH
GEORGE S. TOLLEY

The comment is frequently made that labor market distortions cause spatial misallocations of resources. One line of reasoning is tenuous and is not pursued in detail here. It is sometimes asserted that real wages for identical labor are higher in some places than others due to labor immobilities, and that therefore the real product of the nation could be increased by policies encouraging laborers to move from places where real wages are low to places where they are high. As the first of two major arguments against this view, the idea may be questioned that large geographic differences in real wages are prevalent. Possibly few differences in real wages would be found if, in comparing money wages, adequate allowances were made for geographic differences in costs of living and for differences in human capital among groups being compared. There have been few attempts to make adequate geographic real-wage comparisons. As a second argument, to the extent that geographic differences in real wages do exist, they may represent differences in preferences of labor to live in different regions, or costs of migration including the uprooting of oneself from a familiar environment. It is difficult to argue that social gains can be made from redistributing population to overcome these immobilities. Apparent gains in real output of firms from moving workers

would be more than offset by worker welfare losses and moving costs, resulting in a net decline in national income if properly measured. For the
immobility argument to be valid requires the presence of a market distortion preventing labor from making a preferred move, such as inefficient
provision of labor market information or inefficient capital markets inhibiting individuals from borrowing to move. Whether these preventions of
preferred moves are significant is·at most a speculative matter.

There is another line of reasoning about a spatial misallocations ema-
nating from the labor market which is more direct and appealing. This has
to do with policies deliberately imposed to interfere with labor market
equilibration. In the United States a prime example is legislated minimum
wages. There is every reason to expect that the quantity of labor demanded will fall as the wage is raised above the market clearing level.
Whereas cost of living differences make the market clearing money wage
vary regionally, the usual practice is to impose the same minimum money
wage across regions. Incentives to migrate are affected by this practice,
introducing misallocations in the spatial distribution of resources which
are the concern of the analysis of this chapter.

A two-region model will be considered, where the first region might be
taken to represent the urban North and the second region the urban
South. Climate makes housing and other local goods less expensive, and
smaller city sizes lead to lower rental and daily commuting costs in the
South than in the North. Because of the lower prices in the South, the
same real wage is earned when the money wage is lower in the South than
in the north (see Chapter 12 by Izraeli). In the absence of chronic unemployment in either region, worker mobility ensures that the real wage for
labor of a given skill received in the North W_N is the same as real wages in
the South W_S. But if unemployment exists because of legally imposed
minimum wages, the condition for market equilibrium is $W_N(1 - \mu_N) =
W_S(1 - \mu_S)$ where μ_N and μ_S are the unemployment rates for each region.
When this condition holds, expected real wages in the two regions are the
same. If there were 20% unemployment in the North and no unemployment in the South, a worker would be indifferent between a $4 real wage
in the South and an 80% change of getting a $5 real wage in the North.
Previous concern with this type of phenomenon has centered on adjusting
observed money wages to obtain measures of the social opportunity cost
of hiring a unit of labor. In contrast, the concern here is with aggregative
implications. We wish to find out how much labor moves and to measure
the total effects on national income.

Suppose the labor force consists of various skill groups and includes a
lower-skill group for whom the minimum wage is above the market
clearing level in one or both regions. The demand curves for both kinds of

labor are derived demand curves. The final product produced may be considered a nationally marketed product whose price is given in each region.

Assuming a general homogeneous production function, derived demand elasticities for a region may be calculated for each factor of production. Then assuming that the price of the product is fixed along with prices of all other mobile factors and that the amount of local resources is fixed, the derived demand for this particular type of labor becomes a function of its wage alone. The demand elasticity is

$$\eta = -\frac{(\alpha_2^2 + 2\alpha_1\alpha_2 + \alpha_1^2)\sigma_{12} + \alpha_2\alpha_3\sigma_{13} + \alpha_3\alpha_1\sigma_{23}}{\alpha_2},$$

where the σs are elasticities of substitution and the αs are factor shares. If the elasticities of substitution among the three basic inputs (labor affected by the minimum wage, all other mobile resources, and fixed local resources) are equal to one, and if the share of output attributable to fixed resources and labor affected by the minimum wage are both equal, for example, to 15%, then the elasticity of demand η for this type of labor is about two.

Case I. Minimum Wage Effective Only in the South

A uniform minimum money wage imposed on both regions of the economy might be effective only in one region if it raises wages above market clearing level in the Southern low-money-wage area but not in the Northern high-money-wage area. If one visualizes the minimum wage gradually being raised, since $\eta > 1$, the total wage bill will fall in the South. The expected per capita income will also fall and the result will be an out-migration of laborers from the South to the North, lowering wages in the North and decreasing the initial unemployment caused by the minimum wage in the South. Equilibrium will occur when $W_N = W_S P_S$, where $P_S = 1 - \mu_S$ = probability of being employed in the South. Taking the differential of this condition gives as the relationship between percentage changes (denoted by the overdot).

$$\dot{W}_N = \dot{W}_S + \dot{P}_S \tag{1}$$

The change in employment L in each region is determined by the elasticity of derived demand:

$$\dot{L}_N = \eta \dot{W}_N \tag{2}$$

$$\dot{L}_S = \eta \dot{W}_S \tag{3}$$

The change in employment in the North is by identity related to migration. Let $\gamma = L_N/L_S$ be the ratio of Northern to Southern employment of the type of labor in question. Then

$$\gamma \dot{L}_N = \dot{M}, \tag{4}$$

where $\dot{M}$ is the number of labor force members who migrate out of the South as a percentage of employment in the South in the occupations affected by the minimum wage. Finally, the change in probability of being employed if in the South is by identity related to the change in employment and migration:

$$\dot{P}_S = \dot{L}_S + \dot{M}. \tag{5}$$

Given the commodity price level in the South, an exogenous increase in the minimum money wage translates into an exogenous increase in the real wage. The system (1)–(5) thus determines $\dot{W}_N$, $\dot{P}_S$, $\dot{L}_N$, $\dot{L}_S$, and $\dot{M}$ in terms of the exogenous variable $\dot{W}_S$. The equations can be solved by successively eliminating variables through simple substitutions, giving the following results:

Migration as percentage of initial employment in South
$$\Big\} = \dot{M} = \left[\frac{\gamma\eta(1 + \eta)}{1 - \gamma\eta} \right] \dot{W}_S$$

Unemployment rate in the South
$$\} = (\dot{L}_S + \dot{M}) = - \left[\frac{\eta(1 + \gamma)}{1 - \gamma\eta} \right] \dot{W}_S$$

Employment growth in the North for the occupations affected by the minimum wage
$$\Big\} = \dot{L}_N = \left[\frac{\eta(1 + \eta)}{1 - \gamma\eta} \right] \dot{W}_S$$

National unemployment rate for the occupations affected by the minimum wage
$$\Big\} \quad \text{unemployment rate in South}/ \\ (1 + \gamma) = - \left[\frac{\eta}{1 - \gamma\eta} \right] \dot{W}_S$$

Fall in real wages in the North
$$\} = \dot{W}_N = \left[\frac{1 + \eta}{1 - \gamma\eta} \right] \dot{W}_S$$

where the expressions pertain to labor in the occupations affected by the minimum wage in the South.

As an application, suppose the ratio of population in the North to that in the South is 3, with a minimum wage imposed forcing up the real wage in the South for one-fifth of the work force by 20%. Then given $\eta = -2$, $\gamma = 3$, and $\dot{W}_S = .2$, the foregoing formulas reveal that 17% of the Southern labor force affected by the minimum wage will migrate to the North, 23% of these laborers remaining in the South will become unemployed (an unemployment rate of nearly 5% over all workers in the South), the national unemployment rate will increase by 1.2%, population

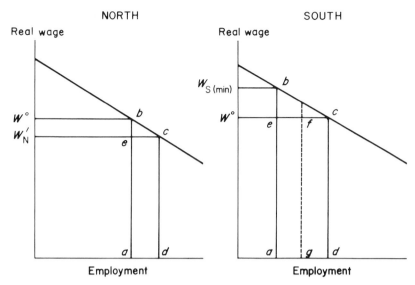

Figure 10-1. Social cost of minimum wage.

in the North will increase by 1.2%, and real wages in the North will fall by 2.9%. In Figure 10-1 without a minimum wage there is equilibrium at the same real wage W^0 in both regions. If a minimum wage is imposed which is effective only in the South, the real wage rises to $W_{S(min)}$ in the South and falls to W_N' in the North. Unemployment in the South develops equal to the distance ad.

The social cost from imposing a minimum wage is equal to the value of lost production due to unemployed labor plus the costs of inefficient spatial labor distribution. In terms of Figure 10-1, the cost is the area $abcd$ in the South less the area $abcd$ in the North, which is also equal to the areas $aefg$ and ebc in the South plus area ebc in the North. Using the expressions derived above, this can be written as

Social cost of minimum wage
$$= W^0([-(\dot{L}_S + \dot{M})] - \tfrac{1}{2}\,\dot{W}_N\dot{L}_N - \tfrac{1}{2}\,\dot{W}_S\dot{L}_S),$$
$$= \left[\frac{-\eta(1 + \gamma)}{(1 - \gamma\eta)} - \frac{\tfrac{1}{2}(1 + \eta)^2\eta}{(1 - \gamma\eta)^2}\,\dot{W}_S - \tfrac{1}{2}\,\dot{W}_S\eta \right]\,\dot{W}_S\,W^0.$$

Given the numerical parameter values being used in this example, the social cost is about 27% of the income previously earned by this segment of the labor force in the South. For example, if this income were $40 billion, then the social cost would be about $11 billion.

The model can be modified to include unemployment compensation. With unemployment compensation, labor will react such that in equilibrium

$$W_N = W_S(1 - \mu_S) + C_S(\mu_S),$$

where C_S refers to the unemployment compensation in the South measured as a percentage of the initial market equilibrating real wage.

Labor will see the unemployment compensation as an increase in its expected income in the South, and consequently the compensation will tend to dampen the migration flow to the North, resulting in greater unemployment and an increase in the social costs of the minimum wage. Conceivably, labor could be attracted out of the full employment North into the South, magnifying direct unemployment costs. Consider a case where real wages are \$2.50 in each region. Suppose that a minimum wage is then imposed raising real wages to \$3 in the South, and welfare compensation is guaranteed for the unemployed, equal in amount to the original real income. Given the same parameters previously used, there will end up being 40% fewer jobs available in the south for this type of labor. Expected income in the South will be [(\$3)(.6) + (\$2.50)(.4)] or \$2.80, which is \$.30 greater than in the North. Consequently, labor will migrate to the South, increasing unemployment there by more than the initial 40%. Such a situation could more than double the loss of \$11 billion suggested earlier.

Case II. Minimum Wage Effective in Both Regions

As the minimum wage is progressively raised, eventually a point will be reached where there is unemployment not only in the South but also in the North. Continuing to include the effect of unemployment compensation, the equilibrium condition becomes

$$W_N(1 - \mu_N) + C_N(\mu_N) = W_S(1 - \mu_S) + C_S(\mu_S).$$

First of all it should be noted that in this situation migration will not affect real output. As labor migrates in response to the new incentives the only thing that will change and eventually bring about an equilibrium is the level of unemployment in each region. Nevertheless the extent of labor migration is still of interest, for at least two reasons. First, if externalities are more prevalent in the congested urban North, then given no production changes associated with migration, net gains could be achieved by relocating labor to the South or by minimizing the flow of labor to the North. External social costs such as congestion and pollution are immediately brought to mind. Suppose also that crime and social unrest are a positive exponential function of the pool of unemployed labor in an area. If the total pool of unemployed labor is greater in the North, the marginal cost of moving an additional unemployed laborer to the North will then exceed the marginal benefit of less crime in the South. Consequently social gains can be achieved by again minimizing the flow of labor to the North.

Second, one needs to consider the costs of welfare compensation, that is, the costs of maintaining the unemployed with some minimum standard of living. If in fact the cost of living and hence the opportunity cost of supporting these people is less in the South, then again society can gain by encouraging migration of the labor force to the South.

As a simple numerical example, suppose that the labor force of low-skilled workers in a city of 6 million population is raised by 2%, or 30,000 unemployed persons, who would not otherwise live there in the absence of the minimum wage law. Suppose that the cost of living is 15% higher in large cities, and that the level of welfare payments in other places of smaller size is \$3000 per family. The cost associated with the spatial malallocation is therefore (\$3000)(0.15)(30,000), or roughly \$15 million. It should be emphasized that this is a very small fraction of the overall costs of the minimum wage system, which include the total value of compensation paid to the unemployed and the additional value of goods and services which could be produced if they were reemployed.

By differentiating the new equilibrium conditions, completing the system in a fashion parallel to the previous case and solving, one obtains

$$k = \frac{[(1 + \eta)(1 - \sigma) - \eta C_N(1 - \beta\sigma) + (1 - \sigma^2)\dot{W}_N]\dot{W}_N}{(1 - \gamma) + (1 - \sigma\gamma)\dot{W}_N - C_N(1 + \beta\gamma)},$$

where

$k = M/L_N$ the percentage increase in the North of that type of labor affected by the minimum wage

$\beta = C_S/C_N$ ratio of welfare compensation in real terms in the two regions

$\gamma = L_N/L_S$ ratio of the sizes of the labor force in the two regions

$\dot{W}_N =$ percentage increase in real wages in the North due to the minimum wage

$\sigma =$ ratio of the percentage increase in the real wage in the North to that in the South, due to the minimum wage

$C_N =$ ratio of real compensation to the level of income earned previous to the minimum wage in the North

$\eta =$ elasticity of demand for the labor group affected.

Given this result the unemployment rate of the labor affected by the minimum wage in each region can be obtained from

$$\mu_N = \eta \cdot \dot{W}_N + k,$$

$$\mu_S = \eta \cdot \dot{W}_N - k.$$

Assume $\sigma = 2$, $\eta = 2$, $C_N = .5$, $\beta = 1$, $\gamma = 3$, and $\pi = .2$. Then if the minimum wage is raised 10% above the market clearing level in the North, the solution for k gives

$$\left\{ \frac{-1 + 2 - (-2)1/2(-1) + (-3)(-2)(-.1)}{4 + .7 - .5(4)} \right\} (.1) = .023$$

indicating that the Northern region will experience 2.3% increase in the type of labor affected and hence a growth in population of about .44%. This migration along with the effect of the minimum wage directly will increase unemployment for this type of labor to 23% in the North (by 4.4% over all workers) and in the South the unemployment rate will rise to 33% (6.6% over all).

It is instructive to examine several other policy variants. In contrast to the foregoing assumption that real welfare payments are the same in both regions ($\beta = 1$), a national assistance plan such as widely discussed in recent years can be considered which would equate nominal welfare payments in the two regions. This would make the real level of compensation in the South greater (say $\beta = 1.3$). In this case $k = 0$, no migration will occur, unemployment in the North will only equal 20% of the affected labor type (4% overall), and in the South it will increase to 40% (8% overall). Because of the lower costs of supporting unemployed workers in the South, there would be nearly a $120 million dollar per year savings in welfare costs.

Policy variants can also be considered changing the nature of the minimum wage. Suppose that a minimum wage were established making real wages equal in both regions. As can be seen from the solution for k, if real unemployment compensation is also equated, net migration will be zero. On the other hand, if no compensation is given in the South, k will equal about 2.6%, Northern cities will grow in population .5%, and unemployment in the North will be considerably higher than in the South (23% versus 12%). If nominal compensation is equated in both regions k will equal -1.6%, that is outmigration from Northern urban areas will be induced and the unemployment differential will be reversed (18% versus 25%).

In general, if β is less than or equal to 1 any overall increase in welfare compensation stimulates a greater movement to the North. If nominal levels of compensation are equated, increases in the overall level of compensation dampen the flow of migration to the North and may even reverse it. The farther real minimum wages are above the market clearing wage holding σ constant the greater will be the migration. However, at extremely high minimum wage levels, σ would probably fall, dampening migration. Table 10-1 summarizes results for combinations of three welfare policies and three minimum wage policies.

As a final extension of this analysis, consider the possibility of impacts being reduced by labor-seeking employment in industries not covered by the minimum wage. The market will equilibrate where

$$W_N(1 - \mu_N) + \max[C_N(\mu_N), W_{N(NC)}\mu_N]$$
$$= W_S(1 - \mu_S) + \max[C_S(\mu_S), W_{S(NC)}\mu_N],$$

where $W_{N(NC)}$ is the Northern wage in noncovered industries and $W_{S(NC)}$ is defined similarly. The migration analysis is changed only in that the wage in the uncovered sector may be used in place of unemployment compensation. $(1 - \mu)$ becomes the probability of working in the covered sector. If this phenomenon existed and was most prevalent in the South either because of a greater opportunity for noncovered employment or because unemployment payments are lower in the South than the noncovered wage, migration results very similar to those reported in Columns 2 and 3 of Table 10-1 would be obtained. However, unemployment in the South will be substantially less if not zero.

The substantive difference then is that there are larger losses from induced migration out of the South inasmuch as labor is being drawn out of use in some productive activity in the South to the North where there is no gain in employment. One can imagine a case where noncovered wages were bid down until $C_S = W_{S(NC)}$. The migration results indicated above

TABLE 10-1
Percentage Migration Rates to the North, k

Wage policy	No welfare in South ($\beta = 0$)	Real welfare payments equal ($\beta = 1$)	Nominal welfare payments equal ($\beta = 1.3$)
Set nominal wages with large real differential ($\sigma = 2$)	6.2	2.3	0
Set nominal wages with small real differential ($\sigma = 1.5$)	3.2	1.0	-1.2
Set real minimum wage ($\sigma = 1$)	2.6	0	-1.6

will be unchanged, only now a 2.3% migration to the North could result in a social loss of considerably over a billion dollars. The market signals are encouraging labor to leave the South where there is certainty of work in an uncovered industry, in exchange for some given probability of earning a much higher wage in the North. But the chance of employment for society is only an illusion, as the probability of increased employment in the aggregate is zero.

With regard to the unemployment results taken as a whole, as one of the major examples welfare compensation was low in the South, and a minimum wage effective just in the South created a social loss of about $5.5 billion. This may approximate the situation when national minimum wages were first introduced in 1938. With significant rises in the minimum wage over the last few decades have come pronounced increases in unemployment of low-skilled workers in Northern cities, suggesting that the relevant case today is the minimum wage being effective in both the South and the North. In this case the social costs connected with failure to utilize labor efficiently mushroom, equalling about $23 billion dollars since labor cannot escape the unemployment. The analysis here, consistent with previous work, suggests that national income costs of the minimum wage are quite large. This finding alone does not have direct urban and regional policy implications. It has been shown here, however, that as a nominal minimum wage is raised, the national income costs of this policy will greatly expand not only because of the direct effect of raising the wage above the market clearing level, but also because coverage will be extended to progressively more areas where the minimum wage previously was not binding.

To the foregoing costs of the minimum wage due to unemployment, one needs to add at least $300 million costs of supporting the unemployed persons attracted to the North. This figure is for direct consumption of the unemployed and does not include social unrest and crime. Measures to reduce the costs resulting from induced regional movements could include raising welfare compensation in the South and, if minimum wages are not eliminated, establishing real rather than nominal minimum wages across regions.

Conclusion

Previous discussions of the spatial effects of the policies considered here have been almost entirely qualitative. The present study gives insights which are quantitative. Surprisingly strong results have been obtained by constructing simple models and applying reasonable numerical parameter values.

Migration flows induced by the minimum wage and by unemployment payments have been found to be substantial. Unemployment payments, as between having small payments in the South and having payments the same in nominal terms in the South as in the North, increased the number of low-skilled laborers in the North by 6%, which amounts to 1% of the North's total population. These are disemployed persons collected together into concentrated groups in the North.

The numbers in the examples could vary several fold and not reverse the indications that minimum wage laws, as currently designed, have profound unintended spatial effects. We have here, in effect, an implicit (and generally unrecognized) deleterious population distribution policy.

VI
LABOR COMPENSATION
AND EXTERNALITIES

11

A Theory of Money Wages[1]

GEORGE S. TOLLEY

Simple Wage Multiplier

If wages in a place are higher than in the rest of the economy, the resulting higher production costs are likely to make prices higher. Prices in turn have a reinforcing effect on wages, since higher prices increase living costs raising the money wage necessary to attract labor. The idea that wages affect, and are affected by, prices, provides a basis for understanding the spatial patterns of prices and wages.

The scope for a cost effect of wages on prices is greater for local commodities than for goods traded between a city and the rest of the economy. If the goods exported from a city to the rest of the economy are widely produced elsewhere, and if the demand for goods imported into the city is small relative to national demand, prices of traded commodities in the city can be taken as essentially given. Prices of imports will be higher by transport costs, and prices of exports will be lower by transport costs, than prices in the rest of the economy. On the other hand, for non-

---

[1] This chapter reproduces a portion of the material first published in George S. Tolley, "The Welfare Economics of City Bigness," *Journal of Urban Economics* **1**, 1974, 324–345.

traded commodities, the latitude for prices to vary within transport costs limits is great, first, because transport costs are high for some goods and, second, because transport costs are infinite for services in as much as services do not physically endure beyond the act of their production.

For a service or a good not transported between cities, a useful definition is that its price equals the sum of wage payments per unit of output plus payments to all other claimants per unit of output. Wage payments may in turn be expressed as wage w times labor input coefficient, that is, $p_L = b_L w + R_L$, where p_L is commodity price, b_L is labor input per unit of output and R_L is payments per unit of output to nonlabor claimants. The subscript L refers to local commodities.

To consider price differences among cities, take the differential of p_L and divide by p_L to obtain: $\dot{p}_L = s_L \dot{w} + r_L$, where s_L ($= b_L w / p_L$) is labor's share of total revenue. This equation expressed the percentage price difference as the sum of the impact of percentage difference in wage plus all other influences.

The reinforcing effect, of prices on wages, is due to labor supply behavior. For human resources, which yield personal services inseparable from owners, switching employment over a very great distance will be accompanied by a change in residence entailing a different location of consumption. Adjustment of labor supplies among different places depends on comparisons by resource owners, not just of money rewards and transport costs, but of differences in prices of goods and services that affect real consumption rewards. If costs of changing employment are negligible relative to capitalized value of wage differences between cities, labor flows will tend to ensure that the same market basket is commanded by an hour of employment everywhere in the economy: $\dot{w} = e_T \dot{p}_T + e_L \dot{p}_L$, where the es are consumer expenditure weights, T refers to an index of goods transported in and out of the city, and as already noted, L refers to commodities not transported in and out. This equation states that wages will be proportional to a cost of living index, that is, the deflated or real wage is the same everywhere.

Substituting the condition for $\dot{p}_L$, that prices of local commodities are affected by wages, into the condition just presented for the percentage wage difference $\dot{w}$ results in an equation where $\dot{w}$ appears on both sides. Solving for $\dot{w}$ gives

$$\dot{w} = [1/(1 - s_L e_L)][e_T \dot{p}_T + e_L r_L]. \tag{1}$$

The first bracket is a multiplier effect of conditions in a city on wages due to wages making prices, and hence wages, still higher. As would be expected, the multiplier is larger, the larger is the share of labor as an expense in producing local commodities s_L and the larger is the consumer expenditure weight for these commodities e_L.

The multiplier explains why differences in wages between cities are accentuated due to local products. On the other hand, the direction of differences depends on the sign of the second bracket, in which the weights e_T and e_L are positive. While possibilities of systematic effects on the price index for traded goods p_T might be investigated, import goods will have higher price and export goods will have lower price than elsewhere. If $\dot{p}_T$ is presumed to be small because of these opposing effects, the prime candidate for explaining the direction of wage differences is the remaining variable in the second bracket, influence other than wages on costs of producing local commodities r_L.

A local commodity whose cost of production tends to vary systematically with city size is housing-plus-access. Travel costs for commuting, shopping, and pleasure, plus residential rents, affect the money wage that must be paid to make people as well off in one place as in another. These costs raise a problem in comparing money wages among cities because travel costs borne depend on where a family resides within a city. People may choose between paying higher rent (or yearly equivalent as owners) and bearing time and money costs of travel. Land pricing makes rent plus travel costs tend to be the same everywhere within the city, with travel savings bid into land values so that moving closer to a place of trip destinations is largely offset by higher rents.[2] Given the substitution possibilities faced by families choosing where to live within a city, payment of rent plus travel costs may be viewed as payment for the single commodity "housing plus access" whose price is generally similar within the city but varies among cities.

In a large city, because of the greater distances to commuting and shopping margins, land has a greater travel savings value at a given distance from trip destination points than in a smaller city, making rent plus travel costs higher in the large city. The effect of greater distances to travel margins, whether for an individual it takes the form of more travel or higher rent, is to make for a positive value of r_L in going to a city of larger size.

Externalities due to congestion and pollution also contribute to higher wages for larger cities via effects on housing-plus-access. Congestion increases the time required to go a given distance making a contribution to r_L over and above the sheer distance contribution. Dirt, discomfort, and disease due to air pollution affect the quality from a given level of expenditure on housing-plus-access and raise r_L. The effects of city size on money wages necessary to attract labor to a city, and in particular those

[2] If everyone's income and tastes are identical, equality of rent plus travel costs within a city is an exact theoretical expectation. Because income and tastes are not identical, some differences, though possibly small, are expected. See Muth [4, pp. 29–34, 39–41]. For other versions of this general model, see Alonso [1] and Wingo [5].

effects due to externalities, will be central later in this chapter. The remainder of this part of the chapter consists of three sections showing how the explanation of wage differences is affected if more general assumptions are made.

Effect of Labor Content of Purchased Inputs
on the Wage Multiplier

The wage multiplier above is based on direct labor costs. To consider indirect labor costs due to purchased inputs, let the local commodity L be disaggregated, and use subscripts i or j for individual local commodities. The revenue identity $p_L = b_L w + R_L$ becomes a set of equations

$$p_i = b_i w + \sum^j a_{ji} p_i + R_i, \tag{2}$$

where b_i is the labor coefficient, a_{ji} is input of the jth commodity used per unit of output of the ith commodity and R_i is all other payments per unit of output. After transposing all prices to the left, the equations are $P[I - A] = B$, where P is the vector of prices, A is the matrix of a_{ji} coefficients, and B is the vector of $wb_i + R_i$ terms. From the solution $P + [I - A]^{-1}B$, the price of each local commodity is

$$p^i = \left(\sum^j b_j M_{ji} \right) w + \sum^j m_{ji} R_j. \tag{3}$$

To consider differences going from city to city, take the differential and express as percentage price differences:

$$\dot{p}_i = \left(\sum^j w b_j M_{ji} / p_i \right) \dot{w} + r_i. \tag{4}$$

Each M_{ji} is the increase in the demand for the jth commodity as a result of a unit increase in output of the ith commodity. The M_{ji}s are identical in concept to interindustry multipliers in regional input–output analysis [2, 3] except that they include only nontraded commodities. As earlier, the coefficient of $\dot{w}$ pertains to impacts on payments to labor assuming as given per unit amounts of labor. In a more extended analysis, effects of higher wages in causing substitutions toward other inputs could be included.

Substituting the solutions of $\dot{p}_i$ into the wage condition

$$\dot{w} = e_T \dot{p}_T + \sum^i e_i \dot{p}_i \tag{5}$$

and solving gives

$$\dot{w} = \left[1\bigg/\left(1 - \overset{ij}{\sum} e_i s_{ji} M_{ji}\right)\right]\left[e_T p_T + \overset{i}{\sum} e_i r_i\right], \qquad (6)$$

where $s_{ji} = wb_j/p_i$. If purchase inputs are not used, M_{ji} is one for $i = j$ and zero otherwise, giving the same value of the first bracket multiplier as in the preceding section. Use of purchased inputs implies positive values of M_{ji} for $i \neq j$, giving a greater value for the multiplier effects on money wages.

Effect of Market Basket on the Wage Multiplier

In Figure 11-1, the market basket chosen as a result of working an extra hour in city A is (x_T, x_L) where an indifference curve is tangent to

$$w' = p_T' X_T + p_L' X_L. \qquad (7)$$

The gain in utility to an owner of human resources from switching an hour of employment from the rest of the economy to City A is $U(x_T, x_L)$ minus $U(x_{T'}, x_{L'})$. The gain may be expressed in terms of observable magnitudes by considering the amount of composite commodity that would be given up to attain this gain, using for convenience a commodity containing one unit of traded goods and an accompanying bundle of nontraded goods defined by a proportion k of nontraded to traded products.

If the expansion path were such that the ratio of X_T to X_L did not change with income and if there were no substitution responses to relative prices, all market basket choices would lie on a straight line $X_L/X_T = k$

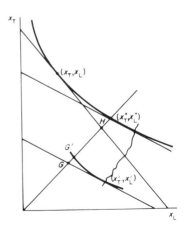

Figure 11-1. The market basket resulting from an extra hour of work in locations of different size.

such as the upward sloping line in Figure 11-1. With kinked indifference curves different from those shown, the point G might be chosen in the rest of the economy, and the point H in City A. The ratios of quantities would be the same in the two parts of the economy and could be used to define the weights in the composite commodity. The cost of a unit of the composite commodity would be $p_T + kp_L$ in City A and $p_{T'} + kp_{L'}$ in the rest of the economy, and the gain from switching employment to City A from the rest of the economy would be

$$[w/(p_T + kp_L)] - [w'/(p_{T'} + kp_{L'})], \tag{8}$$

that is, the difference in amount of the composite commodity purchasable as a result of an hour's employment. The labor supply equilibrium condition, where this gain from switching is zero, would be that the deflated wage rate be the same in City A and the rest of the economy, which is the condition underlying the wage multipliers considered so far. In terms of Figure 11-1, equilibrium would be attained by labor flows changing wages until the points G and H coincided.

More generally, as Figure 11-1 indicates, the same market basket composition will not be chosen. The money wage in the rest of the economy necessary to make a resource owner as well off as in City A is one for which the budget line is tangent to the same indifference curve as (x_T, x_L) enabling composite commodity purchase of (x_T^*, x_L^*) in the rest of the economy. The gain from switching employment, measured as the amount of composite commodity that would be given up to attain it, is represented by a movement from G' to (x_T^*, x_L^*) rather than G to H. So long as the expenditure proportions are different from the proportions in the composite commodity, satisfaction is greater than indicated by the amount of the composite commodity purchasable from an hour of employment at points G and H, because one can with the same money expenditure obtain a more desired combination. Let σ' be the proportionate change in money wage in the rest of the economy necessary to enable purchase of the market basket at G'. The amount of the composite commodity a resource owner would be willing to trade for an hour of employment in City A is then $w(1 + \sigma)/(p_T + kp_{L'})$, and in the rest of the economy is $w'(1 + \sigma')/(p_{T'} + kp_{L'})$. These are amounts of the composite commodity purchasable from an hour's employment plus amount of the commodity that would just compensate a person for being able to choose a more desired market basket. The gain from switching employment to City A is then

$$[w(1 + \sigma)/(p_T + kp_L)] - w'(1 + \sigma')/(p_{T'} + kp_{L'})]. \tag{9}$$

The labor supply equilibrium condition is obtained by setting this gain from switching equal to zero. Solve the equilibrium condition for w/w' and subtract 1, to obtain

$$\dot{w} = e_{T'}\dot{p}_T + e_{L'}\dot{p}_L + (\sigma' - \sigma)/(1 + \sigma), \qquad (10)$$

where $e_{T'}$ and $e_{L'}$ are expenditure weights times $(1 + \sigma')/(1 + \sigma)$. Inserting the price expression $\dot{p}_L = s_L\dot{w} + r_L$ and resolving gives

$$\dot{w} = [1/(1 - s_L e_{L'})][e_{T'}\dot{p}_T + e_{L'}r_L + (\sigma' - \sigma)/(1 + \sigma)], \qquad (11)$$

indicating that the general nature of the wage multiplier is not changed by relative price effects. Later in this chapter the analysis of this section will be used to consider the role of relative prices in labor's response to externalities.

Preferences for Nonreproducible Attributes of a Locality

If factor flows eliminate real differences in renumeration, variation in cost of living should explain the variation among cities in wages paid to labor of a given skill. However, even if refuted by ordinary measures, the assumption in this analysis that labor adjusts to make real wages everywhere the same is not as restrictive as may appear at first sight. The analysis can be redone assuming the labor supply condition to be

$$\dot{w} = e_T\dot{p}_T + e_L\dot{p}_L + \dot{I}, \qquad (12)$$

where $\dot{I}$ has been added to express as a percentage difference in wage rate the amount of money people are willing to take to live in one place as opposed to another after correcting for price differences between places. The expression for $\dot{w}$ taking account of the interdependence of wages and prices becomes

$$\dot{w} = [1/(1 - s_L e_L)][e_T\dot{p}_T + e_L r_L + \dot{I}], \qquad (13)$$

which is the same as the initial result except for the appearance of $\dot{I}$ in the second bracket.

A factual question is whether $\dot{I}$ is zero. The consideration of travel distances and externalities above suggests that it is not easy to establish whether real wages differ. Conceivably the reasons for expecting cost of living difference before introducing $\dot{I}$ explain most money wage variations. High geographic mobility of young people holds down $\dot{I}$, since people choosing where they will work when they enter the labor force act to reduce real earnings differences even though older persons might be willing to forego a substantial amount of income to continue to live where they are.

A nonzero value of $\hat{l}$, if it exists, is evidence of values attached to attributes associated with living in a place that are not included in the list of commodities of the system. For any system with nonzero $\hat{l}$, one can define a counterpart system by introducing an additional nontraded good consisting of these attributes. The value of $\hat{l}$ from the original system reflects differences in the price of this good, while the $\hat{l}$ of the counterpart system is zero. In the counterpart system, the analysis of location of production presented in this paper holds, including the implications that spatial distribution could be efficient in the absence of externalities. The definition of a counterpart system demonstrates that a finding of differences in real wages as usually measured does not prove the spatial distribution of economic activity is nonoptimal. Many discussions take for granted that geographic concentrations of factors earning less in real terms that they could elsewhere indicates nonoptimality. The concentrations raise equity issues not within the scope of this chapter and in any case have been of concern more in policies affecting competition among broad regions than among cities of various sizes.

References

1. Alonso, W. *Location and Land Use*. Cambridge, Mass.: Harvard University Press, 1964.
2. Isard, W. *et al., Methods of Regional Analysis*. New York: John Wiley, 1960.
3. Leontief, W. W. *et al.,* "Economic Analysis in Input Output Framework." *Gokhale Institute of Politics and Economics,* Poona, 1969.
4. Muth, R. F. *Cities and Housing*. Chicago, University of Chicago Press, 1969.
5. Wingo, L. *Transportation and Urban Land*. Washington, D.C.: Resources for the Future, 1961.

12

Externalities and Intercity Wage and Price Differentials[1]

ODED IZRAELI

Differentials in Money Wages and Prices between Cities

It is well known that great variations in money wages and prices of goods exist between different locations within the same country. The variations exist even though there are no legal barriers on mobility, and information about potential earnings and prices in each location is available. The purpose of this chapter is to shed light on why these variations occur.

Attention will be given to a vector of public goods whose supply varies by location. These public goods will be called environmental goods and will be added to the list of regular or private goods. The difference between the regular goods and the environmental goods is that the first have an observable positive market price which is given in every location but may vary between locations, whereas the environmental goods have no explicit market price and their quantity is given in every location, but varies between locations. Food, housing, and clothing are examples of

[1] Portions of this chapter appeared in O. Izraeli, "Differentials in Nominal Wages and Prices between Cities." *Urban Studies* **14**, 1977, 275–290.

regular goods whereas climate and air quality are examples of environmental goods. Environmental goods also include magnitudes influenced by local government such as quantity and quality of public education, probability of fire loss, and security.

Money wages and prices of goods are not two independent variables. Wages, as the main component of firms' cost of production, help determine the price of goods, and the price of goods is a variable affecting labor supply thus helping determine wage. Hence, structural equations explaining prices contain wages, and structural equations explaining wages contain prices. Both types of equations will be of concern in this study, as will the reduced form obtained from considering the simultaneous determination of wages and prices.

The subject of differential incomes between locations is not new in the literature. The most comprehensive recent empirical study (Fuchs [2, pp. 10–16]) found that much variability in money wage exists even after standardizing for color, age, sex, and education. The variation was found to be between different cities which were located in different regions of the country, as well as within each region. The study notes a tendency for money wages after making all standardizations to vary positively with city size. A second study (Hoch [6]) in which a positive correlation between city size and wage was found was a step forward in recognizing that price of goods may be different also according to locations; therefore real income was used. The study tried to explain the positive correlation between city size and real income as compensatory payments for the poor quality of the environment in big cities. The study however did not take into consideration the simultaneous relationship between prices and wages and the direct effect of environmental goods on both.[2] A related literature (Harberger [5]; Tiebout [9]) has called attention to unemployment and community services as conditions influencing the decision of the individual in choice of location. But neither approach has tried to estimate directly the effect of those environmental goods on wages.

Differentials in prices between different locations have received much less attention than money income. Price differences for individual goods traded between areas have occasionally been studied, but there has been almost no consideration of overall differences in prices including both traded and nontraded goods. Aside from the cost of living indices for 39 metropolitan areas, little comprehensive information on prices has been assembled according to location. On the theoretical side, the point noted in the previous paragraph has been made that wages can be expected to

_____

[2] This simultaneous relationship was emphasized by Tolley [10].

affect prices, but the conceptual bases are not developed enough to account for either price level differences with countries or the relationships between wages and prices in the presence of environmental goods.

This chapter advances existing knowledge by analyzing the simultaneous effect of environmental goods on wages and prices. One of the by-products of this effort is to help close the existing deficiency in understanding of effects of city size on the environment.

A MODEL OF WAGES AND PRICES IN A CITY

General Framework

Assume a world of two commodities. The first commodity is an aggregate of the regular goods which will be called Q. People buy these goods in the market, and their expenditures on these goods are equal to their income. That is $PQ = W$, where P is the price of the commodity and W is money income or wage, which implies $Q = W/P$. In other words, the total amount of the regular goods consumed is equal to the money income or wage deflated by the prices of the regular goods prevailing where the person lives.

The second commodity is an aggregate of the environmental goods. Their market price is zero, and their quantity is fixed in every location. The environmental goods will be called Z. In Figure 12-1 the vertical axis measures regular goods $Q = W/P$ and the horizontal axis Z. Assuming a decreasing marginal utility from the environmental good Z, an indifference curve can be drawn between Q and Z, characterized by a negative slope as shown in Figure 12-1.[3]

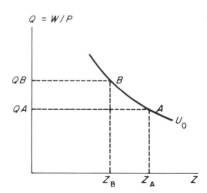

Figure 12-1. Indifference curve between ordinary and environmental goods.

[3] The definition of Z should be as a good which contributes a positive utility, as for example, clean air and not air pollution.

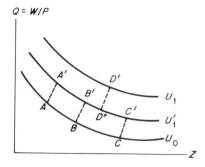

Figure 12-2. Movements toward equilibrium.

Figure 12-2 suggests the mechanism that pushes the system toward equilibrium. Assume that in an initial situation the combinations of W/P and Z in cities A, B, and C are on the same indifference curve U_0, whereas the combination in D is on a curve of higher utility U_1. People will begin to move from A, B, and C to D. Because of the labor movements, one expects that W/P and Z will increase in A, B, and C and decrease in D. Equilibrium will be reached along the curve U_1' in which W/P and Z are higher than before in cities A, B, and C, and lower in D.

Labor supply considerations thus suggest the existence of a first basic relationship, explaining money wages. Money wages can be expected to vary proportionately with prices of regular goods, for given amounts of environmental goods. The magnitude of effects of environmental goods on money wage depends on their marginal rate of substitution for regular goods.

A second basic relationship pertains to differences in prices of regular goods according to location. In order to investigate these differences one can assume that free competition exists in every location and all firms are producing at minimum average cost. As an approximation it may be assumed that price equals minimum average cost. Wages and other remunerated inputs affect costs, and the amounts of environmental goods affect costs because they shift production functions. Thus the price of each regular good may be expressed as a function of the wage level in the location, the prices of other remunerated inputs, and amounts of environmental goods in the location.

The two basic relationships, the one for wages and the other for prices, may be brought together as illustrated in Figure 12-3, which depicts a stable equilibrium. The one relationship stating that wages depend on prices, together with the other stating that prices depend on wages, imply that wages and prices are interdependent. Combining the two relationships into reduced-form equations and solving for wage or price solely in

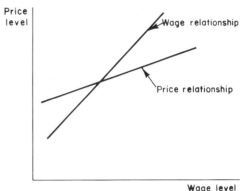

Figure 12-3. Regional wage–
price equilibrium.

terms of environmental goods yields a logically complete explanation of differences in money wages and prices from place to place. When this is done, the ultimate determinant of locational wage and price differences is seen to be environmental goods.

According to the first relationship environmental goods affect worker utility leading to an addition or subtraction from wages necessary to attract labor. Since the second relationship states that prices depend on wages, any effect of environmental goods on utility affecting wages must also influence prices. Similar considerations apply to the effects of environmental goods on firm production costs. According to the second relationship, environmental goods, by affecting firms' production costs, influence the prices of regular goods. Since the first relationship indicates that wages depend on prices, any production cost effects of environmental goods on prices will also influence wages necessary to attract labor.

Because of the interdependence which has been noted, environmental goods have multiplier effects on locational wage and price differences. Consider two cities which are identical in environmental goods except that in one the weather is mild and there is proximity to free public beaches, lowering the wage necessary to attract labor. Suppose this environmental difference is worth 1% of the money wage prevailing in the other city. The money wage in the city with the favorable environment will fall below the wage in the other city by more than 1%. If local labor represents one-third of the production costs in local industries, the costs of production will be made one-third of 1% lower by a 1% lower wage, lowering prices by one-third of 1%. Such a lowering of prices would attract even more labor to the city, further reducing wages. Each reduction in wages continues to lower prices by one-third as much as the lowering of wages. From multiplier theory, the limit to such a process is reached at a wage which is lowered by $1/(1.33)$ or 1.5 times as much as the initial impetus. (Percentage change in W = initial percentage change in W plus the percentage change in prices.) Thus the effect of environmental goods worth 1% of the alternative money wage available to people is a 1.5% wage difference due to the lowering of prices of regular goods.

As an example of a production cost effect, suppose two cities have the same environmental goods except that one is in a mountainous part of the country and the other is in a flat part where transportation costs are lower. If production costs are lowered by 1%, the competitive assumption implies prices will be lowered by 1%. Labor will be attracted by the lower prices until wages have been lowered by 1%, but then prices will fall another .33% further lowering wages, and so on until there is a 1.5% difference in wages between the two cities as in the previous example. The examples could of course be combined for environmental goods that affect both worker utility and firms production costs.

A Wage Equation

An algebraic representation can be derived by assuming a Cobb–Douglas utility function, $U = KQ^\alpha Z^\beta$. Instead of assuming a world of two goods, the regular goods and the environmental goods may be disaggregated:

$$U = K \prod_{i=1}^{n} (Q_i)^{\alpha_i} \prod_{j=1}^{m} (Z_j)^{\beta_j}, \tag{1}$$

where the Qs are regular goods and the Zs are environmental goods. The consumer maximizes utility in a given location by allocating money wage W among the Qs. The condition on the Qs for maximizing U subject to $W = \Sigma P_i Q_i$, obtained by the well-known Lagrangian method, is

$$Q_i = \alpha_i W \bigg/ \left(P_i \sum_{i=1}^{n} \alpha_i \right). \tag{2}$$

Substituting this condition into the utility function gives

$$U = K \left(W \bigg/ \sum_{i=1}^{n} \alpha_i \right)^{\Sigma \alpha_i} \prod_{i=1}^{n} (\alpha_i/P_i)^{\alpha_i} \prod_{j=1}^{m} Z_j^{\beta_j}. \tag{3}$$

Movement of labor can be expected to make wages such that the utility from moving is zero, or $U_A - U_B = 0$ where A and B refer to two different locations. In view of the fact that $U_A - U_B = 0$ implies $\log U_A - \log U_B = 0$, one can take the log of Eq. (3) and insert values for location A, then repeat these steps for location B, set the difference equal to zero and rearrange:

$$\log W_{\mathrm{A}} - \log W_{\mathrm{B}} = \sum_{i=1}^{n} a_i (\log P_{i\mathrm{A}} - \log P_{i\mathrm{B}})$$

$$+ \sum_{j=1}^{m} b_j (\log Z_{j\mathrm{A}} - \log Z_{j\mathrm{B}}), \qquad (4)$$

where $a_i = \alpha_i/\Sigma\alpha_i$ and $b_j = \beta_j/\Sigma\alpha_i$. Equation (4) is a relationship suitable for empirical application which shows that the percentage difference in wages between two locations depends linearly on percentage differences in amounts of environmental goods. The wage equation can be rewritten

$$\log W_{\mathrm{A}} - \log W_{\mathrm{B}} = (\log P_{\mathrm{A}} - \log P_{\mathrm{B}}) + \sum_{j=1}^{m} b_j (\log Z_{j\mathrm{A}}{}^{\bullet} - \log Z_{j\mathrm{B}}), \qquad (5)$$

where, for example, $P_{\mathrm{A}} = \Pi_{i=1}^{n} (P_{i\mathrm{A}})^{a_i}$ is a price index whose value may be approximated by published cost of living indices.

A Price Equation

The second basic relation concerns differences in prices of regular goods between locations. To derive the price equation as determined by supply conditions a Cobb–Douglas production will be assumed for each single good. To illustrate the procedure, let

$$Q_i = \eta_0 L_i^{\eta} G_i^{1-\eta}, \qquad (6)$$

where Q_i is output of good i, L_i is labor, and G_i is all other remunerated factors of production. Equation (6) may be solved for G and divided by Q to obtain:

$$G_i/Q_i = \eta_0^{1/(\eta-1)}(L_i/Q_i)^{\eta/(\eta-1)}. \qquad (7)$$

The total cost is $C_i = WL_i + RG_i$, where W and R are the wages of L and G, respectively. The average cost function is thus $\bar{C}_i = (WL_i/Q_i) + (RG_i/Q_i)$ which in view of Eq. (7) is

$$\bar{C}_i = (WL_i/Q_i) + R(L_i/Q_i)^{\eta/(\eta-1)}\eta_0^{1/(\eta-1)}. \qquad (8)$$

The next step is to find the point of minimum average cost by solving

$$d\bar{C}/d(L_i/Q_i) = W - [R\eta/(1-\eta)]\eta_0^{1/(\eta-1)}(L_i/Q_i)^{1/(\eta-1)} = 0, \qquad (9)$$

which can be solved for L/Q:

$$L_i/Q_i = (1/\eta_0)(W/\eta)^{\eta-1}[(1-\eta)/R]^{\eta-1}. \qquad (10)$$

Substituting this value into Eq. (8)

$$\min \bar{C}_i = (1/\eta_0)(W/\eta)^{\eta}[R/(1-\eta)]^{1-\eta} = P_i \qquad (11)$$

if price equals min $\bar{C}$ as can be expected under the assumption of free competition. The production function shifter η_0 can be disaggregated to show the effects of the environmental goods, which are inputs whose amounts are given to the firm:

$$\eta_0 = \eta_0' \prod_{j=1}^{m} (Z_j)^{\delta_j'}, \tag{12}$$

where as before the Zs are environmental goods. Substituting Eq. (12) into Eq. (11) and adding the level of local sales and property taxes as a factor influencing costs:

$$P_i = (1/\eta_0') \prod_{j=1}^{m} (1/Z_j)^{\delta_j'} (W/\eta_1)^{\eta_1} (R/\eta_2)^{\eta_2} (S/\eta_3)^{\eta_3}, \tag{13}$$

where W as before is money wage of labor, R is price of other remunerated inputs, and S is local sales and property taxes.

To consider the difference in the price of good i between locations A and B, take the logarithms of both sides of Eq. (13) and subtract the resulting condition for City B from the condition for City A:

$$\log P_{iA} - \log P_{iB} = \left[\eta_1(\log W_A - \log W_B) - \sum_{j=1}^{m} \delta_j' \right]$$
$$\times [(\log Z_{jA} - \log Z_{jB}) + \eta_2(\log R_A - \log R_B) + \eta_3(\log S_A - \log S_B)]. \tag{14}$$

Recalling that the price index P_A is $\Pi_{i=1}^{n}(P_{iA})^{a_i}$, multiply Eq. (14) for each good by a_i, sum up, and define $\Sigma_i a_i \delta_j' = \gamma_j$ and similarly for the γs to obtain

$$\log P_A - \log P_B = \gamma_0(\log W_A - \log W_B) + \sum_{j=1}^{m} \gamma_j(\log Z_{jA} - \log Z_{jB})$$
$$+ \gamma_{m+1}(\log R_A - \log R_B) + \gamma_{m+2}(\log S_A - \log S_B). \tag{15}$$

Equation (15) states that the difference in price index between A and B is a weighted sum of the differences in wages, environmental goods, remunerated inputs and local taxes between the two locations. Equation (15) is similar to Eq. (14) but each coefficient is now a weighted average of the coefficients appearing in the equations for the individual goods.

Reduced Form Equations

It is apparent that the two basic equations, the one explaining wages and the other explaining prices, that is, Eqs. (5) and (15), are not independent. A simultaneous relationship exists between them. Substitute Eq. (15) into Eq. (5) and collect wage terms to the left-hand side:

$$\log W_{\text{A}} - \log W_{\text{B}} = [1/(1 - \gamma_0)] \left[\sum_{j=1}^{m} (\gamma_j + b_j)(\log Z_{j\text{A}} - \log Z_{j\text{B}}) \right.$$

$$\left. + \gamma_{m+1}(\log R_{\text{A}} - \log R_{\text{B}}) + \gamma_{m+2}(\log S_{\text{A}} - \log S_{\text{B}}) \right]. \quad (16)$$

The interpretation of Eq. (16) is as follows: The coefficient $1/(1 - \gamma_0)$ is a multiplier which results from the simultaneous interaction of wages and prices. The parameter γ_0 is the elasticity of P with respect to W. Since we deal here with the Cobb–Douglas function, γ_0 is also the share of labor. Therefore $0 < \gamma_0 < 1$ and $1/(1 - \gamma_0) > 1$.

The individual terms on the right-hand side of Eq. (16) show the effects of differences in the amounts of environmental goods, local taxes, and prices of remunerated inputs between the two places. In other words, the equation shows that the ratio of nominal wages between two locations is equal to a multiplier times a weighted average of the ratios of the local conditions. For taxes and remunerated inputs the weights are the elasticities of the price index with respect to each of the factors. The environmental goods are also arguments in the utility function; therefore, their weights are the sums of two elasticities, one from the production function and the other from the utility function.

An example will clarify this point. Suppose that Z is an index of safety or security within the city. Then if all other local conditions are the same in the two places

$$\log(W_{\text{A}}/W_{\text{B}}) = [1/(1 - \gamma_0)](\gamma_j + b_j) \log(Z_{\text{A}}/Z_{\text{B}}). \quad (17)$$

This shows that the difference in security affects the nominal income through two channels. One is through the utility function as reflected in the b_j and the other is through the price index as reflected in γ_j and through it on the nominal wage. To find out each effect separately there is a need to know γ_j and b_j, whereas for the total effect there is a need to know also γ_0.

The reasoning presented here for the reduced form equation for wages also applies to prices. Substituting Eq. (5) into Eq. (15) and rearranging to solve for price gives the reduced form equation for the price level index:

$$\log P_{\text{A}} - \log P_{\text{B}} = [1/(1 - \gamma_0)]$$

$$\times \left[\sum_{j=1}^{m} (\gamma_j + \gamma_0 b_j)(\log Z_{j\text{A}} - \log Z_{j\text{B}}) \right.$$

$$+ \gamma_{m+1}(\log R_{\text{A}} - \log R_{\text{B}})$$

$$\left. + \gamma_{m+2}(\log S_{\text{A}} - \log S_{\text{B}}) \right]. \quad (18)$$

The same kinds of interpretations of effects of environmental goods via utility and via production costs could be given as was done for effects on wages. Furthermore, by substituting Eq. (5) into Eq. (14) it is clear that reduced form equations essentially the same as Eq. (18) could be obtained for the price of each individual good.

AN ESTIMATION STRATEGY

Let lower-case letters refer to differences of logarithms, and measure the differences from the average of the sample of cities for which the estimation will be undertaken. Then Eq. (5), which is the structural equation for wages, can be written:

$$w = b_0 p + \sum_j b_j z_j. \tag{19}$$

It will be noted that in Eq. (5) b_0 was assumed to be one, that is, an increase in prices raises wages proportionately. The possibility will be considered that in estimation $b_0 \neq 1$, because of problems of measuring price index accurately.

Equation (15), which is the structural equation for the price index, can be written

$$p = \gamma_0 w + \sum_j \gamma_j z_j. \tag{20}$$

For convenience, two more zs have been added to stand for r and s, the input price and tax variables, rather than carrying separate notation for these variables.

The reduced-form equations can be obtained by solving Eqs. (19) and (20) for w and p in terms of the zs:

$$w = [1/(1 - b_0\gamma_0)] \left[\sum (b_0\gamma_j + b_j)z_j \right] = \sum_j c_j z_j, \tag{21}$$

$$p = [1/(1 - b_0\gamma_0)] \left[\sum (\gamma_0 b_j + \gamma_j)z_j \right] = \sum_j d_j z_j, \tag{22}$$

where

$$c_j = [1/(1 - b_0\gamma_0)](b_0\gamma_j + b_j),$$

$$d_j = [1/(1 - b_0\gamma_0)](\gamma_0 b_j + \gamma_j).$$

Equations (19) and (20) should not be estimated directly. The inclusion of the mutually dependent variable p in one and w in the other will lead to the familiar problem of least-squares bias. The reduced-form equations do not encounter this problem. A first step is to estimate the reduced-form equations, that is, regress each of the endogenous variables on the exogenous variables. This estimation may be useful for predictive purposes but does not, without further work, give estimates of the underlying structural parameters.

As presented in general form in Eqs. (19) and (20), with no prior information given about any of the bs or γs, the structural equations are not identifiable. The most traditional way to seek identifiability is through assumptions that certain exogenous variables are excluded (i.e., certain parameters are zero). Dividing regression coefficients in the two reduced-form equations,

$$c_j/d_j = (b_0\gamma_j + b_j)/(\gamma_j + \gamma_0 b_j). \tag{23}$$

For any variables excluded from the structural wage Eq. (19), $b_j = 0$ in which case Eq. (23) reduces to $c_j/d_j = b_0$. Thus one has as many estimates of b_0 as there are exogenous variables excluded from Eq. (19). Similarly, for any variable excluded from the price index structural Eq. (20), $\gamma_j = 0$ whence Eq. (23) becomes $c_j/d_j = 1/\gamma_0$. Again there are as many estimates of γ_0 as there are exogenous variables excluded from Eq. (20). The inclusion of input prices and taxes in Eq. (20) and their exclusion from Eq. (19) is thus suggestive of further identifiability possibilities for Eq. (19). There could conceivably be hope of finding environmental variables which are expected to have a pronounced effect on utility but little on the cost of production and vice versa. However, it is easier to be confident about relative intensity of effect of variables than to be willing to hang an entire set of estimates on the assumption that a particular coefficient is precisely zero. Aside from the difficulty in forming such precise a priori notions, there are the usual problems of the lack of ideal measurements of the variables and inevitable omission of some variables, which could lead to nonzero coefficients in the estimation even if one were confident of a zero true coefficient.

As an alternative to the traditional approach to identification, a promising procedure is to make use of the fact that the general order of magnitude is known for the endogenous variable coefficients b_0 and γ_0. Multiply the reduced form coefficient d_j from Eq. (22) by an assumed value of b_0 and subtract the corresponding coefficient c_j in Eq. (21):

$$b_j = c_j - d_j b_0. \tag{24}$$

Similarly, multiply c_j by an assumed value of γ_0 and subtract d_j:

$$\gamma_j = d_j - c_j \gamma_0. \tag{25}$$

If one were sufficiently confident about measurement of price index, the strict implication of the theory that $b_0 = 1$ might be used. The restriction $b_0 = 1$ in Eq. (19) is sufficient to identify the remaining parameters in that equation. These remaining parameters in Eq. (19) can be estimated using the regression coefficients from the reduced-form equations. Rearranging Eq. (24), assuming $b_0 = 1$, gives:

$$b_j = c_j - d_j. \tag{26}$$

As unreasonable as it would be to assume the value of b_0, given existing price measures, is exactly 1, would be to assume that the value is orders of magnitude different from 1. To cover extremes, calculations could also be carried out for values of b_0 of .5 and 2.0. Using these three values of b_0 (.5, 1.0, and 2.0) enables generating three sets of estimates of the remaining b_js using Eq. (24).

The parameters of the structural Eq. (20) for price index remain nonidentifiable even if the restriction of b_0 is assumed to hold. The parameter γ_0 is the elasticity of prices with respect to wages, due to wages being a component of costs. The true value of γ_0 is almost certainly less than 1. With a value of γ_0 substantially greater than 1, any rise in wages would lead to a proportionately greater rise in prices, raising wages proportionately more, and generating explosive differences in wages and prices between different locations. The precise stability condition is that $b_0\gamma_0$ should be less than 1, but as just seen b_0 cannot be very far from 1. If $b_0 = 1$, the stability condition is $\gamma_0 < 1$. On the other hand, the fact that labor is the most important input cost suggests lower bounds for γ_0. In the model presented above with a Cobb–Douglas production function, γ_0 is the labor share. But γ_0 is only the share of local labor in locally produced goods.[4] Therefore three values chosen that almost certainly cover the extremes for γ_0 are .10, .33, and .67. These three values permit generating three sets of estimates of the remaining γ_js using Eq. (25).

An estimation strategy is then to calculate the three sets of b_js and three sets of γ_js and to choose one of each of the sets, so that together the most reasonable overall interpretation is obtained. The criteria for reasonableness are the signs of the structural parameters and relative intensity of effect in the two structural equations, in comparison with a priori notions.[5]

[4] In other words, p is the price of the final product, but the production may take place in several locations. Therefore, if the labor share in the national income is 65–70% and the value added of the production made within SMSA is about 50% of the total value, then γ_0 is the product of share of labor in national income times the share of the value added of the SMSA. Refer also to Tolley [10].

[5] This discussion has mainly restricted itself to the situation where there is one aggregate price index. Instead, one could use measures of prices of individual commodities or subgroups of commodities, in which case Eq. (20) would be replaced by a series of equations. The approach would remain the same as outlined here. A set of three b_js would be calculated for the wage equation, and there would be three sets of γ_{ij}s for each of the individual commodity equations. Applications of this more detailed approach are reported in the Appendix of Izraeli [7].

Previous analyses have mainly attempted to explain geographic differences in money wages in terms of differences in human capital, and there have been almost no serious attempts to explain differences in prices. The objective goal of this section has been to develop an integrated explanation of differences in wages and prices emphasizing environmental goods, holding constant skill level among locations. The next section discusses specific environmental variables and data sources and presents estimates of regression coefficients. It places special emphasis on relationships between population size, the other environmental variables, and urban wages and prices.

Externalities and Intercity Wage and Price Differentials: Some Evidence

The purpose of this section is to develop empirical tests of the theory of money wage and price differentials between urban areas presented in the preceding section. The analysis is based on observations on the variables listed in Table 12-1, for a sample of 67 SMSAs. Following some general comments on the regression coefficients, factors influencing wages, prices, and city size will be discussed individually.

OVERVIEW OF RESULTS

Table 12-2 shows coefficient estimates for the structural and reduced-form wage equations. The wage variable is wage per year for male laborers. The main need is to have a measure of earnings that is influenced as little as possible by wage differences due to factors such as human capital, sex, and other factors associated with skills. Regressions were run using seven other wage measures, including the hourly wage rate of males in some other occupations and median yearly earnings of females and males in different occupations.[6] The results are essentially the same no matter which of these measures is used.

The reduced form results for wages are from least squares regressions of the log of money wages on the logs of the exogenous variables for 67 SMSAs, the maximum number of SMSAs for which data are available. The structural equations for wages were estimated by using the wage rate divided by the price index as the dependent variable (assuming $b_0 = 1$).[7]

---

[6] See Appendix 4 of Izraeli [7].

[7] From Eq. (24), a structural coefficient b_j in the wage equation can be estimated from the reduced form coefficients for wages and prices if b_0 is known. In practice, what was done was to subtract b_0P from both sides of the structural wage Eq. (19) to obtain $W - b_0P = b_jZ_j$. Regressions of $W - b_0P$ on the exogenous variables assuming $b_0 = 1$ are reported in Table 12-2. The estimates are of very low sensitivity to the chosen value of b_0.

TABLE 12-1

Measurement of Variables

Name of variable	Measurement units, year	Sources	Remarks
Wage rate	1. Median earning of male laborers per year 1959, excluding farm and mine workers	*Census of Population,* Vol. I. Table 150, p. 314	
Price index	1. Index of costs based on a low living standard for a four-person family, Spring 1967	*Monthly Labor Review,* April 1969, p. 13	
	2. Cost-of-living index for 39 SMSAs, Autumn 1966	*BLS,* 1570, pt. 1–6	
Population	1. Number of inhabitants in SMSA, 1966	*Statistical Abstract for U.S. 1969*	
Air pollution	1. Sulfates (micrograms per cubic meter), 1966	Air Quality Data 1964–65, 1966, 1967	Because of limitations of the data, part of the observations were from 1965 and part from 1966
Crime, fire, and accident hazard	1. Crimes against persons, 1966 2. Crimes against property, 1966 3. Fire hazardousness, 1966 4. Death rate from accidents 5. Economic loss from each of the four components for the U.S.	(1) and (2) *Statistical Abstract for U.S. 1968, 1969;* (3) *Municipal Year Book 1967, 1969;* (4) *Accident Facts 1968,* p. 65, *N.S.C.;* (5) *Statistical Abstract for U.S. 1969,* p. 144, Table 213	This index is a weighted average of four components. The weights were chosen on the basis of economic damage from each component. The weights are: .08 fire, .67 accidents, .21 crime (property), .04 crime (personal)

Expenditures for services provided by local government	1. Real expenditures of local governments, per capita, in 1967, except fire and police	*Census of Government,* 1967	Deflated by median wage rate of males in all occupations
Real rate of property tax for SMSA	1. Effective rate of property tax (annual tax billed as percentage of sales price)	*Census of Government,* 1967, Vol. 2, Table 21	For missing SMSAs the rate was taken from the county or state
Climate	1. Average temperature during the month of January	*County and City Data Book,* 1967	
Net migration	1. Net rate of migration for regions	*Statistical Abstract of the U.S.,* 1971, p. 35	
Median age	1. Median age of laborers except farm and mine, 1959	*Census of Population,* 1960, Vol. I. Table 123	
Rate of unemployment	1. Rate of unemployment (percent of labor force)	*Statistics on Manpower.* A supplement report to the President, U.S. Dept. of Labor, March 1969, Table D-8.	

TABLE 12-2
Logarithmic Regressions of Median Money Wages of Male Laborers for Sixty-Seven SMSAs[a]

Independent variables	Coefficients in reduced form equations[b]			Coefficients in structural equations[c]		
	1	2	3	4	5	6
(1) Population	.10 (3.7)		.095 (5.0)	.081 (3.7)		.08 (4.7)
(2) Air pollution		.14 (3.4)	.07 (1.9)		.12 (3.3)	.06 (1.8)
(3) Crime, fire, and accident hazard		.04 (.4)	.006 (.07)		.08 (.80)	.05 (.60)
(4) Expenditures for local services per capita		.02 (.2)	−.07 (−.7)		−.03 (−.3)	−.11 (−1.3)
(5) Rate of property tax		.15 (2.7)	.14 (2.9)		.09 (1.7)	.08 (1.8)
(6) Climate		−.48 (−5.9)	−.50 (−7.3)		−.40 (−5.5)	−.42 (−6.8)
(7) Regional net migration		.13 (4.3)	.12 (4.6)		.11 (4.1)	.10 (4.3)
(8) Median age		.60 (1.9)	.54 (2.0)		.42 (1.5)	.38 (1.5)
(9) Rate of unemployment		.03 (.3)	.04 (.5)		.001 (.01)	.01 (.1)
R^2	.18	.59	.72	.17	.54	.66

[a] The t values are given in parentheses. For sources of data, see Table 12-1.
[b] Regression of money wages on the independent variables.
[c] Regression of deflated wages on the independent variables.

This procedure causes some problems in the estimation of the structural equations since price data are available for only 39 SMSAs. The coefficients found for the price equation from the sample of 39 SMSAs were used to project the price index for the entire sample of 67 SMSAs.[8]

[8] If the wage analysis is limited to the 39 SMSAs for which direct price observations are available, the following logarithmic regression equation is obtained:

$$W - P = 3.0 + .06 \text{ population} + .04 \text{ air pollution} - .13 \text{ crime, etc.}$$
$$ (3.1) (1.0) (1.4)$$
$$- .38 \text{ climate} + .09 \text{ migration} + .03 \text{ property tax}$$
$$(5.6) (3.1) (.4)$$
$$- .01 \text{ local services} + .10 \text{ unemployment} + .41 \text{ age,}$$
$$(.16) (1.1) (1.0)$$
$$R^2 = .72$$

TABLE 12-3

Logarithmic Regression for Intercity Variation in Price Index for Thirty-Nine SMSAs^a

Independent variables	Coefficients in reduced form equations^b			Coefficients in structural equations^c		
	1	2	3	4	5	6
(1) Population	.016 (1.8)		.01 (1.8)	−.013 (−1.6)		−.009 −(1.0)
(2) Air pollution		.002 (.1)	−.009 (−.5)		−.03 (−1.5)	−.02 (−1.0)
(3) Crime, fire, and accident hazard		−.02 (−.4)	−.03 (−.8)		.01 (.02)	.02 (.40)
(4) Expenditures for local services per capita		−.07 (−1.9)	−.08 (−2.1)		−.05 (−1.1)	−.04 (−1.1)
(5) Rate of property tax		.05 (−1.6)	.04 (1.1)		.007 (.2)	.02 (.4)
(6) Climate		−.08 (−2.7)	−.08 (2.7)		.07 (2.2)	.07 (2.1)
(7) Regional net migration		.05 (4.0)	.05 (3.6)		−.007 (−.5)	−.004 (−.3)
(8) Median age		.47 (2.8)	.40 (2.3)		.11 (.6)	.15 (.8)
(9) Rate of unemployment		.02 (.5)	.02 (.5)		−.008 (−.2)	−.005 (−.1)
R^2	.08	.51	.56	.06	.31	.34

^{a} The t values are given in parentheses. For sources of data, see Table 12-1.
^{b} Regression of price for independent variables.
^{c} Regression of (price) $P − .33W$ for independent variables.

Table 12-3 shows regression results when the dependent variable is the price index. The reduced-form estimates were obtained by regressing the log of the price index P on the logs of the various exogenous variables. In the structural equation estimates, the dependent variable is $P − .33W$.[9] The sample for the price regressions included only the 39 SMSAs. The price index used was the cost-of-living index published by the U.S. Department of Labor. One problem is that a cost-of-living index may have

---

which is the analogue to Eq. (6) in Table 12-2. As one can see the results are very similar, and the main difference is in the number of significant coefficients, which is larger in the equations based on the larger sample.

[9] This structural equation estimation procedure assuming local labor cost weight $\gamma_0 = .33$ is equivalent to that of Eq. (25), by the same logic as given in footnote 1. The coefficient estimates are of very low sensitivity to γ_0.

different quantity weights for different locations, instead of being a straightforward price index with constant weights. Two considerations help to neutralize the effect of regional differences in proportions of regular market goods consumed on cost-of-living indices. One is that the statistics on cost of living are computed in such a way as to hold utility (real income) constant everywhere.[10] The second consideration is that this analysis disaggregates only to the level of groups of goods and services such as food, housing, and so on, and not to individual goods. In such a case it is plausible to assume that price elasticities of demand for each group of goods are low. If each of these elasticities η_i falls in the range of $0 < \eta_i < 1$ then a change in the consumer cost of one group of goods is in the same direction as the change in price of this group of goods, and it will be of the same proportion if $\eta_i = 0$. Thus the cost-of-living index appears to be a reasonable surrogate for a price index. Cost-of-living indices are computed for low-income, moderate- or intermediate-income, and high-income families. The base for each is the average cost of living in a U.S. urban area given the appropriate level of income.[11] The results in Tables 12-2 and 12-3 are based on the moderate-income price index. Very similar results are obtained if low-income price indices are used.

About 70% of the variability in wage rate and 55% of the variability in price index among SMSAs has been explained. The R^2 is generally higher for the wage equation than for the price equation. To understand the significance of this, consider Table 12-3, Columns 4–6, which present coefficient estimates for the structural price equations. The R^2s in these equations are substantially smaller than in all the other equations. Also, unexpectedly, some of the coefficients raise questions about the reliability of the price index data, that is, the extent to which the price index correctly reflects all the prices that should be included.

Omission of one or more prices from the price index may introduce a bias in the estimation of each independent variable. Let $\hat{P}_t$ be defined as the correct price index, that is,

$$\hat{P}_t = \sum_{i=1}^{n} a_i P_{it},$$

[10] Groom [3] says, "The Budget was designed to represent the estimated dollar-cost required to maintain this family at a level of adequate living, to satisfy prevailing standards of what is necessary for health, efficiency, the nurture of children and for participation in community activities. This is not a 'subsistence' budget, nor is it a luxury budget; it is an attempt to describe and measure a modest but adequate standard of living. This City Worker's Family Budget continues to represent a moderate standard of living for a family of four, consisting of an employed man and his wife (who is not employed outside the home), a girl of 8 and a boy of 12 [p. 7]."

[11] Refer to U.S. Bureau of Labor Statistics Bulletin, 1960–1970, No. 1570, Pt. 1, as well as the Monthly Labor Review, April 1969, pp. 3–16.

where a_i is a constant weight and the P_{it}s are the prices of the individual goods.[12] The index t symbolizes different locations: in the present sample, $t = 1 \cdots 67$. If a price is improperly omitted, the observed index is not $\hat{P}$, but, for example,

$$P_t = \sum_{i=1}^{n-1} a_i P_{it}$$

with P_n omitted. The important point is that $P_n = f(Z_j)$. In other words this error does not have a random distribution over the sample, but rather causes a systematic bias since the omitted price is a function of one of the environmental goods.

A formal presentation follows. In order to simplify the earlier equations, Eqs. (19) and (20), only two explanatory variables will be used, Z_1 and Z_2:

$$W - \hat{P} = b_0 + b_1 z_1 + b_2 z_2, \qquad (27)$$

$$\hat{P} - .33W = \gamma_0 + \gamma_1 z_1 + \gamma_2 z_2. \qquad (28)$$

Suppose that the actual price index fails to reflect some prices which should have been included. In other words, instead of estimating Eq. (28), Eq. (29) is estimated:

$$P - .33W = \gamma_0' + \gamma_1' z_1 + \gamma_2' z_2 \qquad (29)$$

For some of the explanatory variables it can be assumed the expectation $E(\gamma_i' - \gamma_i) = 0$. In other words there is only a random deviation between γ_i' and γ_i. But for other variables it may be the case that $E(\gamma_i' - \gamma_i) \neq 0$, or in other words, that there is a systematic error in the measurement of the price index.[13] Let us assume that the error is in Z_1 only. Then $\gamma_1' \neq \gamma_1$ and all the other coefficients are the same in Eqs. (28) and (29) except for random deviation.

In the wage equation, $W - P$, that is, the log of real wage, was used as the dependent variable, where it will be noted that the price deflator P has measurement error. To consider the result of this, note that $W - P$ can be represented as the sum of the wage deflated properly plus the difference in log of true and measured log of price index, or $W - P = (W - \hat{P}) +$

[12] If $\Sigma a_i P_i^A$ is the price index, it should be divided by $\Sigma a_i P_i^0$ where p_i^0 is a common base for all price indices. Also, it can be assumed that $\Sigma a_i P_i = 1$.

[13] An implicit assumption here is that the wage has no error, or at least a smaller error than the error in the price index.

$(\hat{P} - P)$. Subtracting Eq. (29) from Eq. (28) and adding the result to Eq. (27) gives:

$$(W - \hat{P}) + (\hat{P} - P) = b_0 + (\gamma_0 - \gamma_0') + [b_1 + (\gamma_1 - \gamma_1')]Z_1$$
$$+ [b_2 + (\gamma_2 - \gamma_2')]Z_2. \quad (30)$$

Whenever a systematic measurement error occurs in the price index, Eq. (30) is estimated instead of Eq. (19). In all cases, where $E(\gamma_i' - \gamma_i) = 0$ there will be no bias in the estimation of the ith coefficient. But in case $E\gamma_i' \neq \gamma_i$, the same bias found in the estimation of the price equation will appear also in the estimation of the wage equation for the same coefficients and of the same magnitude, but of opposite sign.[14] A concrete application of this discussion will be made for specific independent variables which will be considered in the following section.

The argument presented here is for omission of a variable correlated with one of the independent variables from the price index. The argument clearly generalizes to a situation where a variable, rather than being completely omitted, is measured with error which being correlated with one of the independent variables.

DETAILED OBSERVATIONS

City Size

The most commonly used measurement of city size is the number of inhabitants within the political boundary of the city or SMSA. Even so it is agreed that city size is only an empirical surrogate for other causal

---

[14] The bias in the reduced form coefficients can be seen by solving Eqs. (24) and (25) for c_j and d_j in terms of the structural coefficients, and by assuming $b_0 = 1$ and $\gamma_0 = .33$.

$$c_j = \frac{b_j + b_0\gamma_j}{1 - b_0\gamma_0} = \tfrac{3}{2}(b_j + \gamma_j) \quad \text{(i)}$$

$$d_j = \frac{\gamma_0 b_j + \gamma_j}{1 - \gamma_0 b_0} = \tfrac{1}{2}(b_j + 3\gamma_j). \quad \text{(ii)}$$

Suppose that the only biased coefficient is that of Z_1. The expression for the biased coefficient from the structural Eq. (30) can be inserted into (i) and (ii) to obtain expressions for the estimated reduced form coefficients:

$$c_1' = \tfrac{3}{2}[\gamma_1' + (b_1 + \gamma_1 - \gamma_1')] = \tfrac{3}{2}(\gamma_1 + b_1) \quad \text{(i')}$$

$$d_1' = \tfrac{1}{2}[3\gamma_1' + (b_1 + \gamma_1 - \gamma_1')] = \tfrac{1}{2}(b_1 + 3\gamma_1) + (\gamma_1' - \gamma_1) \quad \text{(ii')}$$

Comparing Eqs. (i) with (i') and (ii) with (ii') one can notice that there is no bias in the reduced form coefficients in the wage equation due to error in the measurement of the price index. But in the reduced form equation for the price index, it is expected to find a bias in the estimation of the coefficients. The magnitude of the bias is the same as in the structural equation but of opposite sign.

factors that affect wages or prices. This means that city size affects the amounts of some public goods which are available for the residents of the city. These public goods are part of the collection of goods (private or public) that the residents of a city consume. The environmental goods, rather than city size itself, are what affect wages and prices. The residents get or pay monetary compensation depending on whether the contribution of these environmental goods to utility is negative or positive. Suppose the relationship explaining the amount of the environmental goods is:

$$Z_j = f_j(\text{Population, other variables}), \qquad j = 1, \ldots, n, \qquad (31)$$

where Z_j is one of the environmental goods and $\partial Z_j/\partial \text{Pop} \gtrless 0$. Following the approach of using environmental goods as independent variables in explaining wages and prices as suggested earlier, one would prefer to estimate the effect of population on wages or prices by multiplying the effects of population on environmental goods by the effects of environmental goods on wages or prices. The total influence of population on wages or prices is the sum of products of these effects for each environmental good. In equation terms, differentiate Eqs. (19) or (20) by population and substitute partial derivatives of the Z_j with respect to population from Eq. (31) to obtain:

$$\frac{dW}{d\text{Pop}} = \sum_{j=1}^{n} \frac{\partial W}{\partial Z_j} \cdot \frac{\partial Z_j}{\partial \text{Pop}} = \sum_{j=1}^{n} b_j f_j', \qquad (32)$$

$$\frac{dP}{d\text{Pop}} = \sum_{j=1}^{n} \frac{\partial P}{\partial Z_j} \cdot \frac{\partial Z_j}{\partial \text{Pop}} = \sum_{j=1}^{n} \gamma_j f_j'. \qquad (33)$$

This reasoning applies if all the variables are measured accurately. Probably in any empirical study, however, some environmental goods affected by population are omitted or measured imperfectly and there are errors correlated with population in the measurement of some prices. Population is used as a surrogate for these omissions and errors. The interpretation of the population coefficient in the wage and price equations is affected by the existence of a measurement error in the price index. Tables 12-2 and 12-3 show that population has a positive significant correlation with wage rate and a weak negative correlation with price indices in the structural equations. Since on theoretical grounds one would expect environmental goods to affect prices and to affect them perhaps even more significantly than wages, this result suggests that errors in measurement of price have introduced downward bias associated with population in the price equation and upward bias in the wage equation.

Urban economic theory suggests the existence of shortcomings in the construction of the price indexes. In particular, location theory indicates

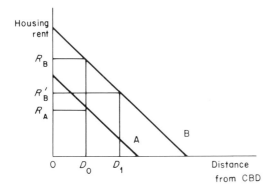

Figure 12-4. Rent–distance relationship.

a relationship between housing prices and distance from central business district ignored in the price index.[15] Figure 12-4 illustrates a rent–distance relationship under very simple assumptions,[16] but it is sufficient to indicate the conceptual problems in the construction of the price index. Land values can be expected to adjust to make consumers indifferent between locations within a city, for example, City A or B in the figure. Any point along a rent gradient expresses the housing rent (or price), given the distance from CBD. However, in practice, housing enters the price index as follows: "The cost of the rental shelter standard was calculated from the average rent in the middle third of the distribution of Autumn 1966 rents. . . . Purchase price . . . represented the average price of the middle third of the distribution of market values for dwellings."[17] In other words BLS tries to compare housing prices at the same *relative* distance from the central business district instead of the same *absolute* distance. In terms of Figure 12-4, the comparison is between points like D_0 and D_1 in locations A and B, respectively. This results in a downward bias of the rent difference between the two locations $[R^B - R^A] > [R^{B'} - R^A]$.

A second error in the price index results from the omission of time and money cost of travel within the area, which are positively correlated with population, since the price index for housing is not measured exactly at the CBD. These errors cause a downward bias in the coefficient of population in the price index equation. If distances were correctly standard-

---

[15] See [1, pp. 114–115].
[16] Usually the vertical axis in a diagram like Figure 12-4 measures the rent per unit of land and not housing. Housing is used here because its price rather than land as such appears in the price index. The use of a straight line instead of a curve implies fixed lot size with respect to distance from center of the city. The relaxing of this assumption makes the illustration more complicated but does not affect the conclusion.
[17] *U.S. Bureau of Labor Statistics Bulletin 1967–1970*, No. 1570, Pt. 1, p. 18.

ized and if the greater time and money costs of travel associated with larger cities were included in the price index, the price index would be more highly correlated with population. In terms of Eqs. (28) and (29), $\gamma_1' <$ γ_1. Concommitantly, as seen from Eq. (4), these errors and omitted factors cause an equivalent upward bias to the coefficient of population in the structural equations for wages. The dependent variable $W - P$ using the price index measured with error rises more with an increase in population than $W - P$ using a correct price index because P fails to respond properly to population. This reasoning explains the negative coefficient of population in the structural equation for prices in Table 12-3 and the strong positive coefficient in the structural equations in Table 12-2.

The responsiveness of wages to population is considered further in Table 12-4. Table 12-4 gives a computation based on Eq. (32). The partial derivatives of wages with respect to environmental goods $\partial W/\partial Z_j$ are based on the regression of Table 12-2, Eq. (6), the structural equation for wages. The derivative of environmental good with respect to population $\partial Z_j/\partial \text{Pop}$, was found by running a simple regression of each Z_j on population.[18] Making use of the multiplicative effect of these two terms for an environmental good, the subtotal in Table 12-4 gives the sum of effects of population on wages due to positive association of population with environmental goods, for those goods where the association is statistically significant. The subtotal is very small in relationship to the .081 coefficient of population in Eq. (4) of Table 12-2, which is the simple correlation between wages and population. This is consistent with the finding that the simple correlation coefficient of population with wages is very similar to the population coefficient in the full structural equation [Eq. (6)], that is, adding variables other than population to the explanation of real wages re-

TABLE 12-4

Effect of Population Change on Wages

	$\dfrac{\partial Z_j}{\partial \text{Pop}}$	$\dfrac{\partial W}{\partial Z_j}$	$\dfrac{\partial Z_j}{\partial \text{Pop}} \dfrac{\partial W}{\partial Z_j} = \dfrac{dW}{d\text{Pop}}$
(1) Air pollution	.20	.06	.012
(2) Local services per capita	.05	−.11	−.0055
Subtotal			.0065
(3) Traveling time	.20	.125	.025
Total			.0315

[18] A regression for each explanatory variable on population was run. In Table 12-4 only those variables with significant coefficients appear.

duces the effect of population very little. The conclusion is that other factors than measured environmental goods must have a larger role in explaining why real wages vary positively with population.

If in Table 12-4, independent estimates for one of the omitted variables, namely traveling time,[19] are added, the sum of products becomes .0315, which is 40% of the population coefficient found in Eq. (6). The interpretation is that if travel time had been included in the price index, the coefficient of population would have been reduced 40% in the structural wage equation.[20]

Air Pollution

In terms of the model developed on pp. 161–168, air pollution is one of the Z_j environmental goods. Tables 12-2 and 12-3 are based on the use of sulfates as a measure of air pollution. This variable is available for all SMSAs. As shown in Table 12-2 for both the reduced form and structural equations, air pollution has a strong positive effect on wages. Using the U.S. average annual wage per year for laborers of $3200, the structural equation estimates imply that a 10% increase in air pollution will require an increase in wages of $19.20 per year. Computations done by Lave and Seskin [8] may serve as a check on reasonableness. Their estimate indi-

---

[19] The estimation of $\partial Z_j/\partial \text{Pop}$ and $\partial W/\partial Z_i$ for the variable of traveling time was done in an indirect way because of lack of data. The first derivation was estimated on the basis of a sample including 32 observations. The sources are: Voorhees [11] and some other scattered data from origin-destination studies done for several cities. The estimation of it is:

$$Zn = -.025 + .20 \text{ population, } R^2 = .70,$$
$$(8.4)$$

where Zn is a logarithm of the average traveling time. The value of $\partial W/\partial Z_j$ was based on the assumption that people evaluate time spent on traveling as time spent on work. In other words, the alternative cost of traveling time is the wage rate. This implies that $\partial W/\partial Z_j = 1/h$ where h is number of hours of work, assumed here to be 8.

[20] Another piece of information may help to explain the residual part of the coefficient of population. The following regression equation suggests a positive correlation between log rent per month and log population in 67 cities.

$$\log \text{rent} = 3.96 + .042 \log \text{population } R^2 = .10.$$
$$(2.6)$$

The effect of population on wages due to higher rents in larger cities is the effect of the price index on wages $\partial W/\partial P$ or 1, times the effect of rent on the price index $\partial P/\partial R$ which can be approximated as the share of rent in the price index of .20 times the effect of population on rent $\partial R/\partial \text{Pop}$, just estimated as .042. Multiplying the three terms together gives .0084, which adds a little more to the explanation of the positive association between wages and population. The rent variable here is median rent per month in each city—not SMSA—and also it probably includes some of the deficiencies that the price index has explained before. But these data may be suggestive of the true relation.

cates that a reduction of 50% in air pollution may save up to $2.08 billion in medical costs. The saving includes forgone earnings and direct medical costs. According to the results in Table 12-2 a reduction of 50% in air pollution would be followed by a reduction of about $96 per year per worker. This change will add up to $2.08 billion if about 25% of the labor force is working or living in places where there is a dangerous amount of air pollution,[21] and if health damage is the only damage that air pollution causes. In view of the fact that 57% of the population is living in SMSAs of 250,000 population or more, almost certainly more than 25% of the labor force is working in places where air pollution is hazardous to health. In other words, it is plausible to assume that this estimation exceeds the one done by Lave and Seskin by a substantial amount.

Three reasons may explain this difference. The first reason is that the present estimation includes compensation for total damage caused by air pollution, whereas health damage is only one component of damage even if it is the most important one. The second reason—as pointed out by Lave and Seskin—is that their estimation of the health damages may be too low. A third reason may be related to the existence of an error in the measurement of the price index. This point may be discussed in relation to findings about effects of air pollution on prices. As shown in Table 12-3, in both the reduced-form and structural equations, the effect of air pollution on prices is small and insignificant. To the extent that air pollution affects mostly things which people care about (and not firms' production costs) and which are not expressed in measured prices, the finding that air pollution affects wages more than prices is reasonable. The possibility of some bias understating the effect in price equation and consequently overstating the effect in wages equation may be noted. Assume that the rent per unit of housing includes payment for the heating system such as interest on the cost of installation and fuel. Also assume that the housing costs are the same in two different locations except that in one a gas heating system is used predominantly, whereas in the other, a coal heating system is used, and suppose that the coal system is cheaper than the gas system and is more polluting as well. Thus by fitting an equation which includes only air pollution as an explanatory variable, and omits fuel cost as an explanatory variable, it might be found that the relationship between rent (or price of house) and pollution will be negative or reduced in value, that is, in polluted areas the use of cheap polluting fuel is lowering the cost of housing producing a bias in the price coefficient.[22] Ac-

---

[21] Not all the populations live in places where the concentration of air pollution reaches a harmful level, therefore, in these places no change in wage will be expected.

[22] See for example, Wieand [12]. He found also weak negative correlation between some measure of air pollution and value of land.

cording to the argument about the relationship between bias in price and wage equations an effect would be to introduce upward bias into the wage coefficient.[23]

Crime, Fire, and Accidents Hazard

Popular discussions of the quality of life in big cities stress the rate of crime and to a lesser extent the high rate of accidents and the high probability of fire. Security or safety will be considered as an environmental good, represented by a weighted average of the three components mentioned above. While measures of the three goods could be included individually in the regressions, none of the three goods alone appears to contribute very importantly to wage rate differences as measured by damages they cause. Moreover, the amounts of the goods tend to vary together. For example, cities with high crime rates may tend to have high accident and fire rates. To avoid these problems, reducing the estimated strength of any one of the goods in the regression, an index of hazard was constructed consisting of an average of the crime, accident, and fire rates for a city, with each rate weighted by a measure of its relative economic damage caused (see Table 12-1 for weights).

People can buy freedom from hazard in two different ways. One way is by buying an insurance policy that may ensure them a certain stream of income. This does not, however, ensure them their own safety. The second way is to avoid the hazard of losing income or property or both and also to avoid the risk of being hurt. This alternative can be bought by moving from a city with high hazard to a city with low hazard. Two effects are expected to occur as one moves between cities with different amounts of hazard. One effect is increases in prices of some goods like auto insurance, home insurance, and other goods and services for which insurance is an input in production. The second effect is an increase in the real wage rate. This increase in real wage should compensate people for the inconvenience connected with living in a place where the probability of being hurt is relatively high. The nominal wage should be higher by the sum of both effects times the multiplier which has been estimated as roughly 1.5 in our model.

In Table 12-3, Eq. (6) (structural price equation) the coefficient of the hazard variable of safety is .02. The coefficient is in the expected direction but its magnitude is small. On the other hand, the corresponding coefficient in a regression, where the dependent variable is transportation cost, is .21 and it is significant at the 5% level.[24] This result can be explained by

[23] See detailed explanation, earlier.

[24] The equation is:

$$P_{\text{Transp.}} = -1.3 - .06 \text{ population} - .03 \text{ air pollution}$$
$$\phantom{P_{\text{Transp.}} = -1.3} (-4.8) \phantom{\text{population} -} (-1.1)$$

the high weight of accidents in the index of safety, and by the fact that auto insurance has a large share among the goods and services which produce the final commodity transportation. The effect of safety becomes very weak in the transformation from transportation index to total price index. (Transportation is only about 10% of total consumption.) A tentative hypothesis is that the weak effect of this variable stems from the fact that other kinds of insurance, such as business insurance, are assumed in the price indices to be the same everywhere. This error will result in an overestimation of the change in real wage found in the wage equation.

In Table 12-2, Eq. (6) (structural equation for wages) the sign for the hazard variable is as expected. The magnitude of the coefficient is larger than in the price equation but is still not significant. In alternative regressions using different wage concepts as dependent variable, the hazard coefficient is significant.[25] In order to estimate the upward bias in the wage coefficient, assume that the effect of hazard on transportation price is taken as a characteristic of its effect on housing (assuming the remaining components food and clothing are not affected by hazard). In this case the true elasticity of the price index with respect to hazard should be the coefficient of hazard found in the transportation equation (footnote 21) multiplied by the share of transportation and housing in the total basket (.3) for an elasticity of .06. Comparing with Table 12-3, Eq. (6), the hazard coefficient in the structural price equation is underestimated by .04. According to the same reasoning used in preceding sections, this bias with changed sign appears in the structural coefficient for wages. Then, for example, the coefficient of the hazard variable in Table 12-2, Eq. (6),

---

$+ .21$ crime, etc. $+ .01$ local services
$\quad$ (3.6) $\qquad\qquad\qquad$ (.2)
$+ .05$ property tax $+ .30$ climate $- .04$ migration
$\quad$ (.9) $\qquad\qquad$ (6.9) $\qquad\qquad$ (−2.1)
$- .27$ age $- .13$ unemployment
$\quad$ (−1.0) $\quad\quad$ (−2.8)
$R^2 = .83.$

[25] For example, when the dependent variable is hourly wages of laborers and helpers, the coefficients of crime, fire, and accidents hazard in the structural equation are mostly in the range of .06 to .15 and are significant:

$$W - P = 1.1 + .05 \text{ population} + .10 \text{ air pollution} + .12 \text{ crime, etc.}$$
$\qquad\qquad$ (3.0) $\qquad\qquad\qquad$ (2.9) $\qquad\qquad\qquad\qquad$ (1.5)
$+ .02$ local services $+ .04$ tax $- 41$ climate
$\quad$ (.3) $\qquad\qquad\qquad$ (.9) $\qquad$ (−6.8)
$+ .08$ migration $+ .18$ unemployment
$\quad$ (3.6) $\qquad\qquad$ (2.7)
$R^2 = .65$

See Izraeli [7, Appendix 4, table 9] for additional regression results.

should be reduced from .05 to .01. The final interpretation would be that a 1% improvement in safety conditions within SMSA should cause a reduction of .06% in the price index, due to lower insurance rates and savings on some protection devices, and a reduction of about .01% in the real wage rate.

Local Government Services

To analyze the effects of local services on wages and prices, assume that people have two alternatives: to buy goods or services in the market as all other private goods, or to get them as public goods provided by the local government. As an example, consider the case of education. In Location A the fact that only a system of private schools exists forces residents to pay direct fees. In Location B, only a system of public schools exists, so residents can use the public system without any direct payment. In this case households would be indifferent between living in Location A, earning higher income and buying all goods and services in the market, and living in Location B, where part of the commodity bundle is provided by the local government, giving up some money income. The value of public services to the residents should thus be reflected in lower prices. On the assumption that most local services are received directly by residents, we expect the effect of public services to be stronger on wages than prices. The variable used in the regressions is total expenditure per capita by local government (omitting police and fire expenditures), deflated by the median wage rate of males of all occupations. A price or cost index for government services would have been an obvious first choice to use as deflator, but one does not exist.[26]

A first observation regarding the magnitude of the effect of local services relates to Table 12-2 Eq. (6) (structural equation for wages), indicating a local services coefficient of $-.11$ and Table 12-3 Eq. (6) (structural equation for prices), where the coefficient is $-.04$. The direction of effects in both equations is as expected, and as previously hypothesized, the coefficient in the wage equation is larger than that in the price equation.

A second observation concerns the magnitude of the coefficient of local services in the wage equation. In 1966–1967 the average amount spent by local government was $293 per capita,[27] times 3.3 persons per

[26] There could be some downward bias in the coefficient in the wage equation, due to the use of a variable in the denominator which is correlated with the dependent variable. Helping to mitigate the problem, the deflator is not the wage rate used as dependent variable in the wage equation, but rather the wage of a broad group of workers.

[27] That is, $338, as reported in *Statistical Abstract* 1970, p. 867, less 14% for fire and police.

household, or $960 per household. Suppose that about two-thirds of the $960, or $640, are spent on services for households and about one-third for firms. The average income per family in the U.S. was $5625 in 1966. Then consider the move of a family which lives in a place where it earns the average wage and receives the average amount of local services to a place where it receives 10% or $64 more in local services. From Table 12-2 Eq. (6) where the elasticity of wages with respect to government services is −.11, a 10% increase in governmental services should reduce wages by 1.1% of $5625 or $62, which is very close to the $64 assumed increase in local services. This is the result expected if the labor market is functioning competitively.

Local Taxes

The main source of revenue for local government is the property tax, which, excluding intergovernmental revenue, accounts for about 50% of general revenue (*Statistical Abstract*, 1970, p. 423, Table 625). The next most important tax is the sales tax. When included in regressions, the coefficients of sales tax rates were insignificant and this variable contributed nil to R^2. Similar results are obtained using a state income tax variable and a variable representing all state and local taxes excluding individual income tax.[28]

Property taxes are indirect taxes imposed mainly on real estate, thus affecting the price of housing. They should therefore be found in the structural equation for prices, but not in the wage equation. Regarding the magnitude of the price effect, consider the extreme alternatives that the elasticity of supply of real estate (land and dwelling units) is close to zero, and that the elasticity of supply is infinite. If the first assumption is correct, the coefficient of the property tax variable in the structural equation for prices will be very close to zero. If the second is true, the price index should increase by the same percentage as the percentage of property tax in the total price index. In Table 12-3 Eq. (6), the coefficient of property tax is .01 with a *t* value less than 1.0. At face value, this result suggests that the elasticity of supply is zero, that is, that the incidence of the residential property tax is on property owners rather than on occupants. However, as shown in Table 12-2, the coefficient is .08 in the structural wage equation rather than zero as expected. This can be explained by recognizing that the effect of property tax does not appear in the total price index equation. As stated previously, such an error in the construction of the price index is expected to result in downward bias in the coefficient of the price equation while in the wage equation an overestimation of the

---

[28] See p. 48 and Appendix 5 of Izraeli [7].

coefficient of the same independent variable will result. The elasticity, and hence the incidence of the tax, therefore cannot be determined through this analysis.

Climate

Wages may be affected by climate (temperature range, sunshine, humidity, and so on), first because people will give up a part of their income to live in a place which has the most attractive natural conditions, and second, because in attractive climates (e.g., neither very hot nor very cold), they can save goods such as housing, clothing, and health care. Ideally, an index of favorable weather might be constructed and used as an independent variable. However, the problem of what variables and weights to use is difficult. A simple index of five weather variables was constructed but it gave less significant results than using individual weather variables. In the absence of a suitable index one is faced with a number of more or less arbitrary measures of weather characteristics such as average temperature, minimum temperature, maximum temperature, "degree-day" measure, average precipitation, percentage of days with sunshine, and others. The weather variable used in the regressions reported in Tables 12-2 and 12-3 is average January temperature. The results for that weather variable are in the expected negative direction and are more significant than for all others tried. The general trend of the results was the same as for degree-days and July temperature.

Assume that in City A the average January temperature is 65° and that people prefer an average of 65° to all other temperatures. Suppose that in City B the average January temperature is 26°. Assuming the average wage per family in City A is $5000 per year and applying the climate coefficient of $-.42$ from the structural wage equation [Table 12-2 Eq. (6)], one expects to find wages in City B to be $1260 higher than in city A.[29] The 26° assumption corresponds to average January temperatures in Chicago, where the average annual heating bill for a dwelling unit is estimated to be $300.[30] In addition to heating, the cold climate leads to construction of sturdier and more highly insulated houses, whose costs may not be fully reflected in the price index. Furthermore, the colder climate results in extra costs for clothing, transportation (such as antifreeze, snow-tires, faster depreciation on cars, and housing), and require compensation for the inconvenience that people experience during the cold winter. All extra costs might well account for the estimated wage difference of $1260.

---

[29] The calculation is: $\Delta W/5000 = -.42 \ 26 - 65/65$, or $\Delta W = .5000 \ (-.42)(-.6) = \$1260$.

[30] Unpublished data from an Environmental Protection Agency study.

Again for the climate variable, we face the phenomenon that most of the explanation comes through the wage equation instead of the price equation. An ideal price index should include all these extra costs, whereas wage differentials should only be reflecting the compensation for inconveniences involved in bad weather. As explained previously, because of mistakes in the construction of the price index, an upward bias is found in the wage coefficient. This may also help explain the sign of the climate coefficient in the price equation, which is opposite to expectation. Another explanation of the climate results, as already hinted, is that a completely satisfactory measure of climate is lacking.

Median Age

Two variables were used to standardize the dependent variables for other economic effects. As explained previously by choosing to regress on the wage rate of a homogeneous group of workers, some of the effects of human capital differences are eliminated. A further consequence of differences in human capital is captured by the age variable, which serves as a surrogate for on the job training. As it turns out, in Table 12-2 Eq. (6), the elasticity of wage rate with respect to age is .38. Assuming that the median age in City A is 33 years, this elasticity implies that a 1-year difference in median age between City A and City B will result in a 1.25% wage difference. But if the median age is 40 years in City A and 41 in City B, the difference in wage will amount only to .95%. These magnitudes of wage difference seem reasonable when compared to other empirical studies of effects of on the job training. Also, the decreasing difference in wage rate as median age increases is a very plausible result.

Labor Market Disequilibrium

Aside from the independent variables which have been reviewed, regional wages and prices may be affected by the extent of labor market disequilibrium. Consider as an alternative to Eq. (6) in Table 12-2, the inclusion of dummy regional variables as explanatory variables for intercity differences in money wages. The theoretical chapter suggests three reasons why regional dummies might explain variations in wages and prices: (a) regional differences in prices of transported goods, (b) climate and other environmental variables having a regional association, and (c) labor market disequilibrium between regions, with labor surplus areas having unfavorable wage differentials not yet eliminated by labor flows. The structural wage regression, the same as Table 12-2 Eq. (6) except using dummy regional variables in place of climate, net migration, and rate of unemployment, is:

$W - P = .5 + .06$ Population $+ .06$ Air Pollution $- .003$ Crime, etc.
$\quad\quad\quad\quad (3.6)\quad\quad\quad\quad (1.2)\quad\quad\quad\quad\quad\quad\quad (-.01)$
$\quad\quad - .06$ Local Services $+ .03$ Tax $+ .41$ Age $+ .18$ North
$\quad\quad\quad (-.8)\quad\quad\quad\quad\quad\quad\quad (.7)\quad\quad\quad (1.7)\quad\quad\quad (3.2)$
$\quad\quad + .31$ Central $+ .31$ West
$\quad\quad\quad (7.3)\quad\quad\quad\quad (6.6)$
$\quad\quad R^2 = .69$ $\hspace{8cm}$ (34)

As seen from comparing Eq. (34) with Eq. (6) in Table 12-2, the difference in R^2 between the two equations is only about .03 and the nonregional coefficients of all regression variables in the equations are very similar.

Equation (34) suggests that the regional dummy effects may be largely due to the more underlying effects for which measures are used in Table 12-2. Climate measurement was discussed earlier. Labor market disequilibrium is reflected in Tables 12-2 and 12-3 by net regional migration and the rate of unemployment. The net regional migration is 1960–1970 net migration between the four geographic regions (Northeast, South, Central, West) in which SMSA is located. The rationale is that labor markets are regional rather than purely local. For instance, a rapidly growing SMSA in a region with large outmigration is expected to have a lower wage than in a similarly growing SMSA in a region with inmigration. The use of regional rather than SMSA migration as an independent variable gives more significant results. In Table 12-2 Eq. (6) the coefficient for net migration is .10. This result is in the right direction since it is expected that as the rate of net inmigration is high the real wage rate will be high too. As for the price equation, no effect of labor market disequilibrium is expected and this is actually what was found in Table 12-3 Eq. (6).

An additional variable, the rate of unemployment, was tried for labor market disequilibrium. Little systematic effect might be expected in a cross section sample such as the present one if unemployment is chronic. Unemployment differences between SMSAs could be chronic due to such factors as differential impacts of minimum wages legislated in nominal terms. In this case, a usual idea is that the expected wage taking account of the probability of unemployment will tend to be the same in different labor markets, so that observed wage rates will be high in labor markets where unemployment is high. Hall [4] has also noted reasons affecting employers and employees relating to intensity of work for expecting such a relation between wage rate and unemployment.

The wage variable in Table 12-2 refers to yearly earnings including both employed and unemployed persons and so already adjusts earnings downward due to unemployment. The unemployment result in Table 12-2 of a small coefficient exceeded several times by its standard error is therefore consistent with the reasoning about expected wage.[31]

INTERPRETATION OF INTERCITY WAGE DIFFERENCES

Up to this point, the chapter has dealt individually with the effect of each independent variable on wages and prices. The aggregate contribution of the separate effects on intercity wage difference can be estimated by computing, given the coefficients from Table 12-2, how much the individual laborer is ready to give up from or add to his real wage, in considering moving from his present location to a new one. These computations are given in Table 12-5 for four pairs of cities. Each pair includes Chicago

TABLE 12-5

Actual and Computed Differences in Real Wages between Four Pair of Cities[a]

	Chicago to New York: Real wage	Chicago to Los Angeles: Real wage	Chicago to Milwaukee: Real wage	Chicago to Dallas: Real wage
(1) Population	233	2	−263	−262
(2) Air pollution	202	−69	−85	−165
(3) Crime, fire, and accident hazard	37	167	−10	96
(4) Expenditures for local services per capita	−445	−203	−167	−18
(5) Rate of property tax	15	−15	232	−78
(6) Climate	−469	−1805	364	−1310
Subtotal	−427	−1923	71	−1737
(7) Regional net migration	348	1201	—	411
(8) Median age	166	−85	−17	−38
(9) Rate of unemployment	25	30	−3	−3
Total	102	−777	51	−1367
Actual	−55	−703	64	−1634

[a] The figures are obtained by first applying the structural coefficients in Table 12-2 to the percentage differences in independent variables between the selected cities and Chicago to obtain a predicted percentage wage effect of each variable. The result is then multiplied by the Chicago wage to express as a dollar difference.

[31] Results when using the hourly wage for persons actually employed are also consistent with the reasoning, since they show a positive relation between unemployment and wage as reported above.

as the present location and a new location which is located east, west, north, or south of Chicago. The subtotal, which appears in Table 12-5, sums up all the effects of the differences in availability of environmental goods. If this sum is positive it means that the new place has less desirable environmental goods than Chicago.

The results may be interpreted with reference to Los Angeles. The subtotal indicates that the individual worker would be ready to give up $1923 per year to obtain the bundle of attributes called environmental goods, which are estimated in this case to be better on a net basis in Los Angeles than in Chicago. Since both SMSAs have about the same population, 6.71 million in Chicago versus 6.76 in Los Angeles, there is need for essentially no compensation due to population differences. It will be recalled that population is considered as an effect on wages because it stands in for transportation cost variables which measurement difficulties preclude from being among the remaining independent variables of the regression. In Los Angeles the concentration of air pollution is 10.0 μg per cubic meter whereas in Chicago it is 14.0 μg per cubic meter. As indicated in Row 2 the laborer is ready to give up $69 to buy the additional amount of clean air which he enjoys in Los Angeles. The same kind of explanation can be applied to all other environmental goods. The sum over all the environmental goods gives an indication of the relative attractiveness of the new place as compared to the old one. In this case, the major overall difference is due to the better climate (winter temperature) in Los Angeles.

A comparison of the environmental subtotal amount with the total predicted difference in real wage gives us an indication as to other economic factors. This can be seen from the three additional variables which appear after the subtotal. Those variables are: rate of regional net migration, median age, and unemployment rate. The major reason the wage is predicted to be $777 lower in Los Angeles in the next to the last row instead of $1923 lower as predicted by considering only the environmental variables is a $1201 positive contribution of regional labor market disequilibrium to the Los Angeles wage as estimated from regional net migration. The total explanation of wage difference is a good one in that the residual between actual and predicted wage difference, indicated by comparing the last two rows of the table, is small.

Table 12-5 has illustrated how to use the results of this chapter to interpret geographical differences in wages. The fact that the figures in the table are on the whole intuitively reasonable strengthens confidence in the conclusions. A tentative conclusion suggested by Table 12-5 is that environmental variables are a greater contributor to intercity wage differences for a given type of labor than other variables, with regional labor market disequilibrium being the only important nonenvironmental contributor.

Conclusion

As can be seen from the statistical results, mainly in Tables 12-2 and 12-3, it appears that people are sensitive to the availability of environmental goods. The variation in the availability of the environmental goods explains most of the variation of wage rate and price index. Not only were significant statistical correlations found, but the reasonableness of the elasticities was encouraging. The main reason for obtaining better results for wages than prices appears to be lack of appropriate data regarding differences in prices between cities.

A major goal of the chapter has been to shed light on the relationship between city size as measured by population and the wage rate and price variables. Previous studies have discussed dW/dPop or dP/dPop, that is, the population effects on wages and prices as important parameters to be estimated. In Table 12-4, dW/dPop was estimated as the sum of products of partial derivatives

$$\sum_{j=1}^{n} \left(\frac{\partial W}{\partial Z_j}\right)\left(\frac{\partial Z_j}{\partial \text{Pop}}\right),$$

the idea being that wages vary with city size only because some environmental goods vary with city size. These environmental goods should if possible be measured explicitly, not only for the purpose of understanding the true relation but also for policy considerations. For instance, if $\partial W/\partial Z_j$ is relatively high and $\partial Z_j/\partial$Pop is relatively low, a change in city size would not solve the problem which Z_j imposes, and a change is required in the amount of Z_j by other means than the change in population.

References

1. Alonso, W. *Location and Land Use*. Cambridge, Mass.: Harvard University Press, 1964.
2. Fuchs, V. R. *Differentials in Hourly Earnings by Region and City Size*. NBER Occasional Paper 101. New York: National Bureau of Economic Research, 1967.
3. Groom, P. "A New City Worker's Family Budget." *Monthly Labor Review* **90** (11), 1967, 1–8.
4. Hall, R. E. "Turnover in the Labor Force." Brookings Panel on Economic Activities, 1972.

5. Harberger, A. C. "On Measuring the Social Opportunity Cost of Labor." Paper presented at a meeting of Experts in Fiscal Policies for Employment Promotion, sponsored by the International Labor Office at Geneva, Switzerland, January, 1971.
6. Hoch, I. "On the Distribution of Urban Population." *Urban Economics Report* No. 62. Chicago: University of Chicago, 1971.
7. Izraeli, O. "Differentials in Nominal Wages and Prices between Cities." Unpublished Ph.D. dissertation, Department of Economics, University of Chicago, 1973.
8. Lave, L. B., and Seskin, E. P. "Air Pollution and Human Health." *Science* **169**, 1970, 723–733.
9. Tiebout, C. "A Pure Theory of Local Expenditures." *Journal of Political Economy* **64**, 1956, 416–424.
10. Tolley, G. S. "The Welfare Economics of City Bigness." *Journal of Urban Economics* **1**, 1974, 324–345.
11. Voorhees, A. M. *et al.* "Factors in Work Trip Lengths." *Highway Research Record* **141**, 1966, 24–39.
12. Wieand, K. F. "Air Pollution and Property Values; A Study of the St. Louis Area." *Journal of Regional Science* **13**, 1973, 91–95.

VII
IMPLICATIONS

13
Overall Assessment of Market Distortions

GEORGE S. TOLLEY
JOHN L. GARDNER
PHILIP E. GRAVES

The purpose of this chapter is to bring together the analyses of the preceding chapters, which have considered particular individual sources of market failure in influencing the location of population and economic activity. In this manner, the book's goal of providing a systematic analysis of how society's ends are served by location decisions, based on analysis of what markets can and cannot contribute to well-being, will be fulfilled.

Estimates will be developed to provide insights on the importance of various distortions in quantitative terms. The orders of magnitude to be presented put major policy issues in perspective and serve to replace vague and qualitative arguments that have characterized much discussion of locational performance.

The Questions

The role of the demand and supply for labor in determining city size was considered in Chapter 1, which included a consideration of how increasing costs associated with commuting, housing, congestion, the environment, and other factors eventually offset locational benefits of an area. An array of different sizes of towns and cities is obtained, the outcome in each case depending on the point at which a balance is reached between the costs and benefits of extra population.

Chapter 1 also noted some of the reasons why the signals for private decisions determining the outcomes might not fully reflect the costs and benefits to society of the decisions. These externalities have been the major focus of the remainder of the book. To bring the analysis together, the idea used in the partial analyses of some of the chapters needs to be applied fully if considering a city in a system of cities comprising a nation. The questions are: What distribution of people and jobs among locations would be expected in the absence of externalities? How do externalities affect this pattern? How much do the effects of the externalities detract from the income of the nation?

The Supply of Resources to a City

Three types of resources used in production may be identified. The first consists of location-fixed resources, such as a locationally advantageous port harbor or transportation nexus. These resources have a great influence on why cities are located where they are and on how large a city grows to be. A city with great natural advantages will tend to be larger than one with fewer advantages, because the extra costs of adding units of complementary resources will not outweigh the benefits until a large city size is reached. The location-fixed resources thus play a role in determining city size, but by their very nature these resources do not flow between cities.

The second type of resource used in a city is physical capital, including houses, factory buildings, and equipment. In an economy with sophisticated capital markets, which includes all advanced economies today, investment in various places will tend to be carried to the point where the monetary return to the investment is the same in all cities.

The third type of resource is labor or, more generally, human resources. Like capital, labor is mobile between cities. A key factor making labor and capital different is that, unlike capital, the owner of labor must be within commuting distance of the place of employment in order to contribute to production. People supplying labor must consume goods available locally. They will tend to migrate in response to real rather than monetary differences in rewards. Particularly because of differences in the costs of producing local goods and services which are not traded between cities, the money cost of living may vary substantially leading to corresponding variations in money wages across cities.

A city grows because of the decisions of its residents who advance to working age not to move away, and decisions of individuals within the country as a whole to move to the city. It is primarily through choices of mobile, young workers that the tendency is brought about for real wages, taking account of amenities and disamenities, to be the same in different places. The money wage needed to bring about this condition may be greatly affected by city size and the environment in each city. A formal condition is that the wage received less the hourly equivalent differential costs of local goods and services including residential land, commuting, and environmental disamenity in the city should be the same as in other towns and cities. Should this condition initially not hold, migration will take place until equilibrium is reestablished or until the less preferred cities disappear (e.g., ghost towns). The notion is that in-migration to more preferred cities will lower the marginal product and consequently the competitive wage and the converse is true for the less preferred cities. Thus, differentially higher costs for residential land, for commuting, and so on will, in equilibrium, be compensated for in the prevailing wage rate.

In small towns these costs which must be added to wages are small, but they increase with increasing city size. The rise in daily travel costs is one of the limiting considerations determining city size. The cost advantages from having some kinds of production in a large city are sufficient to compensate for large daily travel costs, but the rise in costs due to daily travel eventually raises the cost of additional output in the city compared to that in smaller cities. Daily travel costs appear to be one of the reasons why most of the nation's economic activity is not located in one huge city.

Some rough calculations will indicate the order of magnitude of these costs and how they vary with city size. For concreteness, consider a hypothetical city of population 6 million with a work force of 1.5 million employed fulltime at a wage of $10,000 annually. Questions to be examined are how much larger the wage must be in the large city, and by how much more the wage must increase to induce a 1% increase in population size.

When a laborer migrates from farm to city, the edge of the city is moved further out from its center. Anyone living closer in than the edge must pay higher rents due to the commuting advantage of interior residential sites relative to residence locations on the edge. The wages in this city will tend to be what can be earned elsewhere, plus the extra costs of commuting that must be borne if a worker is added in the city. There will be a tendency for money wages in the city to adjust upward as the city grows, relative to money wages in nongrowing places. Suppose that in such a city each worker commuting from the edge of the city would spend an average of 15 minutes per trip longer traveling to work than he would have to from the edges of typical smaller cities. Multiplying by 250 working days per year times two trips per day, and valuing each hour at $3, the extra value of travel time in this city is found to be $375 per year. The wage would have to be larger by enough to yield at least this much additional income in the large city to compensate.

Environmental disamenities provide a second reason why wages must be higher. People in larger cities tend to be subjected to generally higher levels of air pollution, noise, and visual blight, and must pay more per capita to meet water quality standards. The exposition will focus on air pollution for purposes of setting the order of magnitude of this environmental disamenity.

Before the imposition of air quality standards in 1968, a typical level of suspended particulates was 150 μg per cubic meter of air, whereas in smaller cities and towns a representative level was 100 μg. A number of studies of the relationship between property values and air quality indicate that individuals are willing to pay higher rents to escape unfavorable air quality; a rough estimate of the effect is $5 dollars per microgram per family, as a yearly damage value. This presumably reflects damages to health, length of life, deterioration of durable property, and impairment of aesthetic values in the city's environment. Using this damage value, the resident in the larger city experiences a 50 μg difference times $5 = $250 greater damage from air pollution than his counterpart in smaller cities with better air. If air pollution were the only unusually adverse characteristic of larger cities and if the population were stable, the wage in the city of size 6 million would have to be $250 more than in other places of smaller size.

Adding this to the disamenity value of distance, the result is approximately $625 as an estimate of the amount by which wages in the larger city must exceed wages in smaller places to compensate for disadvantages of living there. This is a conservative estimate, in view both of the conservativeness of many of the numerical estimates used in the derivation, and because a number of disamenities have been neglected in this computation. If these figures were correct and if there were no other factors influencing decisions to migrate, an equilibrium could be established with the wage rate $10,000 elsewhere and $10,625 in the large city, since then net gains to a family from moving to the large city would be zero.

Marginal External Costs due to Congestion and Pollution

One might think that since congestion and pollution increase the money wage which must be paid in the large city, their effect is internalized fully, that is, employers have to pay higher wages because of the congestion and pollution, with the result that growth of the city is retarded. However, as brought out in Chapter 1, the key question is whether the greater wage rate fully reflects the costs imposed by hiring an additional worker.

When an additional commuter enters the highway system of an urban area during rush hour, he slows down all the other commuters. Their added time cost constitutes a reduction in the real income of the community. (Because of the way land rents are determined in an urban area, the losses are passed on to the landowners.) For illustrative purposes, suppose that in a city of population 6 million, half of the labor force or 750,000 workers commute to the central employment location. Each one travels an average of 5 miles per trip over congested streets at a speed of 20 miles per hour, and the speed would be 35 miles per hour if there were no traffic congestion. Suppose the average new entrant into the labor force of the city makes five rush hour trips per week over this highway system. The effect of this on traffic speeds and on commuting times for the other motorists can be estimated through the use of the engineering relationship $v = \bar{v} - kq$ where v is the speed under congested condition (20 miles per hour), $\bar{v}$ is the speed under uncongested condition (35 miles per hour), q is the traffic volume (750,000 cars per hour), and k is a constant which is here calculated to be .00002. Recalculating v with $q = 750,000$ cars per hour to estimate the difference in travel time over the 5-mile congested stretch of highway, multiplying by 750,000 the number of motorists who are slowed down, and valuing commutation time at $3 per hour, the estimated value of other motorists' additional commuting time is approximately $140 per year when one additional family moves into the urban area.

The impact of the additional family on damages from air pollution can be computed with the use of data already cited in this chapter. An inference from observations on air quality and metropolitan population size is that the particulate level is likely to rise by .00004 μg per cubic meter when a single family enters. Applying the damage value of $5 per microgram and assuming the number of families in the urban area to be 1.5 million, the result is $300 as an overall damage value. Thus, total additional costs imposed on all other families combined due to air pollution and congestion when a family moves into an urban area of 6 million population are on the order of $440, assuming that other environmental effects are of a lower order of magnitude than those discussed explicitly here.

This result should be considered in relation to the first main conclusion, that wages in this city would be on the order of $625 higher than in other places of smaller size. When an individual moves into this area, if there is an equilibrium of city sizes generally, his personal gain is the

$10,000 wage less $625 urban costs in this city, for which he foregoes the $9375 wage elsewhere. The other families in the large city suffer a combined loss on the order of $440, so that national income is reduced by $440.

This discussion, for simplicity, neglects environmental costs imposed by a resident in his alternative location. If the alternative is a rural area, there may be few costs. If the alternative is a smaller city, the environmental costs are likely to be smaller than in the big city. In any case, the general principle is that the net social cost of adding a person to a city is determined by the difference between marginal external costs in the city and in the place where he would otherwise live.

The Optimum Population Change

Suppose a policy, such as a direct decree or tax incentives, were instituted attempting to restrict the large city to that point where marginal social product in the city was equal to that elsewhere. As the city's size is reduced, there is movement back up the demand curve for labor in the city, increasing the marginal private product of labor. In effect, a slight labor shortage in the city would be created, raising the wage employers are willing to pay for the labor remaining. With a sufficient restriction in city size, the higher marginal private product of labor in the city would just compensate for the higher marginal external costs. At such an optimum point, the total or social product of a worker counting both private and external effects would be the same in the city as elsewhere.

The optimum point depends on the elasticity of demand for labor in the city. Conditions affecting the elasticity are the substitutability of labor for location-fixed inputs and the switch of export-based employment to alternative locations as the cost of production in the city in question is raised by higher wages. Without question the elasticity must be substantial. Based in part on factor share considerations, an elasticity of 3 will be used for illustrative purposes. For instance, for a 1% increase in the labor force (15,000 out of 1.5 million) the marginal private product falls by 33%, or $33, if the initial marginal product is $10,000.

The marginal social product may fall by more than this because the distance which the workers who live farthest away from work must travel each day increases as the city expands. For purposes of illustration, suppose that suburban population densities are 3000 persons per square mile; an addition of 60,000 to the population of a city (15,000 workers assuming one person in four works) would therefore add 20 square miles to its land area. If the city is initially circular with radius 15 miles, the additional 20 square miles will add .2 mile to the radius from its central employment location to the outer margin. Supposing that commutation speeds through this added ring are 30 miles per hour and retaining the $3 per hour time value used earlier, commutation costs from the margin of the city rise by about $20 per year when the margin is changed in this way. Adding to the $33 associated with production of goods and services calculated previously, the result is $53 as the decrease in private marginal product of labor associated with an increase in population of 1% or 60,000. Congestion is also increased slightly as the city grows; using the previous speed relationships, the marginal social product of labor is found to decrease by approximately $1.50 more, or a total of $54.50, as the combined effect on goods and services production, distance from the margin of the city and congestion, if the city grows by 1%. The effect of this change on marginal air pollution damages is negligible.

Thus, all the quantities needed to characterize the optimum population change for this city are in hand. With a population of 6 million, the marginal social product from adding the last family is on the order of $440 less than the wage rate which individuals can earn elsewhere, which they use as a criterion for deciding whether or not to live in the city. This difference can be reduced gradually, at a rate of about $55 for every 60,000 by which the population of the city decreases. There would be gains from restricting the size of this city by as much as 480,000 persons, or 8% of its size, assuming that social and private marginal products are equal to one another elsewhere. The national income gain from this sort of city size restriction would be $26.4 million, or about .2% of the total wage income originating in the city.

Scale Economies

The discussion so far has neglected scale economies which, at least in some ranges of urban size, may be pronounced. A tentative hypothesis, based at least in part on empirical investigation, is that scale economies are great for small towns and cities but are gradually exhausted at larger city sizes. "Lazy-J" cost curves for various indivisible activities would lead to this result.

Specialization of functions increases in production of a wide variety of goods and services as population size increases. This further implies that as cities grow, imperfect competition which is present when there is only one producer of a given item tends to be replaced by a more competitive local market. Intra-city communication and costs of pickups and deliveries are reduced as densities increase in the centers of urban areas as growth occurs. As the size of a labor market grows, the waiting time for employers seeking to fill vacancies and for workers seeking new jobs is reduced, and a better matching of worker skills with needs for production is possible. The hypothesis has been advanced that a greater variety of consumer products is available in larger cities and may contribute to greater consumer satisfaction. A further tentative hypothesis is that the rate of innovation and therefore of technological progress is positively related to size of the city where the inventive process is carried on.

All of these factors constitute one or another form of technological externality. For example, when one person moves to the city, he has a slight impact on production costs for a wide range of activities carried on within the city. These externalities are positive and therefore constitute an offset to the congestion and environmental externalities considered earlier: They narrow the gap between marginal, private, and social products of labor associated with city size. In addition, they tend to lessen the rate of decline of the marginal product of labor as population size increases.

Some exploration of possible magnitudes of these externalities has been carried out. Gardner in Chapter 4 examined scale economies associated with the provision of a variety of public services (fire protection, sanitation, public administration, etc.) by governments in cities. For some of the services, scale economies were exhibited—this confirms findings elsewhere in the literature, summarized by Hirsch [1]. In Chapter 12, Izraeli examined the variation in prices with city size, holding other factors constant. He found an elasticity of prices with respect to population of around $-.03$. In terms of our illustrative example, when a single family enters a city of 1.5 million families, prices tend to decline at a rate of $(.03)/(1.5)(10^6)$. Multiplying this by the total wage income of the city which is $(1.5)(10^6)(10^4)$ gives \$300 as a rough measure of the increased value of goods and services which the residents of the city as a whole can purchase when the one family enters. This is roughly equal to the value of the environmental and congestion externality discussed previously. However, there remains some question as to whether these economies persist as cities grow to sizes such as the 6 million which we have been considering in this book. Because of the hypothesis advanced in this section that they do not, we shall neglect scale economies in the summary calculations later in the chapter.

Local Public Finance Externalities

How is city size affected by the heavy reliance on the urban property tax to provide municipal services? As analyzed in Chapter 8, if larger cities tend to have proportionally greater numbers of wealthy people in comparison to smaller places, tax rates relative to income will be correspondingly less in the larger cities. This creates an artificial incentive for migration of both rich and poor to the larger cities. An equilibrium of city sizes is then reached when the wage rate adjusted for environmental disamenities in the smaller places exceeds the same quantity in the larger places by the difference between taxes in the smaller places and taxes in the larger places.

To carry forward the numerical example with this additional hypothesis, suppose that the 1.5 million labor force in the large city comprises two skill groups, high-skilled workers earning $13,000 per year and low-skilled workers earning $7000 per year. Suppose that environmental damages and travel costs experienced by both high- and low-skilled workers are valued at $500 per capita, and that wages elsewhere are $12,500 for high-skilled workers and $6500 for low-skilled workers. Suppose that the cities would be of equilibrium sizes in the absence of the taxation system described above.

The condition which determines the relative magnitudes of wages in the large city and elsewhere is that the wage plus the per family value of government services less taxes paid must be equal in each place, for each skill group. The tax rates are determined by the level of government services provided, the relative proportions of the skill groups present in the taxing jurisdiction, and their respective wealth levels. Suppose that government service levels are equal in the large city and elsewhere, that the wealth of high-skilled families is three times the wealth of low-skilled families, and that high-skilled workers comprise one-fourth of the labor force except in the large city where the proportion is one-half. Suppose that there is taxable industrial and commercial property in the large city whose value per capita is equal to the wealth level of the high-skilled families, and that in the small city the per capita value of such nonresidential property is equal to the wealth level of the low-skilled families. Under these conditions, it can be shown that wages in the large city will be depressed by 6% for high-skilled families (or $750) and 4% for low-skilled families (or $250). Continuing to apply the elasticity derived previously, it follows that the large city will have 57,100 more high-skilled workers (or 7.5% of the high-skilled labor force) than it would have in the absence of the tax differential, and 24,900 more low-skilled workers (or 3.3% of the low-skilled labor force). The national income loss associated with this misallocation is $21.4 million associated with the high-skilled labor market and $3.2 million associated with the low-skilled, or a total of about 0.2% of the wage income originating in the city.

The problem is further compounded if, as is the case in many large met-

ropolitan areas, high-income people tend to form exclusive suburbs to re-
lieve themselves of the burden of supporting public services to the low-
skilled people of the area. Retaining the same assumptions as before, the
effect is to lower further the tax rate for high-skilled people and widen
their wage differential between this city and elsewhere, while it raises the
tax rate for the low-income people and narrows the wage differential for
them. To illustrate, under the most extreme assumption, that all high-
skilled people form a separate taxing jurisdiction from the low-skilled people, the wage differentials change from 6 to 7% for the high-income groups
and from 4 to 3% for the low-income group. The national income loss is
now $31 million instead of $24.6 million, and the overall population effect
is to make the large city too large by 3500 more workers than before, that
is, too large by 5.7 instead of 5.5%.

Unemployment Compensation and Welfare Payments

The system of transfer payments to support unemployed persons also
has a spatial dimension which tends to provide incentives which make the
largest cities too large. The difficulty originates from the fact that smaller
cities generally tend to have lower prices than larger cities. Initially, imposition of a minimum wage law which fixes the money wage therefore effects a higher real wage in smaller towns than in larger cities. If the elasticity of labor demand is greater than 1—that is, if the proportional increase in the unemployment rate is greater than the proportional increase
in the wage level itself—then there will be incentives to workers to migrate from the smaller city to larger places where the minimum wage law
has not yet taken effect.

There are two types of costs associated with the minimum wage law.
One, the large value of the idle resources and unemployment compensation transfers from working to nonworking people, is a cost of the
minimum wage system in general, and is not properly included as a component of costs of spatial misallocation of resources, which are being quantified here. However, a further cost exists in that the unemployment compensation payments must be higher in large cities than in small towns, in
money terms, because of the higher price levels in large cities, if the
unemployed are to be supported at the same real income levels wherever
they live. There would be a gain in national income if some of these people moved away from the largest cities, even if they remained unemployed.

As a simple numerical example, suppose that the labor force of low-skilled workers in a city of 6 million population is raised by 2%, or 30,000 unemployed persons, who would not otherwise live there in the absence of the minimum wage law. Suppose that the cost of living is 15% higher in large cities, and that the level of welfare payments in other places of smaller size is $3000 per family. The cost associated with the spatial misallocation is therefore ($3000)(.15)(30,000), or roughly $15 million. It should be emphasized that this is a very small fraction of the overall costs of the minimum wage system, which include the total value of goods and services which could be produced if those unemployed were reemployed.

Recapitulation

A graphical and tabular presentation serves to bring the foregoing examples together. Figure 13-1 includes first a conventional marginal product of labor curve (labeled *MP*) whose elasticity is 3, as discussed previously. Beneath this, a private marginal product curve (*PMP*) represents the total marginal product, less the cost of transportation to work and the value of environmental damages. The equilibrium city size of 1.5 million workers (6 million total population) is determined at point *A*, where the private marginal product equals the $9375 level of net wages elsewhere. Finally there is a social marginal product curve (*SMP*) which represents the private marginal product, less the value of external damages imposed on others when one family enters. Optimum city size is determined at point *B*, where the social marginal product equals wages elsewhere, assuming that in these other places the wage equals the social marginal product.

Figure 13-1. Equilibrium and optimum city sizes. (*MP*: marginal product of labor in the factory; *PMP*: received by labor after subtracting rent, commuting, and environmental costs; *SMP*: *PMP* minus external costs imposed by adding a worker.)

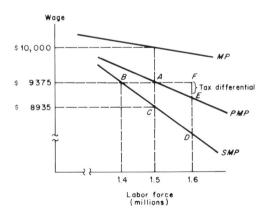

TABLE 13-1
Suggestive Effects of Externalities for a City of Six Million People

Type of externality	Effect on population of the city	National income cost of the city population effect
Pollution and congestion	+500,000	$26 million
Economies of scale	Minor for a city of of this size	Makes small towns too small, but economies are exhausted for larger cities
Local public finance Direct effect	⎧	$30 million
Additional pollution and congestion costs	+400,000	$30 million
Welfare and unemploy- ment compensation	⎩	$15 million

By pursuing a policy of limiting city size, national income could be increased by as much as the area of triangle *ABC*, which is $26 million; a restriction by about 500,000 persons could accomplish this. This does not eliminate all environmental and congestion costs; some portion of the area between the *PMP* and *SMP* curves above line segment *AB* could be eliminated by pursuing policies with respect to these problems within the metropolitan area. The estimates are summarized in Table 13-1.

To show the effects of the property taxation system properly requires two graphs—one for each skill group; however, the construction can be explained adequately in terms of Figure 13-1. The effect of lower taxes in this large city is to create an equilibrium with an even lower wage and greater population than otherwise. The direct national income loss from having this situation is represented by triangles such as *AEF* on the individual labor market graphs. The sum of the areas might be $30 million, in the exclusionary case, and the population size effect is 85,500 workers. The additional environmental damages associated with this excess population, indicated by area *ACDE*, are also $30 million. Finally, additional welfare and unemployment compensation costs from supporting unemployed workers in cities where it is more costly to do so add perhaps another $15 million to national income costs, and the persons attracted to the large city by the combined effects of probability of employment and higher welfare and unemployment compensation payments number at least 100,000 who, it may be noted, are in the unskilled category.

Implications for City Sizes and National Income

The striking results from Table 13-1 are that effects of the externalities on city size are substantial, whereas the national income costs of the city size effects are extremely small. The city is increased in population by more than 10%, whereas the national income cost is only about 0.6% of the income produced in the city. The basic reason for the substantial city population effect is the high elasticity of demand for labor in the city. The production function for many goods is about the same all over the country, so that a small change in wage costs will induce large changes in industry location decisions. The reason for the low national income costs is that, for laborers reallocated, the difference in their marginal products as between locations is a relatively small percentage of their total marginal product.

The specific numbers used and details of the analytical assumptions could vary a great deal and still not alter the basic conclusion.

Reference

1. Hirsch, Werner Z., "The Supply of Urban Public Services," in *Issues in Urban Economics,* H. S. Perloff and L. Wingo, Jr. (Eds.). Baltimore: Johns Hopkins Press, 1968. Pp. 477–525.

14

Policy Conclusions

GEORGE S. TOLLEY
PHILIP E. GRAVES

The major purpose of this book has been to contribute to the objective analysis of effects of decisions affecting where people live and work. In this chapter, the ways in which the results can be used explicitly in contributing to policy will be considered.

The Results in Perspective:
Three Types of Externalities

The organizing concept of the book has been to view the problem of location in terms of externalities. The book broadens the scope for quantitative analysis of policy, but at the same time, there remain externalities which have not been subjected to economic value measurement. In the broadest sense three types of externalities may be identified:

- *Environmental externalities,* such as pollution and congestion, comprise the first type of externalities. The common feature of these externalities is that they have physical effects.
- *Government-induced externalities* result, inadvertently, from gov-

ernment policies which have important spatial dimensions. Chapters 8, 9, and 10 examined the locational misallocations resulting from property taxation, welfare, and minimum wage laws. In each case the private locational decision is distorted by the unintended incentives created by programs aimed at other problems.

• *Broader social goals* constitute a final group of externalities about which little has been said in this book. These include such diverse effects as changes in the distribution of income, racial or ethnic integration, the cohesiveness of society, and prevention of breakdown of the family.

While the book has not dealt directly with the third type of externality concerned with broader social goals, it can help to substantially refocus the discussion, narrow down the range of uncertainty about policy outcomes, and lead to an improved policy-making capability. Of particular importance, it shows that the first two types of externality can be dealt with in quantifiable terms. These are of importance in their own right for many types of policies. They can be juxtaposed along with private costs in considering the total quantifiable cost of policies in a comprehensive quantitative evaluation. A full evaluation can also consider broader goals, which can be quantified in nondollar terms or discussed in qualitative terms. The remainder of this chapter considers more specifically how the results of the book can be used for policy purposes.

Positive Policy Analysis

Policy-making is aided if an attempt is made to present decision-makers with a balanced consideration of effects of policies, quantifying the effects to the maximum extent useful. As brought out in Chapter 1, a defect of much past analysis has been its excessively qualitative nature, as a result of which the weighing of relative importance of various effects can become obscured by rhetoric. In some cases, quantifiable effects can be expressed in a common unit of measure, dollars being typically the most convenient unit of account. Many of the earlier chapters of this book have extended the list of quantifiable effects which would be relevant in any discussion of best city sizes. The examination of pollution and congestion as externalities which increase with increasing city size are cases in point as are the analysis of fiscal externalities.

For some effects expression in a dollar measure might be misleading in view of measurement difficulties. In such cases, the policy effects may be presented to the decision-maker in their best quantified form. Still other effects may not be amenable even to this level of quantification and can be discussed verbally.

Table 14-1 illustrates a methodology for evaluating a policy, a program, or an administrative action which involves a choice among locations. The specific example is for a federal procurement action which might be undertaken in one of two cities. In the absence of externalities, the expenditure for the procurement will be paid out to factors of production in an amount equal to the opportunity cost of what the factors could produce elsewhere, giving an adequate measure of the social cost of the procurement. To these private costs are added externalities which are quantifiable in dollar terms. The techniques of this book have concentrated on the quantification of pollution, congestion, and fiscal externalities. The total of the government expenditure for the procurement plus these externalities gives a total of the costs quantifiable in dollar terms. This total permits a conclusion as to whether externalities quantifiable in dollar terms are sufficiently large and act sufficiently contrary to the comparison of government expenditure cost to reverse the rankings of the two locations. Beyond this, indices of the change in number of people in poverty and of the amount of ethnic and social integration can be constructed. Finally, externalities which are purely qualitative can be noted in the table with very brief verbal reference to the effects to be expected.

The use of this type of tableau could raise the level of discussion of alternatives affecting location, and it could greatly aid those with policy responsibilities in attempting to arrive at coherent decisions.

TABLE 14-1

Comparison of Social Costs of Government Procurement in Two Cities

	Chicago	Tulsa
Government expenditure		
Externalities quantifiable in dollar terms		
Pollution		
Congestion		
Fiscal effects	———	———
Subtotal		
Externalities quantifiable in physical terms		
Poverty		
Integration		
Nonquantified externalities		

Normative Policy Analysis

Policy recommendations involve considerations going beyond the topics considered in this book, including beliefs and values on the role of government and on weights to be attached to various social goals. Any views expressed must therefore be tentative. The following remarks provide an example of how the book might be used to arrive at recommended redirections of policy.

A review of the major policy documents referred to in Chapter 1 indicates that decentralization is almost universally thought well of, for reasons connected with externalities, whereas policies have usually been stated only vaguely. The principal policy approach followed in the past has been public works and loans. Aside from some agency self-evaluation, there has been little attempt to estimate effects of these programs. The benefits depend on how the policies (transportation subsidies, development of public facilities, and new businesses in rural areas) shift production functions. It seems possible that the benefits have been small relative to the expenditures.

The past policy mix is in part explained by a reluctance to undertake really effective population distribution measures and in part by incentives to favor local projects of traditionally high visibility. In practice, there has been a reluctance to consider measures which would have a very large effect on locations of people and jobs. Large effects could be attained by constraining more definitely where people may locate or offering more significant inducements to them to move. A large number of potentially effective measures is available including more explicit consideration of regional effects of federal expenditure policies and various direct subsidies and taxes or other controls on location.

In short, there seems to be an ambivalence in that lip service is given to the desirability of encouraging decentralization and other spatial reorientations, but policy actions actually tend to let decisions in the market determine locations except as affected haphazardly by various policies not explicitly concerned with location. As a nation, we seem to avoid going down the road of really effective measures to influence population distribution. Rightly or wrongly, we may be suspicious of the ability to avoid blunders if government has more power over location. In addition, congressional and executive pressures in the location of activity would become more subject to control.

Is it desirable to adopt a more explicit and logically defensible population distribution policy? If the answer is yes, as we believe it to be, a *first cornerstone* of the population distribution policy could be to eliminate the adverse population distribution effects of existing institutions and policies. Policies inadvertently fostering centralization include the method of state and local government finance, minimum wage policy, and the welfare payments system. They all appear to have large spatial effects leading to greater concentrations of poorer populations in large metropolitan areas as a whole whereas, within these areas, substantially greater suburbanization is being fostered, producing greater income and ehtnic separation. In addition to the more usual arguments given in favor of the following reforms, the reforms may be called for on grounds of improving population distribution: eliminating the minimum wage or neutralizing its locational effects by setting real rather than nominal wages according to regional and city price level variations, and reforming welfare through nationalizing possibly along the lines of the negative income tax.

The foregoing changes pertain to redesigning policies which have reasons for being other than to influence population distribution. Consider finally the implications of this book for measures whose primary purpose is to influence population distribution. The analysis indicates that only small national income or cost differences result from substantial alterations of city size. For instance, if redressing environmental externalities were the only reason for trying to affect population distribution, the trouble might not be justified. The other side of this coin is that there might be little cost to positively pursuing noneconomic goals in population distribution, such as reducing racial separation.

Since it is easily attainable from a cost point of view to change the location of jobs and people to foster the kind of society we want, a *second cornerstone* of population distribution policy could be to face more squarely troublesome questions about mixes of people. Do we want more mixing of income and ethnic groups, with more disadvantaged people in the suburbs and more advantaged people in the central cities? Other questions can be raised: Do we want more of the type of people and values fostered by dispersal and decentralization? Do we want to try to influence the existence of regionalized cultures and the geographic dispersion of political power? If the answer to any of these questions is yes, there remains a fundamental question on which debate will split: Do we believe public decision making can adequately foster these goals?

A prerequisite would be that policy aims be translated to the maximum extent possible into objective norms, providing rules and guidelines to avoid caprice in carrying out the will of legislation. Supposing that major aims in population distribution are to foster greater integration of ethnic and income groups, numerical formulas can be specified indicating contribution of measures to the goals. As simple possibilities, the formulas could measure the effects on racial balance and the effects of the proportion of families with incomes under $3000. The formulas would total all communities affected substantially by a policy measure. An increase in the proportion of nonwhites living in predominately white communities would be given a positive sign, as would an increase in the proportion of whites living in predominately nonwhite communities. The opposite kinds of changes in racial proportions would be given negative signs. Analogous procedures would be followed with regard to proportions of families with incomes under $3000. A specific formula to indicate the contribution of a measure to population distribution objectives would be the population weighted sum of the signed changes in proportions of nonwhites plus the similarly weighted sum for proportions of families with incomes under $3000.

Two types of measures might be contemplated. First, the formulas just described could be used to give points in decisions as to the location of federal expenditures. Second, in revenue sharing the formulas could be used to increase funds to communities showing progress in racial and economic integration. In addition to being objective and having the hope of being more effective than many previous population distribution proposals, these measures have advantages over racial measures such as busing and punitive incentives in that they are carrot rather than stick inducements, thereby reducing the possibility of backlash. More attention to measures such as these could lead to a population distribution significantly, but not necessarily radically, different from what we now have, contributing to national well-being by taking account of societal issues of importance.

Index

DATE DUE